MACMILLAN EXAMS

# DIRECT TO> IELTS

## Student's Book
### with Key

Sam McCarter

MACMILLAN

# Contents map

| Writing | Listening | Speaking |
|---|---|---|
| Task 1: describing line graphs<br><br>Task 2: Discuss both these views and give your own opinion. | Section 1: multiple choice, choose three letters, completing sentences | Part 1: general questions about your country<br><br>Part 2: Describe a view that you like. |
| Task 1: describing pie charts<br><br>Task 2: planning your writing | Section 2: multiple choice, labelling a map | Parts 2 and 3: adjectives of evaluation |
| Task 1: describing a process<br><br>Task 2: describing advantages and disadvantages/measures | Section 3: matching letters to questions, completing a flow chart, completing a summary | Part 3: beginning and developing an answer |
| Task 1: describing tables<br><br>Task 2: expressing opinions/ expressing purpose | Section 4: completing notes with no more than two words/a number | Part 2: Describe a day off from work or study that you remember.<br><br>Part 3: giving examples, reasons and purposes |
| Task 2: expressing opinions, evaluating and organizing<br><br>Task 1: describing bar charts | Section 1: multiple choice, answering questions with no more than two words, completing sentences with no more than two words | Part 2: Describe a leisure activity.<br><br>Part 3: Degrees of certainty |
| Task 1: describing changes in maps<br><br>Task 2: using complex sentences to develop ideas | Section 2: muliple choice, matching letters to questions, completing a table | Parts 1 and 2: answering general questions, Describe a team that you have been part of or would like to be part of. |
| Task 1: describing charts and tables, paraphrasing<br><br>Task 2: expressing opinions, avoiding repetition | Section 3: multiple choice, choosing letters, completing a table | Parts 1 and 2: answering general questions about shopping, Describe a website that you like using.<br><br>Part 3: talking about spending |
| Task 1: describing bar charts<br><br>Task 2: describing causes and measures | Section 4: completing notes with no more than three words/a number, multiple choice | Parts 1 and 2: answering general questions about your culture, Describe a cultural experience or event you enjoyed or didn't enjoy attending.<br><br>Part 3: discussing cultural activities |

# Introduction

*Direct to IELTS* is a short preparation course for students preparing to take the academic version of the IELTS (International English Language Testing System) examination. The course aims to help students in score bands 6–7 and is equivalent to level B2/C1 in the Council of Europe's Common European Framework.

*Direct to IELTS* aims to improve your skills and knowledge of the IELTS exam and to give a boost to preparation for the exam. The Student's Book contains 8 units covering a range of interesting topics relevant to the IELTS examination.

The Student's Book has regular **Exam information** boxes, which give you help on how to tackle various parts of the exam, and **Tip** boxes, which provide guidance on how to answer specific questions. There are also **Grammar focus** boxes which summarize the main features of the grammatical structures being dealt with in the **Language focus** sections. The four main **skills** in the IELTS exam – Listening, Reading, Writing and Speaking – are dealt with in each unit. Each unit contains practice in IELTS Writing Task 1 and IELTS Writing Task 2 with model answers and comments in the answer key. For further practice, there is a **Writing bank** at the end of the book, which contains a model answer with comments, a writing task for you to do and **Useful language** to refer to. At the end of the book there is a section containing **Additional materials** that help you extend and practise what you have learnt.

Each unit contains at least one **Vocabulary** section relevant to the main skills in the unit. These sections seek to activate the vocabulary so that it can be used in conjunction with the other main skills in the unit. The focus in the Vocabulary section is on collocations and words related to a theme. The vocabulary chosen has wide application in preparation for IELTS and in the exam itself.

Each unit also has at least one **Language focus** section. These sections focus on some of the main grammatical structures that are useful at this level and relevant to the IELTS exam. Each section refers you to the relevant part of the **Grammar Reference** for presentation and revision of the structures being dealt with.

At the end of each unit there is a two-page **Review**. The Review contains further practice of the Vocabulary and Language focus sections, as well as the Writing, Speaking and Reading that features in the unit.

Accompanying the course is a **Website**, which has four computer-based tests that can be done in practice mode and in test mode. There are also downloadable workbook-like materials for each unit in the Student's book. The **Grammar reference** section is available as a downloadable PDF.

## The Academic version of the IELTS examination

The IELTS examination tests students' competence in the four main skills: listening, reading, writing and speaking. Note the exam is a test of a candidate's ability to use English language rather than knowledge of English. A score is given for each skill and then a global score is given, e.g. 5, 6, 6, 6 would give a global score of 6 and 6, 7, 7, 7 would give a global score of 7.

## Listening Module (approximately 30 minutes)

The Listening module has 40 questions and lasts approximately 30 minutes.

The module contains four sections with ten questions in each.

### Sections 1 and 2

The first two sections are of a social nature. Section 1 is a conversation between two people and Section 2 is usually a monologue. However, Section 2 can also be a conversation between two people.

### Sections 3 and 4

Sections 3 and 4 are connected with education and training. Section 3 is a conversation involving up to four people and Section 4 is usually a monologue. Note Section 3 can have several people asking a speaker questions where the answers involve long responses. Likewise, Section 4 can have a speaker being asked questions by one person.

Each section is played once only. You answer the questions in the question booklet in the exam as you listen. At the end of the test, you have 10 minutes to transfer your answers to the answer sheet.

The types of questions used are: multiple choice, short-answer questions, sentence completion, notes/form/summary/flow chart completion, labelling a diagram/plan/map, classification and matching.

Your spelling needs to be accurate and you must not write unnecessary words in the answers, for example, words from the exam questions.

## Academic Reading (1 hour)

In the Academic Reading module, there are three passages from various sources such as books, journals, magazines and newspapers. The passages do not require specialist knowledge for you to understand them and at least one of the three passages contains a detailed logical argument.

The range of question types that are used in the Reading module are: choosing suitable paragraph/section headings from a list, identification of information using True/False/Not Given statements, identification of the writer's views/claims using Yes/No/Not Given statements, multiple choice, short-answer questions, sentence completion, notes/summary/flow chart/table completion, labelling a diagram, classification and matching.

## Academic Writing (1 hour)

The Academic Writing module has two tasks. You are advised to spend 20 minutes on **Task 1** and asked to write at least 150 words. For **Task 2** you are advised to spend 40 minutes and asked to write at least 250 words.

### Task 1

Assessment for **Task 1** is based on your ability to summarize, organize and compare data where possible, describe the stages of a process, describe an object or event or explain how something works. Your range of vocabulary, ability to use a range of grammatical structures, accuracy, the coherence of your writing and your ability to complete the task are assessed.

### Task 2

In **Task 2** you are given a point of view, argument or problem to write about. Assessment is based on your ability to write a solution to the problem; present and support your opinion; compare and contrast evidence and opinions; and evaluate and challenge ideas, evidence or arguments.

In both **Tasks 1** and **2** you are assessed on your ability to write in a style that is suitable for the task.

### Speaking Module (11–14 minutes)

The IELTS Speaking module lasts between 11 and 14 minutes and consists of three parts. The exam is recorded.

### IELTS Speaking Part 1

This part of the Speaking module lasts 4–5 minutes. The examiner checks your identity and asks questions about familiar topics, e.g. your hobbies, your studies/work. Lengthy answers are not necessary in this part of the exam.

### IELTS Speaking Part 2

This part lasts 3–4 minutes. You are given a task card, about which you are expected to speak for 1–2 minutes, without any questions or prompts from the examiner. Before you speak you are given one minute to make brief notes.

### IELTS Speaking Part 3

This part lasts 4–5 minutes. You are asked a series of questions by the examiner. The questions are connected with Part 2 and are of a more abstract nature. You need to develop your answers by giving more details, explaining, evaluating and analysing.

The examiner assesses your ability to communicate effectively in English and specifically assesses:

- Fluency and coherence: how well you speak without hesitating and the organization of your answers.
- Lexical resource: the range of vocabulary you use.
- Grammatical range and accuracy: the range of grammar you use, for example the range of structures and complex sentences using connecting words: *because, for instance, and so, but* and so on.
- Pronunciation: how clear and intelligible you are when you speak.

**Sam McCarter**

# UNIT 1 A very modern world

**1** Work in groups and describe the photos A–D. Then answer questions 1–5.

## Exam information

Speaking Part 1 lasts four to five minutes. After checking your personal details, you and the examiner introduce yourselves. The examiner then asks you questions about yourself and your family, hobbies, job, studies and about other familiar topics. In this part of the speaking exam, your answers are usually one or two sentences long.

**1** Do you think it is possible to protect views like this from development where you live? Why/Why not?

**2** What is the effect of protecting or destroying such views for people in your country?

**3** How have views like this changed in your country?

**4** What is the most beautiful view where you live or were brought up?

**5** Speculate what an area you are familiar with was like in the past, and what it will be like in the near and distant future. Use the ideas below to help you.

**a** It may be impossible to stop progress.

**b** The environment has been gradually improved/destroyed. Something has been gained/lost.

**c** The beauty of the landscape/cityscape/skyline is gradually disappearing, as it is not protected.

**d** Few landscapes/cityscapes/skylines of outstanding (natural) beauty are left. It all depends on whether people have the will to protect them.

**e** Progress is vital for our planet.

**f** The changing skyline is the result of higher buildings, because the population is becoming denser. It is really beautiful.

**2** Work in pairs and read the task card. Then read the candidate's short notes below and describe what you think he/she talks about.

> Describe a view that you like.
>
> You should say:
>
> where the view is
>
> when you first saw the view
>
> what the view is like
>
> and explain why you like the view.

**3** 🎧 **1.1** Listen to a candidate speaking and decide whether the candidate uses the notes in exercise 2. Write down synonyms of any of the words that the candidate uses in the spaces provided.

**4** Work in groups and answer the questions.

**1** Does the candidate talk about all the points on the task card?

**2** Does the candidate's answer follow the notes?

**3** Do the notes help to give structure to the candidate's answer?

**4** Do you think it is easier or more difficult to speak using notes?

> Notes
>
> 1 mind            _____
>
> 2 Acropolis       _____
>
> 3 (in the) dark   _____
>
> 4 14 (years old)  _____
>
> 5 breathtaking    _____
>
> 6 worth visiting  _____
>
> 7 not interested  _____
>
> 8 recall          _____
>
> 9 be sorry        _____
>
> 10 reminds        _____
>
> 11 never stop     _____

**5** Choose one of the task cards, A or B. Write short notes about the card. Use the notes in exercise 2 to help you.

**A**

> Describe a neighbourhood in your home town that you like.
>
> You should say:
>
> where the neighbourhood is
>
> when you first visited the neighbourhood
>
> what the neighbourhood is like
>
> and explain why you like the neighbourhood.

**B**

> Describe a walk that you like going on.
>
> You should say:
>
> where the walk is
>
> when you first went on the walk
>
> what the walk is like
>
> and explain why you like the walk.

**Exam information**

In IELTS Speaking Part 2, you have one minute to write notes about the task card.

**6** Work with a partner who chose a different card. Take turns to talk about your card and give each other feedback.

**Additional material: page 102**

# Language focus: Verbs followed by -ing and/or infinitive

1 Look at the following sentences based on Speaking Parts 1 and 2 on page 7. Which verbs are followed by the *-ing* form, the infinitive or both? Is there any difference in meaning?

   1 We watched the sun setting on the Acropolis.
   2 I will always remember sitting there.
   3 I enjoyed looking at the view.
   4 I managed to get a few photographs later in the evening.
   5 We watched the sun set on the Acropolis.

2 Work in pairs and decide which of the following verbs are followed by the *-ing* form, the infinitive or both.

| | | | | |
|---|---|---|---|---|
| enjoy | afford | love | like | continue |
| help | seem | dislike | hate | miss |
| remember | forget | mind | fail | |
| appear | stop | start | | |

3 Complete the sentences with the correct form of the verbs in brackets. Use the infinitive with or without *to* or the *-ing* form once only in each sentence.

   1 Although many young people hate ........................... (study), the changing work environment means many can't afford ........................... (leave) school without qualifications.
   2 I miss ........................... (go) there a lot, so when I am at home I like ........................... (visit) the spot as often as possible.
   3 I don't mind ........................... (work) and studying part-time because I want ........................... (pay) for the course myself.
   4 Most governments have failed ........................... (reduce) crime, which keeps ........................... (rise) continuously.
   5 I was doing development studies at university when I stopped ........................... (take up) a job. Now I regret ........................... (do) so.
   6 Meditation has helped me ........................... (overcome) stress and I like ........................... (meet) people at the class.

7 Life has changed so much in recent decades. Many students used to continue ........................... (study) well into their twenties in the past, but people can't afford ........................... (wait) so long to find a job these days.
8 The city appears ........................... (be) quiet during the day, but actually the extreme heat means ........................... (stay) out of the sun from late morning onwards.
9 I enjoyed ........................... (sightsee) when I was in Russia and managed ........................... (see) some beautiful buildings.

4 In some of the sentences below, the verb form is incorrect. Tick (✓) the correct sentences and correct the verb form in the incorrect sentences.

   1 I miss seeing the changes taking place in my home town.
   2 I try to avoid to buy the latest technology when it first comes out.
   3 I like to work different shifts each day, because it gives my life a lot of variety.
   4 People can't afford not adjusting to the modern work environment.
   5 The pace at which the world is developing means constantly to update one's skills.
   6 It helps finding different ways to relax in the modern world.
   7 Old people enjoy varying their routine as much as younger people do.
   8 It's difficult to find time even to stop thinking in the busy offices where people now work.

5 Write down three places that are worth seeing and three things that are worth doing where you live or have lived. Work in pairs. Take turns to ask each other questions about the places and activities. Use the question words *why/how often/when/what*.

'What kinds of places do you think are worth visiting where you were born/grew up?'

'The most attractive place is the coastline, which is really ...'

Read more about verbs followed by *-ing* and/or infinitive in the online **Grammar Reference**.

## IELTS Listening Section 1

**1** Work in groups. Read the Section 1 questions 1–10 below and discuss what you think the listening will be about.

**2** Predict the answers to questions 1–10. Make short notes about your predictions.

**3** Discuss the importance of predicting the answers before you listen.

It helps you build a picture of the contents of the conversation.

**4** 1.2 Listen and answer questions 1–10.

**Exam information**

Listening Section 1 contains a dialogue of a non-academic nature. The questions usually relate to factual information such as dates, names and numbers. To obtain a good score, you should aim to get all of the answers correct in this section. At the end of the whole exam you have 10 minutes to transfer your answers. When you transfer your answers, make sure you use the correct spelling and the correct boxes.

*Questions 1 and 2*
Choose the correct letter, **A**, **B** or **C**.

> *Example*
> The caller is enquiring about
> **A** a cycling club.
> **B** a walking club.
> **C** a running club.

**1** The club holds walks
**A** once a week.
**B** once a fortnight.
**C** once a month.

**2** Each walk is led by
**A** the group secretary.
**B** a different person.
**C** a group member.

**3** The walks usually last more than
**A** two hours.
**B** half a day.
**C** three hours.

*Questions 4–6*
Choose **THREE** letters, **A–G**.
Which **THREE** things does the woman mention about the Skyline Club newsletter?

**A** the writers
**B** subscriber numbers
**C** the history
**D** newsletter type
**E** the frequency
**F** the future
**G** the length

*Questions 7–10*
Complete the sentences below.
Write NO MORE THAN TWO WORDS AND/OR A NUMBER for each answer.
**7** The next walk is on ..................................... .
**8** The group is meeting at ..................................... am.
**9** The caller's email address is .....................................@thomas.com.
**10** The caller's mobile number is ..................................... .

**5** Look at your notes in exercise 2. How many answers did you predict correctly?

## Reaction

**6** Work in groups. Discuss at least one of the questions 1–4.

**1** Do you think older people are more interested in how cities develop than young people? Why/Why not?

**2** Do you think 3D interactive tours of cities will one day replace tourist trips? Why/Why not?

**3** How do mobiles and the internet allow people to find their way around more easily compared to the past? Is this a positive or negative development?

**4** Do you think that in the near future electronic maps will replace paper maps for everyone? Why/Why not?

## IELTS Writing Task 1

**1** Work in pairs. Make true or false statements about Writing Task 1 below. Exchange your statements with another pair to answer.

The introduction can be a copy of the rubric in the task. (False)

You should spend about 20 minutes on this task.

*The graph opposite shows the proportion of the European population in selected countries who have never used the internet, along with the European Union average.*

*Summarize the information by selecting and reporting the main features, and make comparisons where relevant.*

Write at least 150 words.

Percentage of the population who have never used the internet

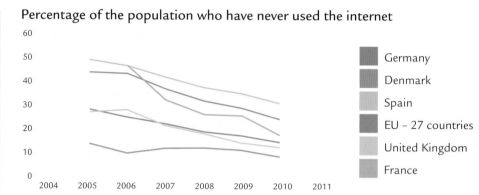

**2** Match 1–6 to a–f. Write a model answer containing five sentences and three paragraphs. Keep 1–6 in the same order and use correct punctuation.

**1** the graph shows the average proportion of the population in the 27 European countries

**2** overall, there is a clear downward trend in the proportion of those who have never accessed the internet

**3** as regards Denmark and the UK, which had the two lowest rates of non-usage of the internet,

**4** Germany followed a similar pattern to the United Kingdom

**5** while France experienced a more marked decline

**6** likewise, Spain, the only country above the European Union average,

**a** from approximately 48 per cent in 2006 to about 18 per cent in 2010

**b** along with selected countries who have never used the internet between 2005 and 2010

**c** with a drop from about 30 per cent to 15 per cent

**d** mirrored the decline of the latter falling to approximately 32 per cent from around 50 per cent

**e** there was a marked fall from approximately 15 per cent to just under 10 per cent and from about 30 per cent to around 12 per cent respectively

**f** with the European average of 27 countries almost halving (from approximately 45 per cent to 25 per cent)

**3** Look at the text in exercise 2 and find evidence for the statements you wrote in exercise 1.

**4** Write your own answer for Writing Task 1 below. Then use the statements you wrote in exercise 1 to check your writing.

You should spend about 20 minutes on this task.

*The graph opposite shows the percentage of internet users in selected European countries playing or downloading games, images, films or music, along with the European Union average.*

*Summarize the information by selecting and reporting the main features, and make comparisons where relevant.*

Write at least 150 words.

Percentage of internet users playing or downloading games, images, films or music

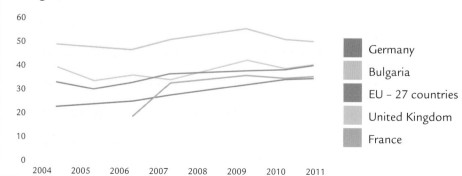

Writing bank: page 109

# Vocabulary: Collocations with nouns

1 Read the extract from IELTS Listening Section 1. What synonyms can you think of to replace the underlined adjective and verb? Use a collocations dictionary if necessary.

Yes. It's worth coming on that one. It's a ... river walk along the south side of the River Thames from London Bridge, looking at the <u>enormous</u> changes that <u>have taken place</u> there in recent years.

2 Complete the sentences using an adjective and a verb in the correct form from the boxes below. There may be more than one answer.

| Adjectives | substantial slow rapid gradual huge enormous economic industrial limited |
|---|---|
| Verbs | improve take place achieve occur make accelerate hinder lead to promote undergo follow |

0 The area where I grew up has undergone substantial/enormous/limited/rapid/huge gradual change over the past decade.

1 Unfortunately, very ............................. progress ............................. in preparing schoolchildren for the modern world.

2 ............................. change ............................. in people's lifestyles at the moment.

3 The introduction of high-speed rail links between cities will ............................. the ............................. development of the continent.

4 A ............................. reduction in traffic can only ............................. if and when the focus of transport moves away from the private car.

5 As cities develop, the ............................. evolution of new ways of living and working will ............................. .

6 ............................. advances in design technology ............................. the world we live in.

3 Transform each sentence in exercise 2 using the words below. Make any changes necessary. You can also change the words in the collocations.

1 slowly   2 enormously   3 economically   4 substantially   5 gradually   6 hugely

1 Unfortunately, preparing schoolchildren for the modern world is progressing slowly.

4 Work in pairs. Discuss how you would answer the IELTS Speaking Part 3 questions below. Use the collocations in exercises 2 and 3 to enrich your answers.

*Discussion topics:*

**Changes to the work environment**

What kinds of changes are taking place in the job market in the modern world?

Do you think that the physical work environment is changing in the modern world? Why/ Why not?

What reasons might employers have for reducing employee workspace in offices?

**Flexible working**

What are the advantages of being able to work flexibly, i.e. at different times of the day?

Do you think it would be a good idea for employees to be encouraged to work from home?

Would there be any disadvantages if certain types of professionals worked from home?

5 Decide how you can begin the answer to each question in exercise 4.

The job market is changing rapidly as growth in ...

6 Change partners and take turns to ask and answer the questions. Give each other feedback about the phrases used from exercises 2 and 3.

**Additional material: page 102**

## IELTS Reading

### Exam information

There are three reading passages in the exam, each containing a minimum of 750 words and each with 1–14 questions. The passages usually become progressively more difficult. To prepare for the IELTS exam, you need to develop your prediction, skimming and scanning skills so you can move around the passage and the questions easily. Learn to survey the whole reading passage and the questions first. Always looks at titles, sub-titles and images. Then skim the passage and the questions. Remember, the questions are effectively a summary of the reading passage. Write your answers on the answer sheet as you do the exam and practise doing so as you prepare for the exam. There is no transfer time at the end.

1 Work in groups. Discuss one or more of the statements below, saying how they relate to you or people you know.

  1 Just under half of all young people (44 per cent) have a social networking profile.

  2 Forty-five per cent of young people said they felt happiest when they were online.

  3 Eighty-four per cent of young people said that the internet brought communities of similar people together.

  4 Young people are highly digitally literate in how they use media and are well connected in a social context.

2 Skim the title of the reading passage and the questions that follow it as quickly as you can. Decide what the topic of the passage is.

3 Scan the reading passage and confirm your predictions in exercise 2.

4 Answer questions 1–13 about the reading passage.

### The Age of the Digital Native or M-Ager

A The internet is a 'natural' space for young people. It is fully integrated into their lives and is as commonplace for the vast majority as walking down their local high street. It is the first place that many of them will go to search for information and provides unparalleled opportunities for communicating and engaging with others. The fact that young people can interact, maintain their anonymity and compare information sources empowers them. It can give them a sense of purpose and control, especially at difficult and challenging times in their lives. At such times, feelings of being in control may on occasion be misplaced and can lead to risk of exposure to unwanted danger. However, the vast majority of young people are able to minimise risk through cross-checking information sources against one another.

B Negotiating the vast amount of information available on the internet presents its own challenges. The ability to locate appropriate information quickly and which is in a language and format that a young person can relate to is not always easy. Equally, as young people's needs have changed so too have their expectations of how they should be able to interact with individuals, organisations and companies.

C Young people today use a variety of digital means to communicate and interact with others at the same time – a mobile phone, a television, a laptop – to build very complex and deep 'tapestries' of connectivity to one another and internet locations. Their life experience and the context in which they use the media inevitably contain many differing behaviours and emphases. At a general level they are often labelled in a variety of ways, the most established terms being 'Digital Natives' or perhaps 'M-Agers' (short for 'Mobile Agers'). The implication in these terms is that this group has grown up surrounded by digital media with access to computers, the internet, mobile phones and digital video games from pre-school age. The Digital Native generation are young people, aged 16 to 24. The internet is a key part of young people's lives today – it is completely natural to them. It is so much a part of them that they can be said to be living hybrid lives, combining the physical and virtual in a seamless network of communication, information, entertainment and sharing.

D For the vast majority of young people, the digital world is a far from isolating experience. It extends reach and connectivity, building on physical or close relationships as well as providing opportunities to interact and build friendships with people who are not geographically close to them. Young people associate the internet with a strong sense of community and as a place where similar people can meet and share together. It is likely that young people have far wider and more varied support communities than previous generations had.

E They are the 'ever on' group. They demand fast and immediate access to both information and friends with the internet ensuring their friends are available whenever and wherever they need them. As access to the internet becomes ever more mobile this trend will continue. Digital Natives are not just different to their parents in using digital media in a natural and hybrid way.

F They are often characterised as being visually literate and as having highly developed visual-spatial skills. Indeed, it has been argued that through this age group we are moving toward a more visual right brain-orientated society with an emphasis on 'creators … and meaning makers' and that young people represent the vanguard. They are experiential, shift their attention from one task to another with great rapidity, are highly digitally literate (in how they use the media) and are well connected in a social context. Importantly, whilst older groups may judge online against an ideal of face-to-face communication (although this is changing), young people evaluate against a wide range of options including instant message, chat, phone, SMS and face-to-face according to their communication needs. These might range from immediacy, message complexity, mobility to cost, privacy, or embarrassment.

**G** This is a response to both the simple presence and availability of technology and to social and environmental change. In combination it demonstrates how young people use today's tools and communication opportunities to connect to the world and to establish and maintain their identities. Although there is much debate, it should be considered that this virtual communication and connectivity is not necessarily to the detriment of more established physically rooted behaviours. Rather, it represents the degree to which, particularly this group, lives hybrid lives – lives that combine digital access and virtual communication into their physical lives.

### Questions 1–5

The reading passage has seven paragraphs, A–G.

Which paragraph contains the following information?

**1** the fact that young people nowadays have more support around them compared to the past

**2** digital natives are at the forefront of a skills shift in society

**3** how the internet is the primary information source for many young people

**4** why digital natives are changing the way they do things

**5** an explanation of the main names to categorize modern youth

### Questions 6–10

Classify the following as relating to

**A** benefits of being connected to the internet

**B** challenges faced by being connected to the internet

**C** neither benefits nor the challenges of being connected to the internet

**6** there is a lot of information available

**7** the information may be available in a few languages

**8** users are able to hide their identity

**9** the information may be available in only one format

**10** it can give meaning to their lives

### Questions 11–13

Answer the questions below.

Choose **NO MORE THREE WORDS** from the passage for each answer.

**11** What does the digital world expand for digital natives?

**12** What standard do older people measure online communication against?

**13** How might young people's lives be described nowadays?

## Reaction

**5** Work in groups and discuss questions 1–3.

**1** Do you think having the opportunity to access the internet at all times makes your life easier? Why/Why not?

**2** Does people being online or texting while talking to friends affect communication? How?

**3** What do you think the effects are of not possessing such skills in the modern world?

> **Tip**
>
> Analyse the phrases 1–5 before you try to find the answers in the text. Underline or circle words that will help you locate the information. Think of synonyms of words. Answer the easy questions first: are 3 and 5 likely to be easier to find than the others?

> **Tip**
>
> In questions 6–10, locate the part of the text that relates to A and B.

## IELTS Writing Task 2

### Exam information

In Writing Task 2, you are required to write at least 250 words on a topic of general academic interest, which does not require specialist knowledge. You are advised to spend about 40 minutes on this task. As Task 2 receives double the marks of Task 1, students are tempted to write their answer to Task 2 first. However, it is better to write Task 1 first and stick to the advised time limits for Tasks 1 and 2. Note you need to write your answer in paragraphs and answer all parts of the question contained in the rubric. You also need to support your ideas by giving reasons and examples, as stated in the rubric.

**1** Match a–f to the boxes.

   **a** word limit

   **b** what you are expected to include in each body paragraph

   **c** view 1

   **d** suggested writing time

   **e** view 2

   **f** three main parts of the task expected

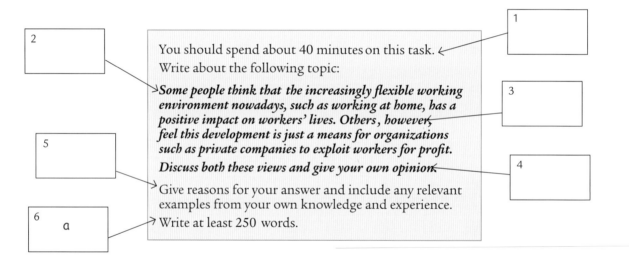

> **1**
>
> You should spend about 40 minutes on this task.
> Write about the following topic:
>
> *Some people think that the increasingly flexible working environment nowadays, such as working at home, has a positive impact on workers' lives. Others, however, feel this development is just a means for organizations such as private companies to exploit workers for profit.*
>
> *Discuss both these views and give your own opinion.*
>
> Give reasons for your answer and include any relevant examples from your own knowledge and experience.
>
> Write at least 250 words.

(boxes labelled 2, 3, 4, 5, 6 a)

**2** Work in pairs. Statements 1–8 relate to the writing task in exercise 1. Decide if the statements relate to the introduction (a), view 1 (b) or view 2 (c).

   **1** Some people feel that the trend towards more flexible working practices for employees is a positive trend. Others have reservations about this phenomenon, arguing that it is just another way for companies to take advantage of workers. a

   **2** Workers have to pay for services such as heating, electricity, lighting and equipment.

   **3** Flexible working gives workers greater freedom.

   **4** With modern technology, a gradual reduction in the number of workers that need to work in one place is happening.

   **5** The changeover to more flexible working is a natural trend in the modern world.

   **6** Space for offices is becoming very expensive, so it suits companies if employees work from home.

   **7** The idea that working from home gives people freedom is an illusion.

   **8** The development may be attractive to employees, but some people quote the negative aspect of such working practices, namely the social impact of people working alone and the increased costs to the workers of having to pay for heating, lighting and so on.

**3** Choose one statement from exercise 2 relating to either view 1 or view 2. Make brief notes about a reason, an example and an impact of the idea in your chosen statement. Compare your notes with another student who has chosen the same statement.

Statement 2

Reason:    they work from home, use their own resources, not the employer's

Example:   they may find their electricity and heating bills increase

Impact:    the employee's costs increase, while the employer's costs fall

**4** Work in pairs. Expand the notes in column A. Create a paragraph relating to statement 1 in exercise 2. Use the items in column B to help you connect the ideas.

| Organization | A Ideas | B Connection |
|---|---|---|
| **Topic** | many employees/workplace/evolve rapidly/people choose place/want to work/time | |
| **Reason** | modern technology/laptops/tablets/latest mobile phones/enable people/change working practices/suit themselves/access workplace wherever | this phenomenon is happening because/as a result of/as a result/ this is because |
| **Example 1** | trainers/accountants/designers/able to access/main place of work/electronically | for example/for instance/take for example/a good example is/a good examples of this |
| **Result** | work/take place/at home/in cafés/hotels/in office space rented by the hour/airports | further/then/the consequence of this is that |

**5** Complete the text with items from the table in exercise 4. Make any necessary changes.

Some people feel that the trend towards more flexible working practices for employees is a positive trend. Yet, others have reservations about this phenomenon, arguing that it is just another way for companies to manipulate the workforce to make more money. I personally think it is a combination of both.

For many employees, the workplace **(0)** .....is evolving......... as people choose the place where they want to work and the time. **(1)** ................................. modern technology such as tablets and mobile phones, which **(2)** ................................. to suit themselves. **(3)** ................................. trainers in any field, accountants, designers or editors, who **(4)** ................................. electronically from anywhere in the world. **(5)** ................................. the work can take place at home, in cafés, in hotels, in office space rented by the hour, or even in **(6)** ................................. .

**6** Write an answer for Writing Task 2 below.

> You should spend about 40 minutes on this task.
>
> Write about the following topic:
>
> *Some people think that changing people's attitudes to other countries and cultures is an important factor in reducing world poverty. Others, however, feel that the most important method is trade.*
>
> *Discuss both these views and give your own opinion.*
>
> Give reasons for your answer and include any relevant examples from your own knowledge and experience.
>
> Write at least 250 words.

**Writing bank: page 115**

# Review

## Language focus: Verbs followed by -ing and/or infinitive

Read part of two conversations. Complete the conversations with the -ing form or the infinitive of the verbs in brackets.

1

**Examiner:**
Do you think it is possible to protect certain views in cities from modern developments?

**Candidate:**
It's difficult to avoid (1) ............................. (alter) views in and around cities, but if we can manage (2) ............................. (save) them then I think it's definitely a good thing. There are many cities like Paris or St Petersburg that could be destroyed if care is not taken (3) ............................. (save) them.

**Examiner:**
Why do you think so?

**Candidate:**
Mmm, protecting cities and their skylines means (4) ............................. (keep) them for future generations to see and enjoy (5) ............................. (look) at. I think it's important to value cityscapes as much as landscapes.

2

**Examiner:**
What do you think your home town will be like in the future?

**Candidate:**
I don't think it'll be recognizable to the present generation. Large parts of it are very old, but the local government have failed (6) ............................. (protect) it up to now and they keep (7) ............................. (construct) new office blocks which are supposed to be modern, but which are very ugly. People there, I think, miss (8) ............................. (live) and (9) ............................. (work) in the old relaxed environment.

## Vocabulary: Collocations with nouns

In some of the sentences below, the word order is incorrect. Tick (✓) the correct sentences and correct the word order in the incorrect sentences.

0  The area I grew up substantial change where has undergone over the past decade.
   <u>The area where I grew up has undergone substantial change over the past decade.</u>

1  Fortunately, progress in educating young people has been made about the substantial demands of the 21st century.

2  The economic development of any region of the world is promoted by innovation as well as natural resources.

3  The evolution has occurred steadily over the past hundred years of transport.

4  Changes that take place tend gradually to achieve more than abrupt transformations.

5  A reduction can only be achieved through substantial education in ignorance.

6  The advances in medicine are improving the enormous lives of everyone in recent years.

7  Too much development of creativity can hinder the control of the way children behave and think.

8  Innovation in technology can promote huge growth in areas of the economy.

## IELTS Reading: Understanding noun phrases

**1** Put a box around the main noun in each phrase below. Underline the prepositional phrase which follows.

**0** | recommendations | <u>about how to increase students' global awareness</u>

**1** the effect of a university education on the earning potential of graduates

**2** the development of different types of vocational courses for young people

**3** the progress made by young people in the field of education in recent years

**4** suggestions about how to promote the growth of creative industries

**5** an awareness of the impact of technology on improving the way that people work

**6** a reduction in the amount of time spent studying for a university degree

**7** an explanation of the relative importance of knowledge and experience

**2** Decide what the noun phrases in exercise 1 mean and what you would expect to find in the paragraph.

**0** recommendations about how to increase students' global awareness

The text or paragraph suggests two or more ways that awareness of the world can be increased among students, probably as a means to improve their own marketability and/ or education.

> **Tip**
>
> As noun phrases are used to summarize information in all parts of the IELTS exam, it is a very useful skill to learn to unpack the meaning so you understand exactly what they mean. Some noun phrases used in headings are short (e.g. *the impact of development*) and some are long, as in the example (between 8 and 11 words).

## IELTS Writing Task 2: The negative viewpoint

**1** The paragraph below develops one of the statements from exercise 2 in Writing Task 2 on page 14. What do you think the purpose of the paragraph is?

**1** to show how working from home benefits employers

**2** to show how working from home benefits employees

> The development may be attractive to employees, but to some people the idea that such working practices give people freedom is an illusion. They quote the negative aspect of these practices, namely the social impact of people working alone and the increased costs of having to pay for heating, lighting and equipment. This benefits companies, because less office space is needed.

**2** Decide where you can add the following words and phrases to the paragraph.

> **1** situation  **2** of home working  **3** In the latter case, the costs can be considerable in both hot and cold climates, and if essentials such as computers or telephones break down.  **4** thus reducing costs for employers  **5** to the workers

**For further practice, go to the Direct to IELTS website for downloadable worksheets.**

# UNIT 2 The past – public and private

## Vocabulary 1: Collocations – multiple combinations

**1** Work in groups. Discuss how the photos relate to methods of bringing history to life.

**2** Decide what the purpose is of each of the methods shown in the photos. Use the ideas 1–5 or your own ideas. Give examples and reasons.

  **1** to carry out a comprehensive study of a particular area by excavating or questioning

  **2** to give people an opportunity to take part in historical events

  **3** to bring historical information to life

  **4** to preserve/showcase historical records of national and international interest

  **5** to restore/exhibit a precious object

**3** Decide whether these words are verbs, nouns, adjectives or prepositions.

> do  carry out  into  search for  take part in  undertake  historical
> groundbreaking  market  compelling

**4** Decide which words from exercise 3 you can use with nouns 1–8 in the table.

do: 2, 4, 5, 6, 7

| Verbs | Adjectives | Nouns |
|---|---|---|
| collect, examine, study | concrete, factual | **(1)** evidence (about/ relating to) |
| make, perform, fund | detailed, thorough, economic | **(2)** analysis (of) |
| keep, update | accurate, brief, detailed, documentary | **(3)** record (of) |
| conduct, fund, support | scientific, close, careful, detailed | **(4)** study (of) |
| carry out, conduct, do, fund | detailed, further, scientific, academic | **(5)** research (on) |
| conduct | detailed, brief, customer, social | **(6)** survey (of) |
| conduct, pursue, lead | close, careful, detailed, thorough | **(7)** investigation (of) |
| study, fund | local, early,  modern, social | **(8)** history (of) |

**5** Complete the following statements using words from exercises 3 and 4. Change the form of the word if necessary. More than one answer may be possible.

  **1** Do you think the government or private industry should ........................... scientific ........................... into history or medicine?

  **2** Is it worthwhile ........................... thorough investigations of every historical artefact discovered? Or could the money be spent on something else?

  **3** Some people think ........................... animal ........................... should be banned. Do you ?

  **4** Social ........................... carried out by researchers can reveal very important information.

  **5** Do you think there is compelling ........................... for global warming?

  **6** It is more difficult nowadays for students to find time to do a thorough ........................... of any subject. Why is this so?

**6** Work in groups. Select at least two questions from exercise 5 and make notes about the reasons and examples. Then take turns to ask and answer the questions.

**Additional material: page 103**

## IELTS Listening Section 2

**1** Skim the questions 1–10 and make a list of at least five items the talk will cover. Make short notes about your predictions.

**2** Work in pairs. Describe where each item is on the plan. Then take turns to describe the route of the path and the places that you can see along it.

**3** 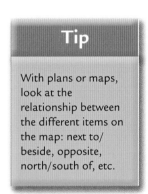 **1.3** Listen and answer questions 1–10.

### Question 1

Choose the correct letter, **A**, **B** or **C**.

**1** According to the speaker, the park has drawn attention to
  **A** local history and research.
  **B** entertainment and local research.
  **C** nature and local research.

### Questions 2–4

Label the plan below.
Write **NO MORE THAN TWO WORDS** for each answer.

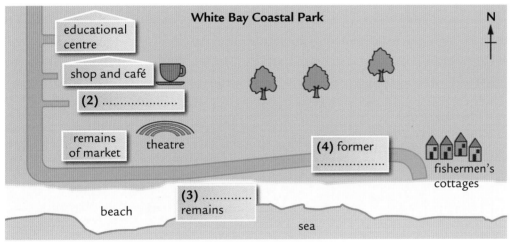

White Bay Coastal Park

educational centre
shop and café
(2) ...................
remains of market
theatre
(4) former ...................
fishermen's cottages
(3) ............... remains
beach
sea

N

> **Tip**
>
> With plans or maps, look at the relationship between the different items on the map: next to/ beside, opposite, north/south of, etc.

### Questions 5–10

Choose the correct letter, **A**, **B** or **C**.

**5** What are the earliest items discovered so far in the excavations?
  **A** weapons
  **B** pottery
  **C** jewellery

**6** Why are certain remains closed to the public?
  **A** to preserve them
  **B** to carry out research
  **C** to renovate them

**7** How far is the beach from the preservation area?
  **A** a very short walk away
  **B** a short drive away
  **C** a long walk away

**8** The beach is famous because of its
  **A** white sand and rocks.
  **B** white sand and shells.
  **C** rocks and shells.

**9** What can be found at the beach shops?
  **A** local photographs
  **B** local artwork
  **C** unusual souvenirs

**10** The entrance ticket allows visitors
  **A** only one visit to the site.
  **B** three more visits a year.
  **C** unlimited visits for a year.

**4** Look at your notes in exercise 1. How many of your predictions were correct?

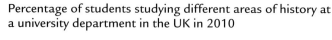

## IELTS Writing Task 1

**1** Work in pairs. Study the pie charts and decide which of the verbs in the box can be used to describe the data. Use the verbs you chose to describe the data in your own words.

account for   consist of   allocate   come from   spend
consume   produce   use   comprise   constitute

Percentage of students studying different areas of history at a university department in the UK in 2000

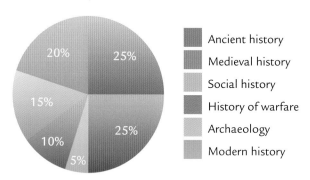

Percentage of students studying different areas of history at a university department in the UK in 2010

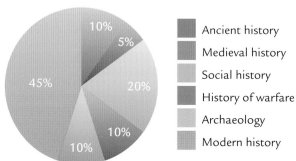

Ancient history
Medieval history
Social history
History of warfare
Archaeology
Modern history

**2** Match 1–7 to a–g to make sentences about the pie charts.

**1** Modern history accounted for

**2** Ancient history comprised

**3** Medieval history and ancient history together made up

**4** The proportion of students studying modern history in 2010

**5** The number of areas in the history department

**6** The study of ancient history amounted

**7** In 2010, medieval history with 5 per cent

**a** 15 per cent of all the students in 2010.

**b** 20 per cent of the students in 2000.

**c** consisted of six in 2000 and 2010.

**d** 25 per cent of the students in 2000.

**e** constituted the smallest proportion of students.

**f** to a much smaller proportion of students in 2010 compared to 2000.

**g** exceeded that in 2000, 45 per cent and 20 per cent respectively.

**3** Write sentences about the charts using the words below. Compare your sentences with other students.

**1** Archaeology/represent/15 per cent/total student body

**2** Social history/make up/smaller proportion/students/in 2000/compared to/2010

**3** History of warfare/constitute/10 per cent/2000

**4** Ancient history/comprise/smaller proportion/student body/2010/compared/2000

**5** proportion/students/studying/archaeology/equal/that/history of warfare/2010

**4** Work in pairs. Describe the pie charts at the top of page 21.

You should spend about 20 minutes on this task.

*The pie charts show a breakdown of sources of income for the upkeep of Castle Keep, an ancient monument, in 1850 and 1950.*

*Summarize the information by selecting and reporting the main features, and make comparisons where relevant.*

Write at least 150 words.

Sources of funding 1850

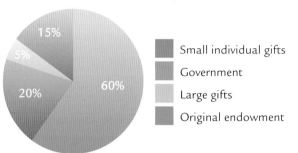

Sources of funding 1950

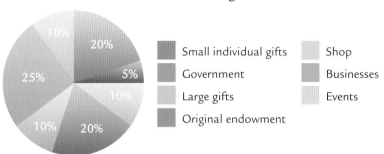

**Glossary:** Original endowment: the original donation or gift to help fund the maintenance of Castle Keep

5 Work in pairs. Complete the answer below describing the pie charts in exercise 4. Use words and phrases from the table.

| Verbs | came from   changed   constituting   accounted for |
|-------|----------------------------------------------------|
| Nouns | the largest proportion of the total   a doubling in the proportion contributed to total income  a reliance on small individual gifts   a much smaller proportion |
| Data  | 15 per cent   20 per cent and 20 per cent respectively   20 per cent |

The charts provide information about where funding for the maintenance of Castle Keep came from in the years 1850 and 1950.

Overall, it is clear that the pattern of income **(1)** ................................. dramatically over the 100-year period with a shift away from **(2)** ................................. to other funding sources. In 1850, for example, small individual gifts **(3)** ................................. 60 per cent of the total funding with large gifts **(4)** ................................. only 5 per cent.

By contrast, in 1950 20 per cent of funding **(5)** ................................. small individual gifts, with businesses forming **(6)** ................................. , followed by small individual gifts and the original endowment, **(7)** ................................. .
For the endowment, there was an approximate 33 per cent rise from **(8)** ................................. in 1850.

As regards income from government sources, in 1950 this consisted of **(9)** ................................. compared to 1850, 5 per cent and 20 per cent respectively, representing a 75 per cent decline, while large gifts saw **(10)** ................................. from 5 per cent to 10 per cent.

Apart from businesses, two new sources of income, the shop and events, together comprised **(11)** ................................. of funding in 1950.

6 Write an answer for Writing Task 1 below.

> You should spend about 20 minutes on this task.
> *The pie charts below show the funding allocation to a range of museums in a European country in 2000 and 2010. Summarize the information by selecting and reporting the main features, and make comparisons where relevant.*
> Write at least 150 words.

Funding allocation to a range of museums in a European country in 2000

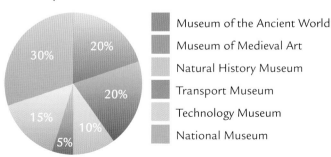

Funding allocation to a range of museums in a European country in 2010

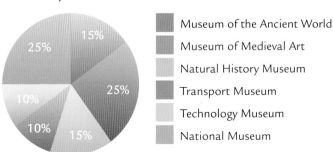

**Additional material: page 103    Writing bank: page 111**

## IELTS Speaking Parts 2 and 3 & Vocabulary 2: Adjectives of evaluation

**1** Work in pairs. Study and discuss the task card.

> Describe a time when you visited a museum you like.
>
> You should say:
>
> > what the museum contained
> >
> > when you visited the museum
> >
> > what type of exhibits you visited
>
> and explain why you liked the museum.

**2** 🎧 **1.4** Listen to a candidate talking about the card and complete the phrases and sentences. Use no more than four words for each answer.

1 museum about ...............................
2 a large exhibition of ...............................
3 The photos were fascinating as they showed ............................... like horses and carts.
4 also rooms with displays of objects that have been found ...............................
5 I've been back to the museum several times, because ............................... .
6 Although the displays and exhibits are ..............................., I found them very effective and quite compelling.

**3** Work in pairs. <u>Underline</u> the words and phrases in exercise 2 which indicate the speaker is evaluating something.

**4** Add the words from the box to the correct place in the table below.

> straightforward  crucial  minor  reasonable  appropriate  unimportant
> ineffective  significant  impractical

| Adjective | Synonym | Opposite |
|---|---|---|
| effective | successful | (1) |
| sensible | (2) | foolish |
| relevant | (3) | irrelevant |
| practical | convenient | (4) |
| trivial | (5) | (6) |
| immaterial | (7) | (8) |
| simple | (9) | difficult |

**5** Work in pairs. Transform the sentences using the words in brackets. Do not change the form of the words in brackets. Compare your answers with another pair.

**0** The changes had an enormous effect on the number of tourists coming to the area. (effective in/bringing)

**The changes were very effective in bringing tourists to the area.**

**1** The changes that took place in my home town made little or no difference to the people. (unimportant)

**2** Taking part in a survey doesn't waste time. (pointless) It's a confidence-building experience.

3 Studying history has little or no relevance for the modern world. (irrelevant)

4 It doesn't make sense to ignore the experience of the past. (sensible)

5 Some people think that relying solely on sponsorship for the arts doesn't work. (impractical)

6 Innovation in industry has had an enormous effect on developing new products. (effective)

7 Do you think qualifications have more worth nowadays compared to the past? (worthwhile)

8 The evidence from the study did not convince people. (unconvincing)

**6** Work in pairs. Make brief notes about one of the task cards. Then take turns to talk about your card.

A

> Describe a place you always wanted to visit when you were younger.
>
> You should say:
>
>> where the place is
>>
>> what the place is like
>>
>> how you first found out about the place
>
> and explain why you wanted to visit the place.

B

> Describe a recent meeting with someone that you think has changed your life for the better.
>
> You should say:
>
>> who the person is
>>
>> when and where you met the person
>>
>> what happened when you met the person
>
> and explain why you think the meeting has changed your life for the better.

**7** Work in groups of three. Choose one of the sets of questions, A or B. Discuss a) possible ideas for each question, b) how to begin each answer and c) examples and reasons to develop each answer.

**A  Communication**

1 Is communication important in people's lives nowadays? Why/Why not?

2 How effective is communication nowadays compared to the past? In what ways?

3 In terms of communication, do you think the introduction of the internet changed the way businesses communicate? Why/Why not?

**B  Personal opinion**

1 Do you think that young people are more confident about expressing their opinions than in the past? Why/Why not?

2 Would it be a good idea to have more language learning outside the classroom to build up confidence in giving opinions in another language?

3 Some people think that learning to be confident in expressing yourself is as much a life skill as learning a language. Do you agree?

**8** Take turns to answer the questions in exercise 7.

## IELTS Reading

**1** Work in groups. Look at the photos and the title of the reading passage. Decide whether the passage is related to a) problems and solutions or b) time.

**2** Read the list of headings i–viii below. List as much information as you can about the contents of the reading passage.

**3** Answer questions 1–13 about the reading passage.

*Questions 1–5*

The reading passage has five sections, **A–E**.

Choose the correct headings for sections A–E from the list of headings below.

**List of Headings**

| | |
|---|---|
| **i** | New developments in sunglasses lenses |
| **ii** | The use of sunglasses in early courts |
| **iii** | How the physical shape of early sunglasses developed |
| **iv** | The introduction of sidepieces on sunglasses |
| **v** | The origins and early history of sunglasses |
| **vi** | Ways in which sunglasses have become trendy |
| **vii** | The arrival of modern sunglasses |
| **viii** | Advertising campaigns for sunglasses |

**1** Section **A**
**2** Section **B**
**3** Section **C**
**4** Section **D**
**5** Section **E**

### The history of a cool image

**A** The history of sunglasses can be traced back to ancient Rome around the year AD 60, where the Emperor Nero is said to have watched gladiator fights whilst holding up polished emerald-green gems to his eyes, thus reducing the effect of the sun's glare. The very first actual recorded evidence of the use of sunglasses can be found from a painting by Tommaso da Modena in Italy, 1352, showing a person wearing sunglasses.

Earlier, around the twelfth century in China, sunglasses were worn by court judges, not to protect their eyes from the sun, but in order to conceal any expressions in their eyes as it was important to keep their thoughts and opinions secret until the end of each trial. These were flat panes of quartz that had been polished smooth and then smoked to give their tint.

It was not until 1430 that prescription glasses were first developed in Italy to correct vision, and these early rudimentary spectacles soon found their way to China, where they were again tinted by smoke to be used by the judges. The frames were carved out of either ivory or tortoiseshell, and some were quite ornate. During the 17th century, prescription glasses were being used in England to help elderly long-sighted people to see better. The Spectacle Makers Company was founded in England, which started manufacturing prescription glasses for the public and whose motto was "A Blessing to the Aged".

**B** The development of sunglasses, however, remained static until the work of James Ayscough, who was known for his work on microscopes in London around 1750. He experimented with blue and green tinted lenses, believing they could help with certain vision problems. These were not sunglasses, however, as he was not concerned with protecting the eyes from the sun's rays.

Prescription spectacles continued to be developed over the next few decades, especially regarding the design of the spectacle frames and how to get them to sit comfortably on the nose. The frames were made from leather, bone, ivory, tortoiseshell and metal, and were simply propped or balanced on the nose. The early arms or sidepieces of the frames first appeared as strips of ribbon that looped around the backs of the ears. Rather than loops, the Chinese added ceramic weights to the ends of the ribbons which dangled down behind the tops of the ears. Solid sidepieces finally arrived in 1730, invented by Edward Scarlett.

**C** Sunglasses, as we know them today, were first introduced by Sam Foster in America, 1929. These were the first sunglasses designed specifically to protect people's eyes from the harmful sun's rays. He founded the Foster Grant Company, and sold the first pair of Foster Grant sunglasses on the boardwalk by the beaches in Atlantic City, New Jersey. These were the first mass-produced sunglasses, and from this year onwards, sunglasses really began to take off.

**D** In 1936, Edwin H Land patented the Polaroid filter for making polarized sunglasses. This type of tint reduces glare reflected from surfaces, such as water. Later in that same year, Ray-Ban took the design of pilots' sunglasses further by producing the aviator-style sunglasses that we know today, using this recently invented polarized lens technology. The edge of the frame characteristically drooped away at the edges by the cheeks in a sort of tear drop shape, to give a full all-round protection to the pilots' eyes, who regularly had to glance down towards the aircraft's instrument panel. The polarized lens reduced the glare from light reflected off the instrument panel. Pilots were given these sunglasses free of charge, but in 1937 the general public were allowed to

purchase this aviator-style model that "banned" the sun's rays as Ray-Ban sunglasses.

**E** In 1960, Foster Grant started a big advertising campaign to promote sunglasses, and pretty soon famous film stars and pop stars started wearing sunglasses as part of their image. The public began to adopt this new fashion of wearing sunglasses, not just to protect their eyes from bright light, but also as a way of looking good. Today, sunglasses are continuing to be improved with efficient UV blocking tints, cutting out all the harmful ultra-violet light. Various coloured tints are now available and, of course, the frame styles are very varied and exciting. Now you can really make a statement with your fashion sunglasses, transforming your image or creating a new one. Designer sunglasses have certainly come a long way in just a few years, and now not only protect our eyes from the harmful sun's rays, but are also an important *fashion accessory* – and it all started nearly 2,000 years ago with the Roman Emperor Nero!

### Questions 6–10

Do the following statements agree with the information given in the reading passage?
Write:

**YES**          *if the statement agrees with the claims of the writer.*

**NO**          *if the statement contradicts the claims of the writer.*

**NOT GIVEN** *if it is impossible to say what the writer thinks about this.*

   **6** The earliest reference to sunglasses can be found in early Roman times.

   **7** Early Chinese sunglasses were worn to correct the wearer's eyesight.

   **8** The work of James Ayscough had a profound effect on the development of modern lenses.

   **9** Prior to 1730, sidepieces on glasses were made of many different materials.

   **10** Sam Foster's sunglasses were the first to be made for a mass market.

### Questions 11–13

Complete the sentences below.
Choose **ONE WORD ONLY** from the passage for each answer.

   **11** The function of the Edwin H Lands Polaroid filter was to lessen surface ......................... .

   **12** People can change their ......................... by wearing trendy sunglasses.

   **13** Designer glasses still offer protection from solar ......................... .

**Tip**

Make sure you read the rubric and note that the statements are about claims made by the writer.

**Tip**

Note the rubric says ONE WORD ONLY.

## Language focus: Using nouns to build ideas

1 Below are some examples of noun phrases from the reading passage. Match the examples 1–6 to the types of noun phrases a–c.

1 cool image
2 this new fashion of wearing sunglasses
3 prescription glasses
4 flat panes of quartz
5 any expressions in their eyes
6 court judges

a (article/determiner) adjective + noun
b (article/determiner) noun + noun
c (article/determiner) (adjective/ noun) noun + prepositional phrase (i.e. preposition + (adjective ) + noun)

2 Find examples of c in Section A of the reading passage. What is the longest noun phrase that you can find?

3 Work in pairs. Add the words in brackets to the correct spaces to create noun phrases.

1 (changes/past/climate/reasons) →
various ................... for ...................
................... in the ...................
2 (products/range/sale/consumer) →
the ................... of ...................
................... on ...................
3 (history/period/country's) →
the most dynamic ................... in the
................... ...................
4 (answer/overcrowding/cities/problem
→ the ................... to the ...................
of ................... in ...................
5 (buildings/types/description)→
a brief ................... of different
................... of ancient ...................
6 (people's/lives/impact/war) → the
................... of ................... on
................... ...................

4 Explain the meaning of the noun phrases in 3.

1 various reasons for climate changes in the past

This refers to a range of reasons given or listed about why the climate changed in the past (rather than now).

5 Transform the sentences below by changing the word in bold into a noun and making any other necessary changes. There may be more than one answer.

0 The price of oranges **rose** dramatically.
1 The population of the world **increased** dramatically in the latter half of the 20th century.
2 The popularity of the radio has **declined** with the advent of new technologies such as CDs, DVDs, iPads and tablets.
3 The Medieval and Renaissance periods in European history were hugely **different** from each other.
4 TV technology has **developed** at a considerable pace in the past decade.
5 The Industrial Revolution **affected** the economic development of the whole world significantly.
6 People were extremely **interested** in the launch of the latest ultra-thin laptop.
7 The establishment of cities **rose** due to developments in agriculture.
8 The archaeologists then **analysed** the data from the site.

0 There was a dramatic rise in the price of oranges.

6 Work in groups. Discuss the impact of one of the following on your life or your country.

1 the cost of living
2 education
3 an awareness of history
4 a lack of awareness of history

www Read more about using nouns to build ideas in the online **Grammar Reference**.

**Additional material: page 104**

## IELTS Writing Task 2

**1** Work in groups. Discuss at least two of the writing tasks below. Think about the content and the structure of the answer for each one.

**A** Making subjects such as history compulsory in schools is the best way to overcome the decline in students studying such subjects at university.

To what extent do you agree or disagree?

What other measures do you think might be effective?

**B** Some people think that studying a practical subject such as science or technology is more relevant nowadays for young people's career prospects than studying the arts. Others think that the arts are more important.

Discuss both these views and give your own opinion.

**C** In the modern world, studying at university is becoming too expensive for many students compared to the past.

What are the causes of this and what measures should be taken to overcome the problem?

**2** Answer the questions below about the writing tasks in exercise 1.

In which essay are you asked to write about:

**1** two points of view and then provide your own opinion?

**2** how far you agree with a particular solution and then suggest other solutions?

**3** the factors contributing to a problem, and solutions?

**4** factors such as the rising cost of living, increased competition for university places and reduction in government support?

**5** such ideas as the value of art and design for industry/architecture, etc.?

**6** measures such as an increase in scholarships, shorter courses, free places at university?

**7** such measures as taking children on field trips, visiting museums and archaeological sites?

**8** the relevance of scientific and technological skills in the modern world?

**3** Match the plan below to one of the writing tasks in exercise 1.

*introduction, evaluation of solution, measure 1, measure 2, conclusion*

**4** Work in pairs. Put the words in italics in the correct order to complete part of the answer for A in exercise 1. Then put the paragraphs in order, using the first three items in the plan in exercise 3.

History could be made compulsory for the first few years of secondary school. During this time lessons could be made interesting and absorbing for students by **(1)** *not just to visits museums,* **(2)** *but of to and historical local national sites interest.* **(3)** *to such as the museums visits transport museum in London* are a good way to encourage even primary schoolchildren to develop an interest in history, because many exhibits are interactive, and engage the students. **(4)** *the such as and modern facilities computers internet* can be used to bring history to life by carrying out simple research into local history or conducting social surveys.

Compulsion regarding history will certainly bring **(5)** *of these the attention subjects to pupils,* many of whom might not have considered it **(6)** *a to worthwhile study subject.* Admittedly, this would in some cases encourage interest in the subject, but on its own as **(7)** *of a encouragement means* it is not enough. For history, there are many strategies that can be implemented to encourage its uptake at university.

When any school subject is made a **(8)** *of the mandatory curriculum part school,* it does not necessarily mean that it will increase enough interest in the subject for students to go on to study it at university. In fact, sometimes it might have the opposite effect.

**5** Write an answer for task B or C in exercise 1.

# Review

## Vocabulary 1: Collocations – multiple combinations

Work in pairs. Match 1–8 to a–h. There may be more than one answer.

1 For young people in the modern world, how relevant is studying
2 Have you ever taken part in
3 Are interactive museums useful for bringing
4 Have you ever done
5 Should the government be solely responsible for carrying out
6 Do you think it's important for students to keep
7 Studying history gives students key academic tools, such as carrying out
8 The internet makes it much easier for students to collect

a a customer/telephone survey? What happened?
b ancient history to their future lives?
c detailed records of their studies inside and outside the classroom? Why/Why not?
d an intensive study of any subject? If so, what?
e sound evidence for their writing compared to in the past. Do you agree?
f scientific investigations such as archaeological digs? Or should private sector involvement be encouraged?
g a close analysis of a problem in all subjects. How far do you agree?
h scientific or historical research to the attention of a wider public? How?

## IELTS Speaking Parts 2 and 3 & Vocabulary 2: Adjectives of evaluation

1 Underline the adjectives of evaluation in the sentences below.

0 Using the latest technology available in any period of history has always been <u>relevant</u> to the economic development of a country.
1 It is sensible to teach even young children about basic research tools like finding things on the internet.
2 Subjects like science and technology are practical for students in today's world.
3 Hobbies such as collecting old coins are trivial pursuits for children.
4 Knowledge of culture is not as important as technology to young people in the 21st century as it has been in the past. However, it is not immaterial.
5 Providing workshops and classes for children in museums and art galleries is a simple way to stimulate pupils' interest in history and the arts.
6 The most significant development in the last hundred years has been the invention of the internal combustion engine.
7 Studying history, especially ancient history, is definitely worthless.
8 Acting out scenes from history is an effective way for students to learn skills for the modern world.

2 Do you agree with the evaluations in exercise 1? If not, change the evaluations to make them true for you. Compare your answers with a partner.

## Language focus: Using nouns to build ideas

Change the words in bold into nouns and combine the sentences. Make any necessary changes.

0 The Inca Empire **spread** along the pacific coast of South America. There were many reasons for this.

There were many reasons for the spread of the Inca Empire along the coast of South America.

1 The Roman Empire **fell**. Various important factors contributed to it.

2 Studying history **affects** young people's critical skills. It must not be underestimated.

3 We can **analyse** world history. It can help us **develop** a better understanding of modern life.

4 The infrastructure of the city was **improved**. It played a major role in economic development.

5 An awareness of history and being able to function in the modern world are **linked**. It is clear.

6 People can **know** many different subjects generally. This is better than **knowing** one field in detail.

7 The relationship between education and happiness has been **researched**. It has been done extensively.

## IELTS Writing Task 2

1 Work in pairs. Discuss Writing Task 2 below.

> *Some people think that the function of studying history at all levels is to teach young people about historical facts and information, while others feel that its main function is to acquaint them with the skills necessary in later life.*
> *Which, in your opinion, should be the main function of education?*

2 Read the first part of an answer for the task in exercise 1. Decide which statements 1–7 are true about the answer. Give evidence for your answers.

The study of history plays an important role in the education process of all young people. While there may be some discussion as to its main purpose in the education system, to impart knowledge or skills for life, I personally feel that the latter is its main function, but that the former is also relevant.

The study of history could not be more relevant nowadays to young people's lives. This is because the modern workplace demands that employees understand the processes of life and skills that studying history teaches them. Take for example learning about how a series of events in history developed and their subsequent impact on people's lives. This process can teach young people about the consequences of changes and developments, which they can then personalize by relating them to developments in their own lives.

At the same time, factual information like dates, names and places can be learnt to help put the developments into context and also to personalize the process. While important, this aspect of learning about history is of secondary importance.

**Statements**

1 Generally speaking, studying history is not important for young people.

2 The fact that people don't agree on the main function of studying history is acknowledged.

3 Acquiring knowledge is more important than learning about processes in studying history.

4 Being an employee nowadays requires more than just knowledge.

5 Studying processes such as urbanization, natural lifecycles or manufacturing products can teach young people about consequences of events and actions in their lives.

6 The part played by learning historical facts is acknowledged, but it is downplayed.

7 Overall, both sides of the argument are supported equally.

3 Write an introduction and first paragraph supporting the teaching of historical facts.

**For further practice, go to the Direct to IELTS website for downloadable worksheets.**

# UNIT 3 The age of information

## IELTS Listening Section 3

**1** Work in groups and describe the photos. Match them to statements 1–4. Do you agree with the statements? Why/Why not?

1 The information age means we can have a paperless work environment.
2 Apps help to package information in a modern way.
3 Books are still very relevant in the modern world.
4 Information overload can be stressful for students.

**2** Work in groups. Answer these questions about writing an essay.

Are you organized?
Do you enjoy the process?
Do you feel overwhelmed?
Do you work on your own?
Do you get frustrated?

**3** Scan questions 1–10 opposite for the following words and phrases. Discuss what you think the listening will be about. Make short notes about your predictions.

1 research habits
2 flow chart
3 journal article search
4 a detailed analysis of the essay title
5 specific targets
6 Organize, reduce time wasting and don't overwhelm yourself with information.
7 struggling with the essay after everyone else has finished

4  1.5 Listen and answer questions 1–10.

**Questions 1–4**

Which of Martha's research habits relate to the following periods?
Write the correct letter, **A**, **B** or **C**, next to questions 1–4.

**A** past
**B** present
**C** future

1 organizing materials during the process
2 making notes on printouts
3 collecting too much data
4 reducing the research time

**Questions 5–7**

Complete the flow chart below.
Choose **NO MORE THAN TWO WORDS** for each answer.

**Advice on doing a journal article search**

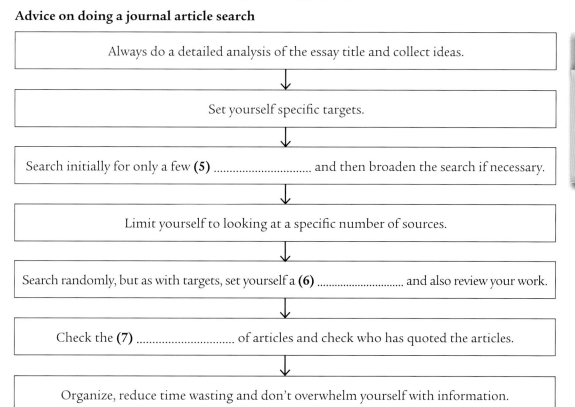

| |
|---|
| Always do a detailed analysis of the essay title and collect ideas. |

↓

| |
|---|
| Set yourself specific targets. |

↓

| |
|---|
| Search initially for only a few **(5)** ............................ and then broaden the search if necessary. |

↓

| |
|---|
| Limit yourself to looking at a specific number of sources. |

↓

| |
|---|
| Search randomly, but as with targets, set yourself a **(6)** ........................... and also review your work. |

↓

| |
|---|
| Check the **(7)** ........................... of articles and check who has quoted the articles. |

↓

| |
|---|
| Organize, reduce time wasting and don't overwhelm yourself with information. |

**Tip**

Check the grammar used in the flow chart. Circle the main information before the spaces to be completed.

**Questions 8–10**

Complete the summary below.
Write **NO MORE THAN TWO WORDS** for each answer.

David's essays may receive **(8)** ........................... , but he feels that he makes work for himself and ends up struggling with the essay after everyone else has finished. Martha thinks that David is good at constructing **(9)** ........................... and usually has very good **(10)** ........................... .

5 Look at your notes in exercise 3. How many of your predictions were correct?

6 Work in groups and discuss these questions.

   1 Is it difficult to change your study/work practices? Give reasons and examples.
   2 Is technology forcing people to study in different ways? If so, how?

## IELTS Speaking Part 3 & Language focus: Prepositions

**1** Complete the extracts below from IELTS Listening Section 3. Then underline the verbs and prepositions.

1 And I think I've just about succeeded ........................................ doing so.
2 But now I'm so used to putting notes and materials ........................................ order as I do it.
3 ... stick ........................................ a narrow range of key terms to search for.
4 No, just aim ........................................ it and ...
5 ... and often seem to be struggling ........................................ the essay when everyone else has finished.

**2** Work in groups. Match the prepositions to the verbs 1–15. Think of an example sentence for at least 5 of the items. Use a dictionary, if necessary.

| in   from   on   with |

| | | |
|---|---|---|
| **0** differ in, from | **6** elaborate | **12** comply |
| **1** specialize | **7** coincide | **13** suffer |
| **2** associate | **8** insist | **14** depend |
| **3** benefit | **9** concern | **15** distinguish |
| **4** result | **10** argue | |
| **5** stem | **11** arise | |

My brother and I differ greatly. He is quiet and calm, and I am very loud.

**3** Complete the sentences using the correct form of the verbs in exercises 1 and 2.

1 Having access to the internet for studying can ........................................ in information overload.
2 To ........................................ in life people need qualifications proving they have the necessary knowledge and skills.
3 A sedentary lifestyle ........................................ with modern illnesses such as obesity and diabetes.

4 Everyone in work can ..................................... from upgrading their professional knowledge.

5 Studying to gain qualifications nowadays ..................................... considerably from the situation 20 years ago.

6 The causes of a problem cannot always ..................................... from the effects.

7 Many social and related problems ..................................... from illiteracy and innumeracy.

8 People generally ..................................... with the constant changes in the modern information age.

9 If universities ..................................... on everyone having a qualification that includes general knowledge, it would help to raise standards.

10 Too many jobs in the modern world ..................................... on gaining knowledge rather than experience.

**4** Work in pairs. Select one claim from exercise 3 and discuss whether it is true or false. Give reasons and examples.

**5** Work alone. Write 50–75 words about the claim you chose. Compare your answer with your partner.

**6** Read the Speaking Part 3 questions below and think how to begin the answer, using the phrase in brackets. Compare your answer with a partner.

**Information and studying**

0 In what way is technology shaping the way students organize and use information to prepare themselves for the modern workplace? (benefit from)

> Students
> nowadays are
> benefitting from having the
> ability to organize and retrieve
> information more easily than previous
> generations of students. And this
> is affecting how they work and
> develop their ideas.

1 Do you think accessing information and knowledge was the same in the past as it is now? In what way(s)? (differ from)

2 How do you think people in the future will acquire information and knowledge? (benefit from)

3 University education is often criticized for teaching knowledge that is irrelevant to the modern world. How far do you agree? (associate with)

**Information overload**

4 What advantages have devices such as mobiles and tablets brought to young people? (result in)

5 With so much information available, is it becoming more difficult for young people to specialize in a particular field? (suffer from)

6 Do people in employment and students suffer from information overload? What are the causes of this development? (stem from)

7 In terms of gaining knowledge, how is the present different from the past for students? (differ from)

**7** Work in groups of three: candidate, examiner and monitor. Take turns to ask and answer at least three questions from exercise 6. Develop the answers in your own way.

Read more about prepositions in the online **Grammar Reference**.

**Additional material: page 104**

## IELTS Writing Task 1

**1** Work in pairs. Describe how you think one of the following is developed. Think of at least 5 stages.

1 a new car   2 a mobile phone app   3 a TV documentary

**2** Complete the following stages in the development of a language app for a mobile phone. Use the words in the box.

| testing | design | refining | uploading | submission |
|---|---|---|---|---|
| approval | conception | production |

1 the ............... of the idea for the app

2 the ............... of a proposal

3 the ............... of the proposal

4 the ............... of the prototype

5 the ............... of the prototype

6 the ............... of the prototype

7 the ............... of the prototype

8 the ............... of the app

9 the sale of the app

**3** Rewrite the stages in exercise 2 using the present simple passive.

1  The idea for the app is conceived.

**4** Work in pairs and compare your answers. Describe what happens at each stage, using exercises 2 and 3 to help you.

**5** Describe the diagram for Writing Task 1 below in your own words.

> You should spend about 20 minutes on this task.
>
> *The diagram below shows how a language app for a mobile phone and tablet is made.*
> *Summarize the information by selecting and reporting the main features, and make comparisons where relevant.*
>
> Write at least at least 150 words.

### Grammar focus

* To form the passive, we use *to be* in the same tense as the active verb + the past participle of the active verb.

*At the next stage, they design the car.* (active)
*At the next stage, the car is designed.* (passive)

* When you describe natural and manufacturing processes, it is common to use the passive voice without an agent. This is because you are only interested in the stages of the process rather than the person or agent who performed the action. If the person or agent is important, you can mention them at the end of the sentence, introduced with *by*.

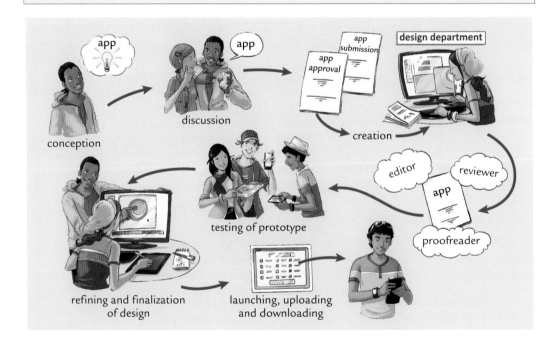

conception

discussion

app submission

app approval

design department

creation

editor

reviewer

app

proofreader

testing of prototype

refining and finalization of design

launching, uploading and downloading

**6** Work in pairs. Discuss how you could complete the text in your own words. Use the diagram in exercise 5 to help you.

The illustration shows the process of producing a language app for mobile phones and tablets. Generally speaking, **(1)** ..................................... : the creation of the concept of the app and its development, the production of a prototype and the launching of the app on the web. **(2)** ..................................... is conceiving the idea for the app.
**(3)** ..................................... , it is discussed with interested parties and a proposal is submitted to the publishing company involved in developing the app. After that,
**(4)** ..................................... where it is approved both conceptually and financially.
**(5)** ..................................... · **(6)** ..................................... , the contents of the app are checked, edited and reviewed. **(7)** ..................................... , which is tested and refined.
**(8)** ..................................... , the last stage is the launching of the app.
**(9)** ..................................... , the app then is sold, downloaded by members of the general public and used.

**7** Complete the text in exercise 6 with a–i.

**a** when the design is finalized
**b** the next stage is the writing of the app itself
**c** the proposal undergoes a process
**d** before being tested electronically
**e** the initial stage in the process

**f** the production process involves three main phases
**g** a prototype is then produced
**h** after being uploaded onto various websites on the internet
**i** once the concept is arrived at

Learn more about Macmillan's new IELTS app.
www.macmillaneducationapps.com

**Additional material: page 105**

**8** Write your own answer for Writing Task 1 below.

You should spend about 20 minutes on this task.

*The diagram below shows how newspapers are recycled.*

*Summarize the information by selecting and reporting the main features, and make comparisons where relevant.*

Write at least at least 150 words.

**Tip**

Remember to use the present simple passive and appropriate linking words such as *when, then, next, where, before, after, as soon as.*

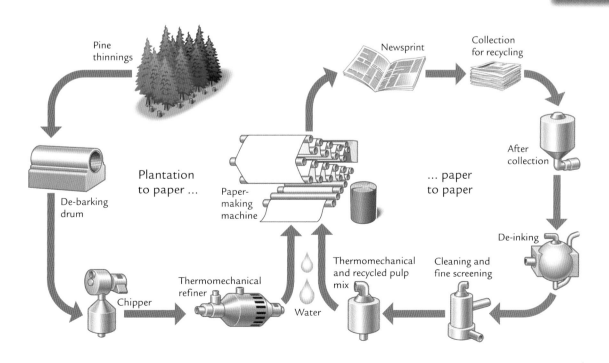

## IELTS Reading

**1** Work in groups and discuss the effect of the following on your life and studies.

- the modern information age
- slow reading
- fast reading
- jumping from one web page to another

**2** Work in pairs. Divide the text into two and select at least 5 words or phrases which your partner can scan for. Then work out the meaning of the words and phrases you chose.

**3** Answer questions 1–13 about the reading passage.

### The art of slow reading

If you're reading this article in print, chances are you'll only get through half of what I've written. And if you're reading this online, you might not even finish a fifth. At least, those are the two verdicts from a pair of recent research projects – respectively, the Poynter Institute's Eyetrack survey, and analysis by Jakob Nielsen – which both suggest that many of us no longer have the concentration to read articles through to their conclusion.

The problem doesn't just stop there: academics report that we are becoming less attentive book-readers, too. Bath Spa University lecturer Greg Garrard recently revealed that he has had to shorten his students' reading list, while Keith Thomas, an Oxford historian, has written that he is bemused by junior colleagues who analyse sources with a search engine, instead of reading them in their entirety.

So are we getting stupider? Is that what this is about? Sort of. According to *The Shallows*, a new book by technology sage Nicholas Carr, our hyperactive online habits are damaging the mental faculties we need to process and understand lengthy textual information. Round-the-clock news feeds leave us hyperlinking from one article to the next – without necessarily engaging fully with any of the content; our reading is frequently interrupted by the ping of the latest email; and we are now absorbing short bursts of words on Twitter and Facebook more regularly than longer texts.

Which all means that although, because of the internet, we have become very good at collecting a wide range of factual titbits, we are also gradually forgetting how to sit back, contemplate, and relate all these facts to each other. And so, as Carr writes, "we're losing our ability to strike a balance between those two very different states of mind. Mentally, we're in perpetual locomotion".

Still reading? You're probably in a dwindling minority. But no matter: a literary revolution is at hand.

First we had slow food, then slow travel. Now, those campaigns are joined by a slow-reading movement – a disparate bunch of academics and intellectuals who want us to take our time while reading, and re-reading. They ask us to switch off our computers every so often and rediscover both the joy of personal engagement with physical texts, and the ability to process them fully.

"If you want the deep experience of a book, if you want to internalise it, to mix an author's ideas with your own and make it a more personal experience, you have to read it slowly," says Ottawa-based John Miedema, author of *Slow Reading* (2009).

But Lancelot R Fletcher, the first present-day author to popularise the term "slow reading", disagrees. He argues that slow reading is not so much about unleashing the reader's creativity, as uncovering the author's. "My intention was to counter postmodernism, to encourage the discovery of authorial content," the American expat explains from his holiday in the Caucasus mountains in eastern Europe.

And while Fletcher used the term initially as an academic tool, slow reading has since become a more wide-ranging concept. Miedema writes on his website that slow reading, like slow food, is now, at root, a localist idea which can help connect a reader to his neighbourhood. "Slow reading," writes Miedema, "is a community event restoring connections between ideas and people. The continuity of relationships through reading is experienced when we borrow books from friends; when we read long stories to our kids until they fall asleep." Meanwhile, though the movement began in academia, Tracy Seeley, an English professor at the University of San Francisco, and the author of a blog about slow reading, feels strongly that slow reading shouldn't "just be the province of the intellectuals. Careful and slow reading, and deep attention, is a challenge for all of us."

But what's clear is that our era's technological diarrhoea is bringing more and more slow readers to the fore. Keith Thomas, the Oxford history professor, is one such reader. He doesn't see himself as part of a wider slow community, but has nevertheless recently written – in the *London Review of Books* – about his bewilderment at the hasty reading techniques in contemporary academia. "I don't think using a search engine to find certain key words in a text is a substitute for reading it properly," he says. "You don't get a proper sense of the work, or understand its context. And there's no serendipity – half the things I've found in my research have come when I've luckily stumbled across something I wasn't expecting."

Some academics vehemently disagree, however. One literature professor, Pierre Bayard, notoriously wrote a book about how readers can form valid opinions about texts they have only skimmed – or even not read at all. "It's possible to have a passionate conversation about a book that one has not read, including, perhaps especially, with someone else who has not read it," he says in *How to Talk About Books that You Haven't Read* (2007), before suggesting that such bluffing is even "at the heart of a creative process".

### Questions 1–5

Complete the summary using the list of words and phrases, **A–J**, below. You may use any letter more than once.

Two recent research projects both suggest a sizeable proportion of the population no longer have the concentration to read articles **(1)** ................................. . Another report suggests that the same applies to reading books, with one lecturer revealing that **(2)** ............................... and another that junior colleagues did **(3)** ............................... using a search engine rather than reading **(4)** ................................. of a document completely. Nicholas Carr suggests that our online habits and constant exposure to news are having an impact on the way we engage with **(5)** ................................. of articles.

| | | |
|---|---|---|
| **A** the whole document | **B** their analysis of sources | **C** reading process |
| **D** to the end | | **F** most of the way through |
| **G** reading lists had to be shortened | **E** shorter books had to be used | |
| | **H** their resources | **I** burst of words |
| | | **J** the contents |

### Questions 6–10

Look at the following statements (questions 6–10) and the list of writers below.

Match each statement with the correct writer(s), **A–D**. You may use any letter more than once.

6  Reading gives readers the opportunity to find things by accident.

7  Slow reading is a way for readers to establish links with the people who live around them.

8  Our ability to gather facts together and then synthesize them is disappearing.

9  Rather than being about releasing the reader's creative ability, slow reading is connected with revealing the writer's.

10  For readers to combine a writer's ideas with their own, slow reading is required.

### List of writers

**A** Keith Thomas    **B** Nicholas Carr    **C** John Mediema    **D** Lancelot Fletcher

### Questions 11–13

Complete the sentences below.

Write **NO MORE THAN TWO WORDS FROM THE PASSAGE** for each answer.

11  Keith Thomas has written about his ............................... at fast reading among academics.

12  According to Pierre Bayard, Readers can have ............................... about things they have only glanced at or not even read.

13  Pierre Bayard also says that pretending to read a book is at the core of a ........................... .

**Tip**

Read the summary and predict what some of the answers might be. The answers are likely to be at the beginning of the text or throughout the whole text. Check to see if there is anything, such as a name, that helps you locate the beginning or the end of the part of the text summarized.

**Tip**

Always read the rubric carefully.

**Tip**

Put a box around the names. This helps you to focus on the relevant part of the text.

# Vocabulary: Verbs related to connections

1 Read these extracts from the reading passage. What is the connection between the ideas in each extract: a) a cause and effect, b) a transformation or c) a link without any cause/effect or transformation?

1 our hyperactive online habits are damaging the mental faculties we need to process ...

2 ... slow reading has since become a more wide-ranging concept.

2 Categorize the verbs below according to whether they relate to a) a change/ transformation, b) a cause/effect relationship or c) a connection without any relationship indicated.

link  translate  connect  associate  transform  affect  develop  correlate  liaise  involve  correspond  belong to  conflict with  match  combine  interfere with  create

3 What is the noun form of each verb in exercise 2?

4 Use 1–6 and a–f to form questions. There may be more than one answer. In pairs, compare your questions and decide what kind of connections the questions are asking about, using a–c in exercise 2.

1 Is the wealth of a country connected with
2 Has education at all levels been transformed by
3 Does knowledge have the power to affect
4 Is there a correlation between
5 Is success in life bound to
6 In what way does being exposed to a wealth of information from all over the word conflict with

a people's lives?
b the accumulation of wealth and the level of education?
c technological expertise?
d the wider availability of knowledge nowadays?
e traditional values?
f the quality of one's education or who one knows?

1 Is the wealth of a country connected with technological expertise?

5 Work in pairs. Prepare answers to three questions from exercise 4, including examples and reasons. Change partners and take turns to ask and answer your questions.

This question is talking about c) a connection without any relationship indicated. There is a link, but no cause and effect relationship is indicated.

6 Write three sentences about your own country, talking about recent changes, what the changes are linked to and the possible causes and effects of the changes. Compare your answers in pairs.

## IELTS Writing Task 2

1 Work in groups. List the similarities and differences between writing tasks A and B below. Compare your answers with another group.

A

You should spend about 40 minutes on this task.

*Over the past few decades, with the help of the internet an unimaginable amount of information has become widely available to the general public.*

*What do you think are the advantages and disadvantages of this development?*

Give reasons for your answer and include any relevant examples from your own knowledge and experience.

Write at least 250 words.

**B** You should spend about 40 minutes on this task.

*Over the past few decades, with the help of the internet an unimaginable amount of information has become widely available to the general public. In what ways has having more information available affected people's lives? Is this a positive or negative development?*

Give reasons for your answer and include any relevant examples from your own knowledge and experience.

Write at least 250 words.

**Tip**

Make sure you analyse Task 2 questions carefully. As you prepare for the exam, practise working out what organization is required for the different question types. Note you will lose marks if you do not complete the task that is set, even if your grammar, vocabulary, accuracy and coherence is very good.

**2** Work in groups. Look at the following ideas, which are sorted into positive and negative. Decide whether they relate to writing task A, B or A and B. Add ideas of your own.

**Positive**
1 useful for students
2 accessible information
3 lots of information available
4 saves time and energy
5 convenient
6 efficient

**Negative**
1 being overwhelmed by information
2 not being able to discriminate between information
3 not having time to check whether the information is true
4 not having time to understand fully
5 not being able to read and examine the information closely
6 difficulty making choices
7 lack of skills at sifting and organizing information

**3** Decide which writing task in exercise 1 the summary below relates to.

1 Introduction stating the focus of your essay:

Recent years have seen/increasing volumes of knowledge/public domain/such a flood of information/impact on people's lives/positively/negatively/but harmful trend

2 Introduce a positive effect: accessible information

3 Introduce a negative effect: being overwhelmed by information

4 Introduce another negative effect: not being able to read and examine the information closely

5 State whether the development is positive or not: some positive/but largely dangerous trend

6 Write a conclusion about positive/negative effects/impact/increasing volumes of knowledge

**4** Write an introduction and conclusion for the summary in exercise 3 using the notes provided, or your own words.

**5** Complete the sentences about information with your own ideas.

1 Having access to information on the internet outside library hours makes life …
2 The availability of knowledge in electronic form nowadays results in …
3 Studying is often associated with …
4 Students and workers alike can suffer from …
5 Studying and writing essays at university depend on …
6 Information overload stems from …
7 If anyone is faced with too much information, …
8 The way information is packaged in software such as apps is …
9 Many libraries and museums around the world are linked to …

**6** Write at least 250 words for writing task B in exercise 1. Use the summary in exercise 3 to help you.

**Writing bank: page 116**

# Review

## Language focus: Prepositions with verbs

**1** Complete the questions with the correct prepositions. Then answer the questions.

1 How does your experience of learning languages differ _____ your parents' generation?
2 Would you like to specialize _____ a particular field at university? If so, what?
3 How have you benefited personally _____ using technology?
4 Has being given the wrong information ever resulted _____ problems for you?
5 Where does your interest in studying English stem _____ ?
6 Does anyone in your family insist _____ a particular career for you?
7 Do you find it difficult complying _____ rules?
8 Do you suffer _____ nerves during oral exams?
9 In your case, does speaking English depend _____ natural ability, hard work, or a bit of both?
10 Do you enjoy arguing _____ controversial subjects in class?

**2** Compare your answers with other students.

## IELTS Writing Task 1

**1** Find examples of 1–10 in the text in exercises 6 and 7 on page 35.

1 complex sentences using conjunctions
2 the use of the passive without an agent
3 the use of the active
4 the order of the steps reversed
5 the use of adverbs to signpost the steps
6 the use of signposts in noun phrases
7 the use of a preposition plus gerund (x2)
8 the use of the present simple tense
9 the overview
10 a paraphrase

**2** Match the verbs in the box to the processes 1–5. You can use the verbs more than once. Then write about the stages of one process using the verbs.

| select   design   include   write   add   apply   pay   upload   monitor |

**1**
preparing an information leaflet on health
select (information), write, ...

**2**
writing a newspaper article

**3**
the creation of a web page

**4**
the carrying out of a research project

**5**
the creation of a garden

1 The selection of information, the writing of the information, ...

**3** Write down the stages involved in recycling a computer. Change the verbs into noun phrases.

The computer is:

dumped/transported to a recycling centre or a factory/various reusable components are removed/the plastic is crushed/it is recycled/components such as metal are reused; or it is renovated/repaired/resold/donated/reused

1  the dumping of the computer, ...

**4** Work in pairs. Choose another process in exercise 1. Make a list of the verbs to describe it, then the stages of the process. Write a brief description of the process.

**5** Compare your answer with other students.

## Vocabulary: Verbs related to connections

**1** Work in pairs. What is the most likely connection between the ideas: a) a cause and effect, b) a transformation or c) a link without any cause/effect or transformation?

1  reliable information/better choice
2  footballers/huge salaries
3  happiness/good health
4  money/people's lives
5  water shortages/human activities
6  technology/the way we read
7  rote learning/good memory

In 1, I think the connection is a). For example, if you have reliable information about a product you want to buy, it will result in a better choice when you go to the shop or buy it online.

**2** Link the ideas in exercise 1 using verbs from page 38.
There may be more than one answer. If so, think of an explanation for the differences in meaning between the alternatives.

1  a) Reliable information about products such as computers results in better choice for consumers.

1  b) Reliable information about products such as computers is associated with better choice for consumers.

In sentence 1a), the relationship between the ideas is one of cause and effect. Sentence 1b) shows that the ideas are linked but does not mention if the relationship is one of cause and effect, or otherwise.

**3** Work in pairs and compare your answers.

**For further practice, go to the Direct to IELTS website for downloadable worksheets.**

# UNIT 4 Leisure and the environment

## Vocabulary: Leisure and entertainment

**1** Work in groups. Describe the photos A–E. Do they represent typical leisure activities among you and your friends and in your country?

**2** Do any of the activities in the photos have an impact on the environment? If so, how?

**3** Answer the questions below using an adjective or noun plus the word *leisure* or *entertainment*. If necessary, use the words in the upside-down box below.

    **0** What do you call time people have for leisure?   leisure time

    **1** What do you call a place where people watch something and enjoy themselves?

    **2** What do you call activities that people pursue in their free time?

    **3** What is the term for a place to which people go to do sport?

    **4** What is the sector of the economy devoted to people's enjoyment called?

    **5** What is the term for entertainment that takes place outside in public places?

    **6** What kind of entertainment is not too heavy or serious?

    **7** What do you call things that you buy for use in the gym or on the beach?

    **8** What kind of amusement is enjoyed by people generally?

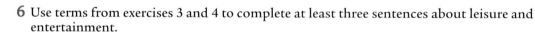

> entertainment industry    light entertainment    entertainment venue
> popular entertainment    ~~leisure time~~    leisure activities/pursuits    leisure goods
> leisure centre    street entertainment

**4** Match a–h to your answers in exercise 3.

    **a** such as weight machines and games  7

    **b** such as musicals rather than operas

    **c** such as a concert hall like Carnegie Hall in New York

    **d** with facilities such as a swimming pool or sports equipment

    **e** like busking or drawing on pavements

    **f** for example, companies making films and putting on plays for profit

    **g** for instance, going to the gym or reading

    **h** like soap operas and game shows on TV

**5** Work in pairs. Give another example for 1–8 in exercise 3.

**6** Use terms from exercises 3 and 4 to complete at least three sentences about leisure and entertainment.

    **0** ... is/are hugely enjoyable because ...

    Light entertainment such as musicals are hugely enjoyable because they are light and do not need much effort.

    **1** ... such as hobbies like ... is/are really relaxing.

    **2** ... bring(s) enjoyment to a lot of people.

    **3** ... increase(s) people's general well-being by ...

    **4** ... provide(s) young people with exciting opportunities ...

    **5** ... such as shopping ...

    **6** ... make(s) free time ...

    **7** ... can make ...

**7** Work in pairs or small groups. Swap your sentences and take turns to ask and answer questions about them.

> Why do you think ...?

> What makes you think ...?

> In what way?

> How?

**Additional material: page 105**

## IELTS Speaking Part 2

**1** Work in pairs. Discuss what you would describe for the task card below.

> Describe a day off from work or study that you remember.
>
> You should say:
>
> where you went
>
> with whom you spent the day
>
> what activities you did
>
> and explain why you remember the day off.

**2** 🎧 **1.6** Listen to a candidate talking about the task card in exercise 1. Write down as much information as you can about the items below and then compare your answer with a partner.

We borrowed bicycles from friends **(1)** ...............................................

When we got tired **(2)** ...............................................

We were able to stop for lunch before going on and it was **(3)** ...............................................

Reasons for remembering the day:

I remember the day well because **(4)** ........................................... and because **(5)** ...............................................

We saw **(6)** ...............................................

**3** Listen again and count the number of times the candidate hesitates. In pairs, discuss the questions below.

   **1** Why is the candidate hesitating?

   **2** Do these hesitations interfere with the fluency and the comprehension of the talk?

   **3** What can be done to reduce hesitations?

**4** Work in pairs. Take turns to talk about the task card in exercise 1.

> **Tip**
>
> Spend one minute writing notes before you speak. Glance at your notes as you talk.

# Language focus: Comparative and superlative adjectives

**1** Read the extracts from IELTS Speaking Part 2. Look at the words in bold. What structures are used?

  **1** It was much **more peaceful** than the city.

  **2** The people on the boats were **friendlier than** the people in the city.

**2** Work in pairs. What are the comparative and superlative forms of the adjectives 1–8?

  **1** easy         **5** poor

  **2** hot          **6** quiet

  **3** effective    **7** bad

  **4** expensive   **8** common

**3** What are the opposites of the adjectives in exercise 2?

  1 difficult

**4** What are the comparative and superlative forms of the adjectives from exercise 3?

  1 more/less difficult, most/least difficult

**5** Make a list of rules for making comparative adjectives using the adjectives in exercises 2, 3 and 4.

  You can add '-er' to adjectives with one syllable to create the comparative form, e.g. quiet → quieter.

**6** Make sentences which reflect your opinion. Use the prompts below and words from the Useful language box to help you.

  **0** urban/rural/peaceful

    I find a rural environment much more peaceful than an urban setting.

  **1** cities/countryside/friendly

  **2** chess/video games/interesting

  **3** days out/long breaks/exciting

  **4** leisure pursuits such as team sports/ activity/thrilling

  **5** outdoor sports/leisure centres/ rewarding

  **6** film/entertaining/ever

  **7** book/activity/boring

  **8** computer skills/crucial/skills/one

  **9** young people/video games/films/ harmful

  **10** active/passive/leisure pursuits/physical well-being/beneficial

**7** Work in groups of three and compare your sentences. Choose one sentence each and discuss the sentences, giving reasons and examples.

 Read more about comparative and superlative adjectives in the online **Grammar Reference**.

## IELTS Speaking Part 3

**1** Work in pairs. Read the questions relating to 'Leisure time' below. Discuss possible answers, giving examples, reasons and purposes. Then take turns to ask and answer the questions.

**Leisure time**

Do you think it's good to have days off during the week? Why/Why not?

In terms of relaxation, is it better to have long or short breaks from work?

What are the benefits of going away for long breaks?

**Time and work**

Which should be more important to people: earning money or having time to spend with friends and family?

People seem to spend more hours at work than in the past. Why do you think this is?

How can work affect people's leisure time?

**2** Change partners and take turns to answer both sets of questions. Give each other feedback about developing the answers using examples, reasons and purposes.

## IELTS Listening Section 4

**1** Work in groups. Use the headings in 1–10 below to predict the contents of the talk.

**2** Decide what type of answer is required for 1–10 below: a noun, an adjective, a noun phrase or a number.

**3** 🎧 **1.7** Listen and answer questions 1–10. Check your answers in pairs and make corrections.

*Questions 1–10*
Complete the notes below.
Write **NO MORE THAN TWO WORDS OR A NUMBER** for each answer.

### LEISURE AND ENTERTAINMENT

**Past predictions**
Making projections: **(1)** ...................................................................
Many past predictions: very odd
All fields including railways and electric light

**Quotes by**
Darryl Zanuck: the inability of **(2)** ................................................. to maintain its market share
Thomas Watson: the lack of a world market for computers
Ken Olson: there was no need for people to have a computer at
**(3)** .....................................................

**Statistics relating to media in the UK and the USA**

Mobile phones – 2002
Number of UK mobile phones per 100 people: **(4)** ...............................................
Comparable figure for the USA: only **(5)** ...........................................

Personal computers – 2004
Noticeable gap in ownership between both countries
UK: **(6)** ............................................... per 1,000 people – ranked 12th
USA: 762.2 per 1,000 ranked **(7)** ...............................................

**Predictions about the future**
Entertainment
The area with the most significant advances in the leisure and entertainment industries:
**(8)** ...............................................
HD television, 3D TVs, more sophisticated sound systems – widely available, cheaper and more attractive to families
Impact: will not lead to a **(9)** ............................................... in cinema attendance
Mobile to take over from credit cards, travel cards, tablets and the
**(10)** ............................................... eventually

**Exam information**

Listening Section 4 is usually a monologue of a talk or a presentation. Sometimes there may be a presenter introducing a speaker. Note there is no break in the middle of the listening test as in the other three listening sections. Also, the content is more formal than the other three sections.

**Tip**

When people give examples when speaking they often use *like, such as, for example, for instance.*

## IELTS Writing Task 1

**1** Work in groups. Discuss which of the situations in the photos is likely to put the most pressure on the environment in the future.

**2** Find three sentences below which do not contain the simple future with will. Decide whether it is possible to rewrite them using the simple future with will, and whether this changes the meaning.

1   Entertainment will become more important in our lives in the future than now.
2   It is expected that the number of tourists will continue to increase.
3   There is a chance that leisure pursuits such as outdoor skiing will have disappeared by the middle of the century.
4   It is forecast that leisure time will decrease as people are forced to work longer.
5   The characters in video games are projected to become almost lifelike in the very near future.
6   In the future, people will be transported to the moon for holidays.
7   The world will have changed dramatically by the end of the century.

**3** Make predictions about the future using these notes. When you have completed the sentences, discuss with a partner whether they surprise you or not.

1   According UN/global population/to between 7.8 and 10.5 billion people/2050
2   Egypt's population/and the populations of Ethiopia/Sudan/the remaining countries/Nile basin/project/double by 2050
3   UK/population/to 73 million/2050/according/Office for National Statistics
4   As urban areas, particularly smaller towns and cities/continue grow/size/about 5 billion people/expect/live/cities/by 2030

**4** Read the writing task below and look at the table. Then complete the sentences.

> *The table below shows the projected demand in hectares for developed land for various purposes in England between 2011 and 2030.*
> *Summarize the information by selecting and reporting the main features, and make comparisons where relevant.*

### Grammar focus

* To form the future simple we use *will/shall* + infinitive without *to*. We use it to express predictions and speculations about the future.

* To form the future continuous we use *will* + *be* + present participle. We use it to describe an action in progress in the future.

* To form the future perfect we use *will/shall* + *have* + past participle. We use it to describe an action that will be completed by a certain time in the future.

Projected demand for land for future development

| | Hectares | | | | |
| --- | --- | --- | --- | --- | --- |
| | 2011 | 2015 | 2020 | 2025 | 2030 |
| **Total Demand for Developed Land** | **5,171** | **6,051** | **5,760** | **5,492** | **5,155** |
| Industrial & Commercial | 582 | 974 | 825 | 791 | 801 |
| Residential | 3,235 | 3,520 | 3,442 | 3,277 | 3,021 |

**Glossary:** Hectare: 10,000 square metres

1 The demand for developed land is expected to peak in 2015 at ....................................... hectares, with ................................... property making up the largest proportion of the land required.

2 By ................................... , it is estimated that 801 hectares will be required for ................................... purposes, while for residential purposes the proportion of land is expected to be considerably larger at ................................... hectares, which is approximately two-thirds of the total demand for developed land.

3 The table shows how much land will be needed for future ................................... and ................................... construction on land that is already in use between 2011 and 2030.

4 By ................................... , the demand for land for ................................... and ................................... purposes will have risen to 3,277 and 791 hectares respectively.

5 Overall, it is clear that the greatest demand for developed land comes from ................................... property.

6 The demand for developed land from the industrial and commercial sector is expected to hit a peak in 2015 at ................................... hectares, before falling back again.

5 Work in pairs. Answer the questions about the statements in exercise 3 and the table.

1 Which sentence provides an overview of the data?

2 Which sentence can be used as an introduction?

3 What synonyms of the word *project(ed)* are used in the sentences? What other synonyms do you know?

4 Which tenses are used in the sentences? Which sentence contains an example of the future perfect? Why is it used?

5 Which sentence contains the longest noun phrase and what is it?

6 Which sentences contain comparisons?

7 In which sentence is there more than one clause?

6 Write your answer for Writing Task 1 below.

> You should spend about 20 minutes on this task.
>
> *The table below shows the projected demand in hectares for undeveloped land for various purposes in England between 2011 and 2030.*
> *Summarize the information by selecting and reporting the main features, and make comparisons where relevant.*
>
> Write at least 150 words.

Projected demand for land for future development

| | Hectares | | | | |
|---|---|---|---|---|---|
| | 2011 | 2015 | 2020 | 2025 | 2030 |
| **Total Demand for Undeveloped Land** | 4,450 | 5,218 | 4,960 | 4,751 | 4,481 |
| Industrial & Commercial | 330 | 702 | 576 | 545 | 549 |
| Residential | 2,191 | 2,373 | 2,313 | 2,206 | 2,030 |
| Transport & Utilities | 911 | 1,084 | 1,024 | 977 | 916 |
| Community Services | 485 | 526 | 514 | 491 | 452 |

## IELTS Reading

**1** Work in groups. Read the title of the reading passage and look at the photo. Decide what the topic of the passage is.

**2** Discuss the questions.

  **1** What is the impact of people doing recreational activities in the snow in mountainous regions? Consider:

  - plant life/vegetation
  - animals
  - taking plants, etc. as souvenirs
  - rubbish
  - overuse of certain areas
  - noisy machines

  **2** What steps can tour operators and individuals take to reduce this impact?

**3** In which part of the text you would expect to find the solutions to a problem: the beginning, middle or end? Why?

**4** Answer questions 1–13 about the reading passage.

### The impact of snow-dependent recreational activities

While many of the good environmental practices for promoting sustainable mountain tourism involve avoiding or minimizing negative impacts to ecosystems, tour operators can also go beyond simply reducing negative impacts and seek opportunities to benefit biodiversity and nature conservation efforts by contributing to improving the state of the environment at a local, regional or national level. Such actions can be particularly important in countries or regions where capacity and resources for environmental conservation may be limited.

Snow-dependent recreational activities include cross-country, downhill and glacier skiing, heli-skiing, snow scootering, snowboarding, tobogganing, snowshoe walking and sledding.

The mountain areas that support these activities often contain the most fragile ecosystems, with many unique species requiring specific environmental conditions and relying on sparse habitat and food sources. Even small changes in landscape contours, vegetation coverage and distribution, natural water flows, or soil, air and water quality can have significant effects on habitat, wildlife and species diversity.

In the highest mountain ecosystems, snow cover protects the vegetation below it to some extent. However, repeated, harsh or intensive use of the same areas or areas with minimal snow cover can easily damage the sensitive vegetation beneath, inhibiting growth and recovery in already short growing seasons. Such areas are also vulnerable to soil compaction, which makes surfaces more impermeable and creates greater surface water runoff, leading to erosion and inhibiting vegetation growth. Watercourses may be modified through the creation of channels from repeated sledding, skiing and use of snow transport vehicles and the development of artificial slopes. Excessive water use for snow making machines can also alter natural water flows.

Heavy use can reduce habitat and food sources for local fauna, and cause wildlife to relocate. Animals are also likely to relocate away from areas adjacent to snow-based activities, as they are loud, abrupt and involve fast movements. Species may also be affected by predation or competition through the introduction of exotic flora or fauna species carried on equipment, clothing, transport vehicles or sled animals.

Poorly positioned artificially created slopes (for downhill skiing in particular) and associated infrastructure often involve the clearing of large areas of already sparsely distributed vegetation. Many alpine ecosystems are small and concentrated in particular geographic areas, and this clearing can easily lead to significant reductions in biodiversity and habitat, as well as remove natural barriers and protection from avalanches. Land-clearing for associated tourism infrastructure such as lodges, accommodation, restaurants and entertainment also contributes to the problem.

There are many reasons why tour operators should care about the mountain environment. The high concentration and number of visitors and levels of noise and activity that often result from snow-based activities and infrastructure can detract from the natural landscape, serenity, seclusion and "wildness" of mountain areas that attract many visitors to these areas. Secondly, low-pollution and trash-free environments are more attractive to all visitors and higher levels of vegetative cover will protect habitats, improve the visual attractiveness of areas, and increase natural protection against avalanches. Likewise, the loss or relocation of flora and fauna as a result of the effects of snow-based activities will reduce the opportunity for all visitors to see and experience mountain wildlife.

Tour operators can take a range of steps to lessen the impact of tourists on the mountain environment. For example, to help preserve the environment the use of motorized transport should be minimized and sharing transport vehicles and infrastructure with other tour operators or accommodation providers should also be considered. It is also possible for accommodation and transport providers to demonstrate good energy, waste and water practices (particularly for snow making). To prevent contamination, all trash where possible could be taken away with the travellers and sled animals, and equipment and clothing kept free of seeds and other exotic organisms. On its ski-mountaineering trips across South Georgia Island, for example, Geographic Expeditions requires that all waste be carried out in heavy-duty plastic bags on sleds and disposed of on the ships that support the expedition.

To maintain tour business revenue and viability, operators may need to consider decreasing their dependence on snow-based activities and diversifying tours to include non-snow-based nature and adventure activities. High-quality and unique mountain landscapes, flora and fauna are a direct asset for the development of such nature-based activities. They also support the well-being and lifestyle of local communities. Nature-based and cultural activities can supplement and diversify tour products and can provide revenue all year around.

*Questions 1–5*

Choose the correct letter, **A**, **B**, **C** or **D**.

1 According to the writer, tour operators

**A** already try to lessen the impact of tourism.

**B** make no attempts to reduce the impact of tourism.

**C** make only a few attempts protect the environment.

**D** try to hide the impact of their business on the environment.

2 Why are environmental improvements by tour operators beneficial?

**A** They provide much needed financial support for development.

**B** They help areas without sufficient means to protect the environment.

**C** They increase state revenues to fund employment projects.

**D** They help with the management and exploitation of natural resources.

3 Leisure pursuits that rely on snow

**A** contain the most interesting plant species.

**B** use special machines to protect local habitats.

**C** use up the food resources of local communities.

**D** frequently expose ecosystems to harm.

4 Which of these statements is true about any alteration in the local environment?

**A** Vegetation loss affects natural water flows.

**B** The area recovers quickly from any activity.

**C** The influence on the area is considerable.

**D** The impact on the vegetation is minimal.

5 According to the writer, snow at the highest altitudes

**A** can safeguard all of the plant life under it completely.

**B** damages most of the plant life below it.

**C** provides plant life underneath it with some protection.

**D** has a destructive impact on the local ecosystem.

*Questions 6–8*

Complete the sentences below.

Choose **NO MORE THAN THREE WORDS** from the passage for each answer.

6 The over-production of artificial snow can change ............................. .

7 Snow-based activities can drive ............................. away from their normal habitat.

8 The creation of artificial slopes can result in a fall in ............................. and ............................. .

*Questions 9–13*

Complete each sentence with the correct ending, **A–H**, below.

9 Tourists are attracted to

10 The impact of tourism can be reduced by

11 Geographic Expeditions ensures

12 Diversification may be needed for

13 Nature-based and cultural activities bring in

**A** an income throughout the year.

**B** the mountain environment's natural state.

**C** the excitement of dangerous ski slopes.

**D** a constant flow of research.

**E** the pooling of resources.

**F** the protection of the tourism business.

**G** richer types of tourists.

**H** the removal of all rubbish.

5 Before you check your answers, discuss them in pairs. If you disagree, check the evidence in the text. Then compare your answers with other students.

### IELTS Writing Task 2

**1** Read the extract from the reading passage. Which part of the sentence expresses a purpose? What other structures can be used to express purpose?

To maintain tour business revenue and viability, operators may need to consider decreasing their dependence on snow-based activities and diversifying tours to include non-snow-based nature and adventure activities.

**2** Work in pairs. Decide what the purpose of the following leisure pursuits is. Add other possible pursuits.

1 playing board games
2 watching TV
3 going on holidays
4 playing team sports
5 going to concerts
6 going hill walking
7 reading
8 socializing
9 playing video games

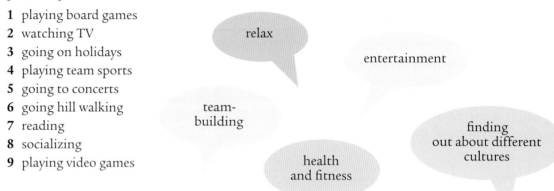

relax

entertainment

team-building

finding out about different cultures

health and fitness

**3** Work in pairs. Decide which statements contain a purpose and underline the word(s) that introduce(s) the purpose.

1 The government needs to subsidize leisure centres so that people will be encouraged to adopt a more active lifestyle.
2 Chess is a useful activity for elderly people as it helps them to keep mentally active.
3 To bring performances such as plays and musical concerts to a wider public, they should be supported financially by the government.
4 People, especially young people, should be educated about the benefits of sport in order to help promote fitness and reduce health costs.
5 Free access to gyms could be made available to the public for a period of time such as a week or a month so as to attract people to such facilities.
6 People can be encouraged to relax by listening to music.
7 Promoting involvement in out-of-school games is beneficial for young people.
8 Tourists travel abroad to have a break and relax.
9 Leisure breaks should be taxed to discourage overuse of air travel.
10 People often participate in evening classes such as drama and music classes in order to meet new friends as well as to learn something.

**4** Discuss Writing Task 2 at the top of page 51. Answer the following questions.

1 What is the main purpose of subsidizing entertainment and leisure facilities?
2 Are there other purposes? If so, what are they?
3 Is using subsidies in this way beneficial? How? To whom? Give reasons and examples.
4 How could such subsidies be harmful?
5 Could other methods be used to achieve the purposes mentioned in 1 and 2 above? If so, what? Give reasons and examples.
6 What is the impact of not subsidizing entertainment and leisure facilities?
7 Could the money be better spent on other areas? If so, how?
8 To what extent do you agree with the statement in the task?

You should spend about 40 minutes on this task.

Write about the following topic:

***Entertainment or leisure activities should be subsidized by the government.***
***To what extent do you agree or disagree?***

Give reasons for your answer and include any relevant examples from your own knowledge and experience.

Write at least 250 words.

**5** Write an introduction for the writing task in exercise 4 using the items below or your own ideas. Then write three topic sentences to begin the three main body paragraphs of the answer.

supporting activities such as entertainment and leisure pursuits

using public money

wasteful

I accept ...

financial help

lead to

a lack of appreciation of the facilities provided

clearly

many benefits

financial subsidies

> ### Tip
>
> A topic sentence summarizes the main idea of a paragraph. Use a topic sentence at the beginning of a paragraph to show what the paragraph is about. Then use examples and reasons to support your topic sentence.

**6** Work in pairs. Give reasons and examples for each topic sentence in exercise 5. Compare your answers with other students.

**7** Write an answer for Writing Task 2 below.

You should spend about 40 minutes on this task.

Write about the following topic:

***Some people think that the latest technology for home entertainment such as sophisticated TVs, high-speed internet connections and tablets are having a negative impact on people's lives, especially young people.***
***To what extent do you agree or disagree?***

Write at least 250 words.

**8** Select at least three of the items below to check in your answer. Compare your answer in pairs.

- clear purpose
- clear opinion
- examples
- reasons
- organization

**Writing bank: page 118**

# Review

## Vocabulary: Leisure and entertainment

**1** Work in pairs. Think of a purpose you associate with each photo.

**2** Match each photo to as many of the purposes 1–8 as possible. Compare and discuss your answers with other students.

**1** to enjoy themselves

**2** to meet new friends

**3** so that they can learn something

**4** to improve the quality of their lives

**5** to keep themselves physically and mentally fit

**6** to improve people's general health

**7** to promote well-being

**8** to relax

A: 1, 2, 4, 5, 6, 7, 8

## Language focus: Comparative and superlative adjectives

**1** Write down three activities you have done in the past week. Match each activity to as many adjectives in the box as possible. Then write a sentence comparing the activity with the previous week or month.

| long | delicious | good | boring | heavy | happy | cheap |
|---|---|---|---|---|---|---|
| expensive | enjoyable | interesting | friendly | slow | | |

Things I have done in the past week

1 cooked a meal (delicious, cheap)

2 went window-shopping (happy, cheap, enjoyable)

3 Skyped my brother in New Zealand (happy, slow)

**1** Last week I cooked a delicious meal for my parents. It was much cheaper than the meal I prepared for them last month – I bought that from a takeaway!

**2** Compare your activities with at least one other student.

## IELTS Speaking Part 3

**1** Work in groups. Prepare at least three questions about topics 1–4. Use the prompts below.

Do you think ... ?
In terms of ... , do you think ... ?
Some people think that ... What is your opinion?
Why do you think ... ?
How does/do ... ?
What are the main (benefits/effects/causes) ... ?
What is the main purpose of ... ?

1 the effect of leisure activities on people's health
2 the subsidizing of recreation and leisure by the government
3 the need for more open spaces for recreation in cities
4 a comparison between the need for time and the need for money

**2** Work with a student from another group. Take turns to ask and answer your questions.

## IELTS Writing Task 1

**1** Work in pairs. Look at the table and write one sentence for each age group and 'All ages'.

Projected population by age 2010–2035, United Kingdom

Thousands

| Age group | 2010 | 2011 | 2016 | 2021 | 2026 | 2031 | 2035 |
|---|---|---|---|---|---|---|---|
| 0–14 | 10,872 | 10,958 | 11,674 | 12,324 | 12,448 | 12,234 | 12,117 |
| 15–29 | 12,471 | 12,535 | 12,527 | 12,097 | 12,276 | 12,985 | 13,543 |
| 30–44 | 12,725 | 12,645 | 12,595 | 13,411 | 14,092 | 14,013 | 13,664 |
| 45–59 | 12,126 | 12,323 | 13,152 | 13,050 | 12,436 | 12,391 | 12,986 |
| 60–74 | 9,163 | 9,285 | 9,853 | 10,472 | 11,121 | 11,940 | 11,981 |
| 75 & over | 4,905 | 4,990 | 5,470 | 6,282 | 7,446 | 8,202 | 8,918 |
| **All ages** | **62,262** | **62,735** | **65,271** | **67,636** | **69,820** | **71,766** | **73,208** |

It is predicted that the 0–14 age group will increase in size from 10.872 million in 2010 to 12.117 million in 2035.

**2** Work in groups. Discuss the impact of the population increase on one or more of the following.

- the environment
- people's personal space
- stress levels
- pollution
- food and water
- open spaces for recreation and leisure

**For further practice, go to the Direct to IELTS website for downloadable worksheets.**

# Unit 5 A healthy world

## Vocabulary: Collocations related to health

**1** Work in groups. Describe the photos and explain how they are all connected with health.

**Exam information**

IELTS Speaking Part 1 lasts 4–5 minutes. The candidate and examiner introduce themselves and the candidate's name is checked. The examiner then asks questions about the candidate's family, home, work, hobbies and a wide range of topics of general interest. You are not expected to give long detailed answers in this part as there isn't enough time.

**2** Discuss and then answer two or more of the IELTS Speaking Part 1 questions below.

   **1** Do you try to maintain a healthy lifestyle? How? Why?

   **2** Is it difficult to try to keep healthy? Why?

   **3** What is the main purpose of keeping healthy?

   **4** Is there anything that you do which you think is not healthy? If so, what?

   **5** What could you do to be healthier?

**3** Decide whether the words in the box are nouns, verbs or adjectives and then use them to complete the sentences. Check your answers with a partner.

| service | care | financed | eating | way | education | lifestyle |
| --- | --- | --- | --- | --- | --- | --- |
| | | economic | | expenditure | public | |

**1** Healthy ..................................... is one factor involved in maintaining a healthy ..................................... of living.

**2** Health ..................................... needs to take place at an early age, in fact, as early as primary school.

**3** To promote a healthy ..................................... , fatty foods should be banned in schools and work canteens.

**4** The cost of health ..................................... systems is increasing around the world.

**5** Running a health ..................................... absorbs considerable funds in many countries, but it is worthwhile expenditure.

**6** The ..................................... health of a country depends on human resources as much as material wealth such as oil and minerals.

**7** Should healthcare systems be ..................................... by the public or by the private sector?

**8** The health ..................................... in some countries far exceeds that in other countries.

**9** ..................................... health is concerned with the well-being of the general population.

**4** Decide whether you agree or disagree with statements 1–5.

   **1** It is better to focus health spending on curing illnesses than on prevention.

   **2** A lot of things in the modern world such as different types of technology harm us as much as help us.

   **3** Trying to keep healthy requires a lot of time and money.

   **4** The modern world encourages people to be lazy.

   **5** Doctors and nurses deserve to be paid more than celebrities such as footballers and film stars.

**5** Work in groups of three. Each choose one statement from exercise 4 and lead a discussion about the statement.

## IELTS Speaking Part 2

**1** Work in pairs. Choose and then rank the three healthiest activities in the list below. You may also add activities of your own. Consider whether any of the activities could also be unhealthy.

   **1** jogging on a regular basis

   **2** swimming every day

   **3** going to the gym daily

   **4** doing volunteer work

   **5** walking every day

   **6** using the Wii

   **7** skateboarding

   **8** cycling

**2** Compare your answers with another pair of students. Give at least one reason why you consider each activity to be healthy.

**3** Spend one minute making notes for one of the task cards below.

**A**

> Describe a leisure activity you do which you consider to be healthy.
>
> You should say:
>
>    what the leisure activity is
>
>    when and where you do the leisure activity
>
>    who you do the leisure activity with
>
> and explain why you consider the leisure activity to be healthy.

**B**

> Describe a leisure activity you do or you used to do which you consider to be unhealthy.
>
> You should say:
>
>    what the leisure activity is
>
>    when and where you did the leisure activity
>
>    who you did the leisure activity with
>
> and explain why you consider the leisure activity to be unhealthy.

### Tip

Keep your notes to a maximum of 12 words. Use individual nouns, verbs, adjectives and adverbs, as they are easier to think about than phrases. Decide what is the best way to organize your notes so you can glance at them easily while speaking.

**4** Compare your notes and your organizational strategy with a student who chose the same card. Take turns to talk about the card for two minutes. Give feedback on your partner's reasons and the organization of the answer.

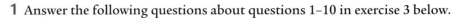

## IELTS Listening Section 1

**1** Answer the following questions about questions 1–10 in exercise 3 below.

   **1** What does the example tell you about the subject of Listening Section 1?

   **2** Are there other references to this in the other questions?

   **3** What do you think the caller was asked in question 1?

   **4** Who do you think gives the information in question 2?

   **5** What do you think is the most likely answer for question 3, considering volunteers will be new to the organization?

**2** Work in pairs and compare your answers. Then ask each other questions about questions 4–6.

**3**  **1.8** Listen and answer questions 1–10.

*Questions 1–3*
Choose the correct letter, **A**, **B** or **C**.

**0** What does the caller want to talk about?

   **Ⓐ** an advert for volunteers

   **B** the travel expenses for volunteers

   **C** the location of the offices

**1** The caller saw the advert

   **A** on a website.

   **B** in the local paper.

   **C** in a shop window.

**2** How many volunteer programmes are there?

   **A** three

   **B** four

   **C** five

**3** The first volunteer scheme involves

   **A** dealing with telephone enquiries.

   **B** answering members' letters.

   **C** keeping a database up-to-date.

*Questions 4–6*
Answer the questions below.
Write **NO MORE THAN TWO WORDS AND/OR A NUMBER** for each answer.

**4** What do volunteers help raise in scheme two?

**5** What can volunteers do for old people in scheme three?

**6** What do volunteers not deal with?

*Questions 7–10*
Complete the sentences below.
Write **NO MORE THAN TWO WORDS** for each answer.

Application process

   **7** With the application, a CV and the names of ............................... are needed.

   **8** Volunteers have an induction course which lasts a ............................... .

   **9** The application can be completed and submitted ............................... .

   **10** The minimum volunteering hours per week is ............................... .

## Reaction

**4** Work in groups. Is volunteering a good thing to do? Why/Why not? What other types of volunteering can you do?

*You can volunteer to help the environment, ...*

# Language focus: Degrees of certainty & IELTS Speaking Part 3

**1** 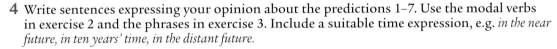 **1.9** Listen to a student answering a question about health in the future and answer the questions.

    **1** What is the examiner's first question?

    **2** Is the candidate sure about the near and distant future? How does the candidate show this?

    **3** What is the examiner's second question?

    **4** Does the candidate express his prediction about the future?

**2** Decide whether the sentences express necessity/lack of necessity, (weak) possibility, probability, certainty or impossibility.

    **0** The world might be free of stress in the future. **weak possibility**

    **1** It's likely that children will be encouraged to do more exercise at school in future.

    **2** Too many adverts about food on TV may be harmful to people's health.

    **3** Governments need to invest more money in healthcare.

    **4** In 50 years' time, food shortages should be a thing of the past.

    **5** In future, the world could be more worried about the lack of clean water than oil.

    **6** Cities will definitely be more overcrowded than now at the end of the century.

    **7** It will be impossible for people to become ill in the near future.

    **8** In the distant future, people will not need to work.

    **9** Working less can reduce stress and make people happier.

**3** Where possible, rewrite the sentences in exercise 2 using the phrases in the box. There may be more than one answer.

> It is possible that ... will   it will be possible for   it will be impossible for
> it is likely/unlikely/probable/certain that ... will
> it won't be necessary for

**4** Write sentences expressing your opinion about the predictions 1–7. Use the modal verbs in exercise 2 and the phrases in exercise 3. Include a suitable time expression, e.g. *in the near future, in ten years' time, in the distant future.*

    **1** Robots will look after children and old people.

    **2** Machines will replace doctors and nurses.

    **3** All medicines will be free.

    **4** People will no longer work.

    **5** We will live in a stress-free world.

    **6** People will live twice as long as today.

    **7** Machines will repair people's bodies in their homes.

**5** Think of one idea for each question below.

**Diet and exercise**

Do you think people worry too much about diet and exercise nowadays? Why/Why not?

Some people think that each individual has a responsibility to look after his/her health. How far do you agree?

How can people be encouraged to take more exercise?

**Technology and health**

How do you think technology will improve our standard of living in the future?

In the future, do you think it's likely that technology will replace doctors and nurses?

Do you think it's dangerous to rely on machines in areas such as health? Why/Why not?

**6** Work in groups of three and compare your ideas. Take turns to ask and answer the questions in exercise 5. Use modal verbs and phrases to express certainty.

 Read more about degrees of certainty in the Grammar Reference.

## IELTS Writing Task 2

**1** Work in pairs and read the writing tasks A–C. Decide which one

    **1** asks you to give your opinion about a statement.

    **2** asks you to choose between two alternatives.

    **3** presents you with two views and asks you to discuss both of them and give your own opinion.

**A** Some people think that healthcare should be free for everyone and that it should not depend on people's ability to pay.

To what extent do you agree or disagree?

**B** Some people feel that healthcare provision should be free, while others believe that healthcare should be paid for by the individual.

Discuss both views and give your own opinion.

**C** Some people think that the healthcare system should focus on curing disease and illnesses. Others believe that the true function of a healthcare system should be to prevent diseases and illnesses through health education and preventive measures.

What, in your opinion, should be the main function of a healthcare system?

**2** Reasons 1–8 relate to task A in exercise 1. Categorize the evaluations as positive or negative. Do you agree with the evaluations? Why/Why not?

| Reasons | Evaluations |
| --- | --- |
| **0** impact on other services | damaging/harmful **negative** |
| **1** cost of providing such a service | prohibitive/impossible |
| **2** basic human right | essential/valid/crucial/achievable |
| **3** investment in people | economical/effective/highly desirable |
| **4** cost of medicine | impossible/extravagant/too expensive |
| **5** correlation between health/prosperity | productive/sensible/integral |
| **6** open to abuse | wasteful/uneconomical |
| **7** not taken seriously | wasteful/inefficient |
| **8** healthy population | valuable/invaluable/an asset |

**3** Answer the questions using the ideas and evaluations in exercise 2.

> I agree that free healthcare could have a damaging impact on other services. For example, if too much is spent on health, there might not be enough money for education or for the police service.

    **0** In what way can you evaluate the idea of free healthcare?

      Free healthcare is highly desirable.

    **1** How *worthwhile, possible, (un)desirable*, etc. is it? (very/highly/extremely)

    **2** Why is it worthwhile, possible, (un)desirable, etc.?

    **3** What is the purpose of free healthcare/not having free healthcare?

    **4** What example(s) can you give to justify your answer?

    **5** Do you have you any doubts/reservations about free healthcare? If so, what?

    **6** What is your conclusion about free healthcare?

**4** Compare your answers in pairs.

**5** Discuss how far the plan at the top of page 59 matches the questions in exercise 3. Add any other possible linking devices to the plan.

**Plan**

| Organization | Ideas | Linking devices |
|---|---|---|
| **1 Topic** | free healthcare = essential/basic human right | because/as/since/the reason for this is |
| **2 Reason** | no discrimination rich/poor = equality | because/as/since/the reason for this is |
| **3 Purpose** | providing free healthcare makes general population healthy | to/in order to/so that/so as to |
| **4 Example** | not suffering because of lack of money, productive/prosperous | for example |
| **5 Result** | healthy society = physically/socially productive, generate wealth, pay for healthcare | as a result |
| **6 Reservation** | increasing costs | may not always/however |
| **7 Conclusion** | still fundamental right | yet/nevertheless |

**6** Write a sentence for each item in the plan in exercise 5. Add ideas and any specific examples where appropriate, using *such as, like, for instance.*

1   There is no doubt that free healthcare is essential because it is a basic human right, just like education.

**7** Compare your sentences with the rest of the class.

**8** Write an answer for Writing Task 2 below.

> You should spend about 40 minutes on this task.
>
> *Some people think that the main influence on young people's diet is advertising rather than family and friends.*
>
> *To what extent do you agree or disagree?*
>
> Give reasons for your answer and include any relevant examples from your own knowledge and experience.
>
> Write at least 250 words.

**9** Work in pairs. Swap your answers and underline the adjectives of evaluation in your partner's answer.

**Additional material: page 106**

**Writing bank: page 118**

## IELTS Reading

**1** Work in groups and discuss the statements 1–3.

**1** Adding electronic devices or gadgets to our bodies is dangerous.

**2** Technology has always caused problems and we never learn from our mistakes.

**3** Any gadget or device which improves healthcare is beneficial.

**2** Find words in the reading passage that mean the same as 1–6.

**1** devices (paragraph A)       **4** parts (Paragraph F)

**2** available (paragraph B)     **5** likely (Paragraph G)

**3** combining (paragraph C)     **6** follow (Paragraph J)

**3** Answer questions 1–13 about the reading passage.

**'Electronic Tattoos'**

**'Electronic Skin' attaches Gadgets to Body**

**A** He may have had a laser in his watch and a radio in his lighter, but even James Bond didn't sport gadgets tattooed to his skin. Now he could, thanks to the development of ultrathin electronics that can be placed on the skin as easily as a temporary tattoo. The researchers hope the new devices will pave the way for sensors that monitor heart and brain activity without bulky equipment, or perhaps computers that operate via the subtlest voice commands or body movement.

**B** Stretchy and bendy electronics have been around for a few years. One approach is to write circuits onto materials that are already flexible, such as ink on paper, so gadgets can be folded and put away. Another is to make the circuits themselves flexible. In 2008, for example, engineers at the University of Tokyo created a conductive material that looked a bit like a fishnet stocking. Made of carbon nanotubes and rubber, it could stretch by more than a third of its natural length, possibly enough to make robots become more agile.

**C** The problem with these past attempts, says materials scientist John Rogers of the University of Illinois, Urbana-Champaign, is that none of them has been as stretchy and as bendy as human skin. That's a shame, because scientists have had grand visions for integrating the skin with electronics, from medical sensors to music players or cell phones that you can literally wear on your arm.

**D** Now, Rogers and his colleagues at Urbana-Champaign and other institutions in the United States, Singapore, and China have come up with a form of electronics that almost precisely matches skin's mechanical properties. Known as epidermal electronics, they can be applied in a similar way to a temporary tattoo: you simply place it on your skin and rub it on with water. The devices can even be hidden under actual temporary tattoos to keep the electronics concealed.

**E** "The skin represents one of the most natural places to integrate electronics," says Rogers, whose group's paper appears online today in *Science*. "As the largest organ in our body, and our primary sensory mode of interaction with the world, it plays a special role."

**F** The new technology is the product of advances in several areas. One is in the active circuit components—transistors, diodes, and other inherently stiff semiconductors—which Rogers's group has flattened and shrunk to the size of the tiniest bumps and wrinkles on the skin. Another is in the material on which these components are arranged: a sheet of rubbery "elastomer" that mimics the mass, thickness, and elasticity of the skin. Like an extra-clingy plastic wrap, the elastomer sticks to the skin naturally, using only the weak, short-range, attractive forces that always exist between neighboring molecules for adhesion. It can stay attached for over 24 hours almost anywhere on the body.

**G** The third important ingredient is the circuit's arrangement. Place the components and wires too close and they will stiffen the device, making it liable to tear. So Rogers's group uses a computer program to predict all the stresses and strains that arise with different designs and then picks the one that keeps elasticity at a maximum.

**H** In one experiment, the group applied a device the size of a postage stamp to a person's chest to pick up the electrical signals produced by the heart. The measurements agreed "remarkably well" with those produced by a hospital electrocardiogram, the researchers say, without relying on potentially uncomfortable gels or tape. In another

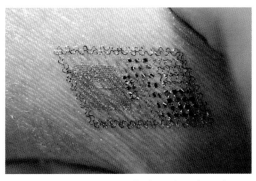

Electronic tattoo. Wearing high-tech gadgets has never been so easy, thanks to the latest advance in bendy electronics.

experiment, the group applied a device containing a microphone to a person's throat and fed the signal to a computer. The computer could recognize four different words: "up," "down," "left," and "right." This technology could eventually help people with some disabilities control computers, the researchers say.

I  Physicist Siegfried Bauer of Johannes Kepler University in Linz, Austria, agrees that epidermal electronics have important medical applications. However, he notes that the technology needs to be tested with a range of skin conditions, from dry to sweaty. "Circuits must allow for transpiration and breathing," he says.

J  Rogers and his colleagues have separately demonstrated that they can add other useful features to epidermal electronics. Solar cells could one day power the devices without an external source; meanwhile, signals recorded by the devices could be transmitted to a base station wirelessly with antennas. In the long term, Rogers believes the technology could provide an electronic link to the body's most subtle processes, including the movement of enzymes and antibodies, to track the path of disease. "Ultimately, we think that [our] efforts can blur the distinction between electronics and biology," he says.

## Questions 1–6

The reading passage has ten paragraphs, A–J.

Which paragraph contains the following information?

1  various potential uses of epidermal electronics with future additions

2  examples of trials on epidermal electronic devices

3  a criticism of early examples of electronic gadgets

4  the function of human skin

5  the possibility of light health sensors

6  how epidermal electronic gadgets can be covered up

## Questions 7–10

Classify the following statements as referring to

 A  circuit components      B  elastomer      C  circuit arrangement

7  It can be used on any part of the skin.

8  The size has been reduced to match the structure of the skin.

9  The maximum elasticity is maintained.

10  Little force is needed to ensure adhesion to the skin.

## Questions 11–13

Do the following statements agree with the information given in the reading passage? Write:

**TRUE**        *if the statement agrees with the information*

**FALSE**        *if the statement contradicts the information*

**NOT GIVEN**   *if there is no information on this*

11  Siegfried Bauer doubts whether skin electronics have any useful function to perform in the medical field.

12  Solar cells are a possible energy source for the devices in the future.

13  Rogers plans to conduct further research into the relationship between biology and electronics.

## Reaction

4 Work in pairs. Discuss whether you think the devices described in the reading passage have potential for use in the future, inside and outside the medical field.

## IELTS Writing Task 1

**Tip**

As you prepare for IELTS Writing Task 1, number the points on the chart you want to write about. You can also write verbs or phrases on the chart. You can practise writing overviews by covering the data and making general notes about what you remember. Then use the notes to write an overview. In the exam, you should spend about 1–2 minutes looking at the data and quickly numbering what you are going to write about.

**1** Study Writing Task 1 below and locate information related to the following in the chart.

   **1** the main difference between the boys and the girls

   **2** the main similarity between each age group in boys and girls

   **3** the trend related to age for each year in boys and girls

   **4** the trend related to years in both age groups

   **5** the highest consumption in girls and boys

You should spend about 20 minutes on this task.

*The bar chart below shows the average proportion of children in EU countries reporting daily fruit consumption.*

*Summarize the information by selecting and reporting the main features, and make comparisons where relevant.*

Write at least 150 words.

Average proportion of children in EU countries reporting daily fruit consumption, 2001–02 and 2005–06

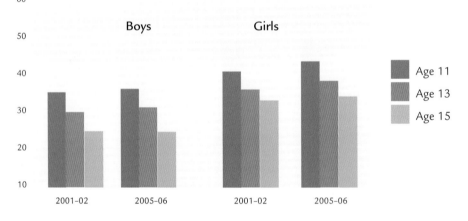

**2** Work in pairs and compare your answers.

**3** Match a–e to 1–5 in exercise 1.

   **a** Among boys and girls alike for both years, the younger children are, the more fruit they eat.

   **b** While the consumption of fruit barely rose among boys between both years, for girls it was most marked among 11-year-olds.

   **c** The highest consumption of fruit among girls was in those aged 11 in 2005–06 and in the same year among boys of the same age group.

   **d** The same pattern is found across both genders and in both periods, with fruit consumption clearly declining with age.

   **e** In conclusion, it is clear that girls tended to eat more fruit than boys, with 11-year-olds eating the most in both years, 2001–02 and 2005–06.

**4** Add data from the chart to at least two of the sentences in exercise 3.

   a  Among boys and girls alike for both years, the younger children are, the more fruit they eat, just over 35 per cent and 36 per cent and approximately 40 per cent and 45 per cent respectively.

**5** Write an introduction using these words.

   chart   information   proportion   children   age group   gender
   consume   fruit   two periods

**6** Write an answer for Writing Task 1 below. When you have finished, swap your answer with a partner. Underline the number of comparisons your partner makes.

> You should spend about 20 minutes on this task.
> *The chart below shows the number of practising physicians per thousand people in selected countries in the EU, along with the EU average. The chart also shows the change in percentage terms of physician density between 2000 and 2008.*
> *Summarize the information by selecting and reporting the main features, and make comparisons where relevant.*
> Write at least 150 words.

> **Tip**
>
> Always remember to support what you say by providing data. Remember you do not have to quote all the data.

**Practising physicians per 1,000 population**

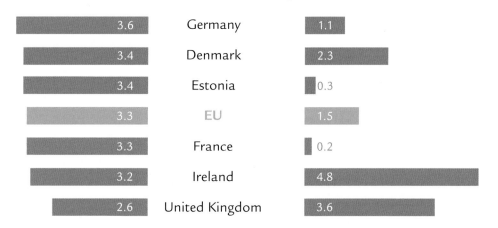

| 2008 (or nearest year available) | | Change 2000–08 (or nearest year available) |
|---|---|---|
| 3.6 | Germany | 1.1 |
| 3.4 | Denmark | 2.3 |
| 3.4 | Estonia | 0.3 |
| 3.3 | EU | 1.5 |
| 3.3 | France | 0.2 |
| 3.2 | Ireland | 4.8 |
| 2.6 | United Kingdom | 3.6 |

**7** Check your answer for mistakes and then make a checklist of the features of your answer. Work in pairs and take turns to describe your answer using the checklist.

   • paraphrase of the introduction
   • examples of data
   • comparison
   • ...

**Writing bank: page 113**

# Review

## Vocabulary: Collocations related to health

**1** Complete the sentences in your own words. Then compare your answers with another student.

1 In order to promote a healthy lifestyle among …
2 The best way to keep health costs down is to …
3 It is likely that healthcare in the future …
4 Health professionals such as doctors and nurses should be paid more than …
5 Healthcare should be financed by …
6 Running a health service requires …
7 The economic health of any country …
8 Health expenditure in my country …

**2** Write five sentences about your own lifestyle. Explain them to a partner.

## Language focus: Degrees of certainty

**1** Rewrite the sentences about the future using the words in brackets.

1 I might study medicine at university. (possible)
2 People probably won't have a lot of personal space. (unlikely)
3 In the future, the world should be a better place to live in. (likely)
4 People won't need to work long hours each week. (unnecessary)
5 In my home country, the next generation of young people should have a better standard of living. (probable)
6 It won't be possible for people to live in the countryside. (impossible)
7 Finding a good job may become very difficult in coming years. (possible)

**2** Work in pairs. Take turns to say the sentences or your answers in exercise 1. Your partner then transforms the sentence.

**3** Write at least three sentences about possible developments in your country in the near future or distant future. Write about health, transport, education or technology.

**4** Compare your sentences with other students.

### IELTS Writing Task 2

**1** Work in pairs. Study the Writing Task 2 question below from page 58 and write at least two adjectives to evaluate each function of healthcare systems, 1 and 2.

> *Some people think that healthcare systems should focus on curing disease and illnesses. Others believe that the true function of a healthcare system should be to prevent diseases and illnesses through health education and preventive measures. What, in your opinion, should be the main function of a healthcare system?*

1 Focus on cure: desirable, …
2 Focus on prevention: worthwhile, …

**2** Compare your adjectives with those below. Do the adjectives favour prevention or cure?

Focus on cure: wasteful, uneconomical, impossible, extravagant, too expensive, wasteful, inefficient

Focus on prevention: essential, valid, crucial, achievable, economical, effective, highly desirable, productive, sensible

**3** Give a reason and an example to support the evaluations in exercise 2. Use the following ideas if necessary.

less expensive

saves money

quicker

people take more responsibility

people probably happier

not all diseases can be prevented

**4** Write a paragraph supporting either prevention or cure. Use the adjectives and ideas above, or your own ideas.

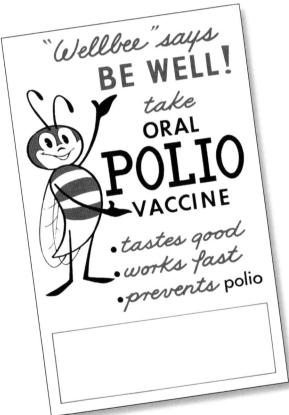

 **For further practice, go to the Direct to IELTS website for downloadable worksheets.**

# UNIT 6 Shaping the world and beyond

## Vocabulary: Words related to space and place

**1** Work in groups. Describe the photos A–D and explain how they are linked to the title of the unit. Give examples from your own country and experience.

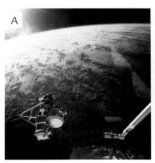   

**2** Circle the incorrect alternative in each question.

1 Is there any *room/space/place* for more satellites around the earth?

2 Is there *room/space/a gap* for any more rice terraces in photo C?

3 Is there much *gap/distance/room* between the buildings in photo B?

4 Which of the images is related to man's attempt to control his *surroundings/environment/setting*?

5 Are cities the best *spaces/locations/places* for people to live and work?

6 Can human beings bring *order/organization/systems* to the world around them through cooperation or individually?

7 Does infrastructure such as bridges and roads seek to bring order to the *chaos/organization/disorder* of nature?

8 Why do we need *systems/infrastructures/organizations* such as a satellite and transport networks? What other networks can you think of?

**3** Work in pairs and compare your answers. Then answer three of the questions giving reasons and examples. Compare your answers with another pair.

**4** Make adjectives from the alternatives in exercise 2. Use these endings: *-al, -ious, -y, -t, -ed, -ly, -tic, -atic.* You may not be able to use all the alternatives.

1 roomy, spacious

**5** 🎧 1.10 Complete the dialogue in your own words. Then listen and check your answers.

**Examiner:** Do you think we rely **(1)** ..................................... such as satellites?

**Candidate:** Yes, I think there is a tendency to do so. For example, if the **(2)** ..................................... on cars or a communication satellite broke down for a long time, it would have a huge impact on social order. It would result not only in financial costs for businesses, but it could also lead to loss of life and **(3)** ..................................... . In fact, I think it would be **(4)** ..................................... .

**Examiner:** In what way?

**Candidate:** Well, while GPS systems are not used that much in my country, **(5)** ..................................... would be affected and maybe other communications, so supermarkets might not be able to order food, which could lead to **(6)** ..................................... , and people in **(7)** ..................................... might be cut off. I think we should always ...

**6** Work in groups and discuss one of the following, giving reasons and examples. Compare your ideas with groups who chose a similar item.

- an example of a network or system that you use frequently
- an example of chaos when a system or network broke down

- a scientific place or location that is helping the development of the world
- a landscape in another world you'd like to visit
- a setting or location that fires your imagination

## IELTS Speaking Parts 1 and 2

**1** Make a list of the questions an examiner might ask a candidate in Speaking Part 1 relating to:

1 name  **What is your name?**
2 hobbies/interests
3 infrastructure changes that affect people's behaviour in your home town
4 technological developments, e.g. CCTV in the town
5 space in your town for future development
6 facilities for young people
7 new systems/infrastructure such as broadband
8 changes to physical surroundings such as satellite dishes and mobile telephone masts

**2** Work in pairs. Take turns to ask and answer your questions from exercise 1.

**3** Work in pairs and discuss how one or more of the types of teams/groups below affect people's lives.

- space scientists
- computer software designers
- research scientists
- engineers

**4** Work in pairs and discuss the task card below. Use the notes 1–3 to make lists. Compare your answers with other students.

> Describe a team that you have been part of or would like to be part of.
>
> You should say:
>
> when you joined/would like to join the team
>
> what the team was/is
>
> why you joined/would like to join the team
>
> and explain why you enjoyed/would enjoy being part of the team.

1 types of teams that you can belong to: _____
2 benefits/purposes of joining teams: _____
3 what makes being in teams enjoyable: _____

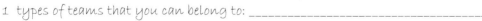

**5** Spend one minute making your own notes for the task card in exercise 4, selecting words where appropriate from the list in exercise 3. Then take turns to talk about the card.

**6** Give feedback about the reasons/purposes used by your partner. Were they clearly signposted?

### IELTS Listening Section 2

**1** Scan questions 1–10 below and find evidence for a–g. Compare your answers in pairs and discuss what you think the listening will be about.

**a** The listening section is about organizing some kind of event.

**b** Money is discussed.

**c** There are plans to invite large numbers of people.

**d** Different parts of the school buildings are going to be used for specific purposes.

**e** The organization of the event is divided among different teams.

**f** The teams have different targets.

**g** The targets have deadlines.

**2** (🎧) **1.11** Listen and answer questions 1–10.

*Questions 1–3*

Choose the correct letter, **A**, **B** or **C**.

**1** The running costs for the celebration have been exceeded by

| A | B | C |
|---|---|---|
| 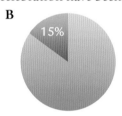 50% | 15% | 25% |

**2** The celebration will be attended by
  **A** no special guests.
  **B** several well-known people.
  **C** many former pupils.

**3** The number of invitations printed will be
  **A** 2000.
  **B** 3000.
  **C** 5000.

*Questions 4–6*

What does the speaker say each of the locations is going to be used for?

Write the correct letter **A**, **B** or **C** next to questions **4–6**.

| **A** displays | for student work and college | **4** | sports block | _____ |
|---|---|---|---|---|
| **B** | for refreshments | **5** | arts block | _____ |
| **C** the | for organizations from outside college | **6** | science block | _____ |

*Questions 7–10*

Complete the table below.

Write **NO MORE THAN TWO WORDS OR A NUMBER** for each answer.

| Team | Action | Dates |
|---|---|---|
| John's | **(7)** ................................. arrangements finalized | 29th of this month |
| **(8)** ......................... | History displays ready | 10th of next month |
| Angus's | Student displays completed | **(9)** ........................... M |
| Sara's | Selection of the design of the **(10)** ............................ | 14th May |

# Language focus 1: Hypothesizing

**1** Work in pairs. Read the extracts from Listening Section 2 and decide whether they are examples of first, second or third conditionals.

  **1** I think if we [1] **hadn't had** the individual meetings up to now, things [2] **wouldn't have gone** so smoothly.

  **2** If more [3] **were** to turn up, that [4] **'d be** great.

  **3** If anyone [5] **has** any questions about this, they [6] **'ll** be able to see me afterwards.

**2** Match the parts of the sentences 1–6 in exercise 1 with a–f.

  **a** future with *will*
  **b** past perfect
  **c** *would* + infinitive without *to* in the result clause
  **d** verb in the subjunctive in the *if* clause
  **e** a present tense (present simple)
  **f** *would* + *have* + past participle for an imaginary result

**3** Expand the notes in italics to complete the sentences. Check your answers in pairs.

  **0** *If I/play more team sports/school*, I'd have been much more of a team player at work.

  > If I had played more team sports at school, I'd have been much more of a team player at work.

  **1** Provided international space scientists pool their resources, *more more/breakthroughs/occur*.

  **2** Unless primary schoolchildren are taught basic scientific processes through projects such as learning about space travel, *they/be/disadvantage/later on/life*.

  **3** *If/be/fewer rules and regulations*, more young people would set up their own businesses.

  **4** Even if we managed to explore the moon and other planets in the near future, *not be/possible/exploit them easily*.

  **5** If international governments cooperated on standardizing electronic products, *many/scientific goods/such as/computer hardware/be cheaper*.

**4** Discuss the Speaking Part 3 questions below. What is each question asking you to do?

  - Is it asking you to evaluate something?
  - Is it asking you to give several criteria, factors or characteristics and explain?
  - Is it asking you to compare several items or ideas?

  **Working in teams**
  **1** What do you think makes someone a good team member?
  **2** Do you think we are part of different types of teams throughout our lives? In what ways are these teams different?
  **3** How easy is it to work together with people as part of a team?

  **International cooperation**
  **4** How important is it for countries to be able to work together in areas such as space research?
  **5** In terms of priority, do you think governments should cooperate on eradicating poverty or on space exploration? Why?
  **6** Do you think countries will work together on major scientific projects more in the future, or less?

**5** Match the answer below to one of the questions about working in teams in exercise 4.

  > It's not always easy, certainly, but if people want to get on in life, they will have to learn to work together.

**6** Write a statement using *if, provided, unless* or *if ... not* for each of the questions 1–6 in exercise 4. Compare your answers with a partner.

**7** Work in groups of three. Take turns to ask and answer the questions 1–6 in exercise 4.

## Grammar focus

* To form the first conditional we use *If* + present simple + future with *will*. We use it to talk about things that are probable in the future.

*If travel companies arrange trips to the moon, many people will pay to go there.*

* To form the second conditional we use *If* + past simple + *would* + infinitive without *to*. We use it to talk about situations in the present or the future which are imaginary or which are unlikely.

*If the moon were colonized in the near future, very few people would live there.*

With the verb *to be*, the subjunctive is used: *If I were you, I'd work as a research scientist.*

* To form the third conditional we use *If* + past perfect + *would have* + past participle. We use it to describe situations or events that didn't happen in the past.

*If international governments had cooperated on space research from the outset, space travel would have been more advanced by now.*

 Read more about hypothesizing in the online **Grammar Reference**.

IELTS Writing Task 1

## Grammar focus

* To form the passive, we use *to be* in the same tense as the active verb + the past participle of the active verb.

*Scientists help society enormously.* (active) *Society is helped enormously by scientists.* (passive)

* We use the passive to focus on the action, rather than the person doing the action. We also use the passive when we do not know or it is not important who the person doing the action is.

* We do not use intransitive verbs in the passive. *The spaceship rose into the sky.* NOT *The spaceship was risen into the sky.*

* We do not use stative verbs like *look, have, seem* in the passive. *The astronaut looks worried.* NOT *The astronaut is looked worried.*

**1** The maps show changes in the area around Welton between 1995 and 2012. Make a list of changes between the two maps.

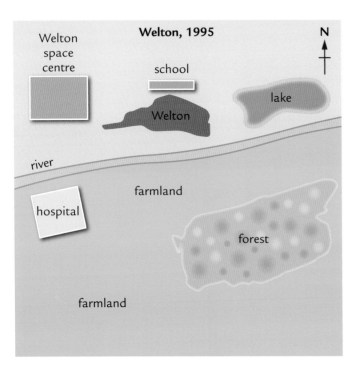

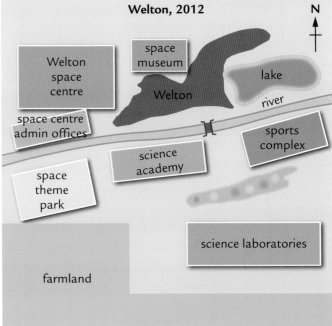

**Tip**

In the exam, number the changes on the maps, starting at the top left-hand corner.

**2** Decide which sentences below contain factual mistakes. Then correct them. Compare your answers in pairs.

1 The town increased in size slightly with the forest in the southwest almost disappearing.
2 The hospital north of the river was turned into a space theme park.
3 Some of the farmland south of the river vanished.
4 Some of the farmland made way for the construction of science laboratories, and some for the construction of a science academy.
5 A bridge was built across the river linking the new developments in the south to the north.
6 The lake remained the same, but in 2012 it is partially surrounded by the village.
7 Part of the forest was given over to the creation of a sports complex.
8 The area changed beyond all recognition with the expansion of the space centre and additional facilities and the disappearance of large parts of the farmland and the forest.

**3** Identify the verbs in the sentences in exercise 2. Decide whether they are transitive or intransitive. Decide which verbs can be used both transitively and intransitively.

Transitive: *A bridge was built ...*

Intransitive: *The town increased in size slightly  ...*

**4** Write sentences about the following.

  **1** an introduction mentioning the transformation of the area

  **2** the replacement of the school with the space museum

  **3** the shrinking of the forest to construct the science academy and the sports complex south of the river

  **4** the expansion of Welton space centre in the northwest by 2012

**5** Follow the same procedure as in exercise 1 for the maps below.

**6** Write an answer for Writing Task 1 below.

> You should spend about 20 minutes on this task.
>
> ***The diagrams below show the transformation of the area around Tumbledown between 1995 and 2010.***
>
> ***Summarize the information by selecting and reporting the main features, and make comparisons where relevant.***
>
> Write at least 150 words.

**Grammar focus**

\* Transitive verbs are always followed by an object. *The scientists built a new space rocket.*

\* Intransitive verbs do not have an object. *The transformation occurred very slowly.*

\* Some verbs are both transitive and intransitive. *The astronauts flew the spaceship to Mars.* (transitive) *The spaceship flew across the sky.* (intransitive)

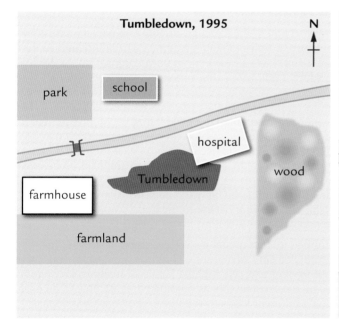

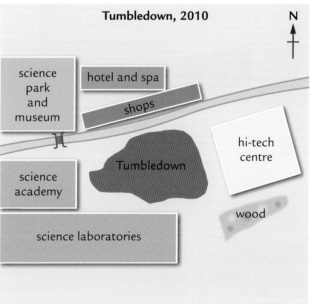

**7** Work in groups. Compare your answers using the checklist below.

- Does the introduction paraphrase the rubric?
- Have you used paragraphs?
- Have you written at least 150 words?

- Have you used transitive and intransitive verbs correctly?
- Have you used the passive correctly?
- Have you checked the answer for mistakes?

**Additional material: page 107**

## IELTS Reading

**1** Read the title of the reading passage. Discuss questions 1–4 in groups.

   **1** There is an enormous amount of debris in space around the earth. Where do you think it comes from?

   **2** What do you think happens when fragments of the debris collide just like cars?

   **3** How do you think the debris in space can be got rid of?

   **4** Do you think the debris could be dangerous? How?

**2** Skim the passage and the questions that follow and check your answers in exercise 1.

**3** Think of at least one synonym of the words *debris, fragments, dangerous*.

**4** Answer questions 1–14 about the reading passage.

### Cleaning up Earth's orbit: A Swiss satellite to tackle space debris

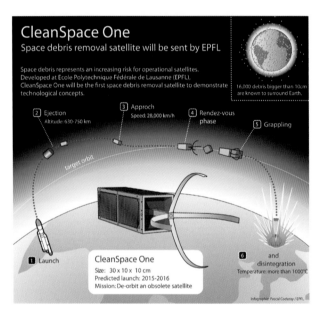

*The growth of debris orbiting the Earth – primarily jettisoned rocket and satellite components – is an increasingly pressing problem for spacecraft, and it can generate huge costs. To combat this scourge, the Swiss Space Center at EPFL (École polytechnique fédérale de Lausanne) is announcing today the launch of CleanSpace One, a project to develop and build the first installment of a family of satellites specially designed to clean up space debris.*

The Earth's orbit is full of all kinds of floating debris; a growing crowd of abandoned satellites, spent rocket stages, bits of broken spacecraft, and fragments from collisions are rocketing around the planet at breathtaking speeds. NASA keeps close tabs on at least 16,000 of these objects that are larger than 10 cm in diameter. When an operational spacecraft such as a satellite collides with one of them, serious, costly damage can result; often the satellite is completely destroyed. And the collision itself then generates thousands more fragments, further exacerbating the problem.

"It has become essential to be aware of the existence of this debris and the risks that are run by its proliferation," says Claude Nicollier, astronaut and EPFL professor. To move

beyond mere rhetoric and take immediate action to get this stuff out of orbit, the Swiss Space Center at EPFL is launching CleanSpace One, a project to build the first prototype in a family of "de-orbiting" satellites.

### One satellite, three technological hurdles

The cleanup satellite has three major challenges to overcome, each of which will necessitate the development of new technology that could, in turn, be used down the road in other applications.

After its launch, the cleanup satellite will have to adjust its trajectory in order to match its target's orbital plane. To do this, it could use a new kind of ultra-compact motor designed for space applications that is being developed in EPFL laboratories. When it gets within range of its target, which will be traveling at 28,000 km/h at an altitude of 630–750 km, CleanSpace One will grab and stabilize it – a mission that's extremely risky at these high speeds, particularly if the satellite is rotating. To accomplish the task, scientists are planning to develop a gripping mechanism inspired by a plant or animal example. Finally, once it's coupled with the satellite, CleanSpace One will "de-orbit" the unwanted satellite by heading back into the Earth's atmosphere, where the two satellites will burn up on re-entry.

Although its first model is destined to be destroyed, the CleanSpace One adventure will not be a one-shot deal. "We want to offer and sell a whole family of ready-made systems, designed as sustainably as possible, that are able to de-orbit several different kinds of satellites," explains Swiss Space Center Director Volker Gass. "Space agencies are increasingly finding it necessary to take into consideration and prepare for the elimination of the stuff they're sending into space. We want to be the pioneers in this area."

The design and construction of CleanSpace One, as well as its maiden space voyage, will cost about 10 million Swiss francs. Depending on the funding and industrial partners, this first orbital rendez-vous could take place within three to five years.

### About space debris

16,000 objects larger than 10 cm in diameter and hundreds of millions of smaller particles are ripping around the Earth at speeds of several kilometers per second. From the beginning of the Space Age, Earth's periphery has been increasingly encumbered by all kinds of debris, primarily concentrated in Low Earth Orbit (less than 2000 km in altitude, where the International Space Station is orbiting) or Geostationary Orbit (35,786 km in altitude). Many of these objects are spent rocket stages or satellites that have broken up in orbit. If they collide with another orbiting object, say a functioning satellite, they can cause massive damage, or even destroy it. The financial consequences of these collisions are enormous, particularly for insurance companies involved in the space sector; a sum currently estimated at $20 billion to insure existing satellites.

Cases such as this one are bound to increase in number. Even in the immensity of outer space, the increasing density of human-generated waste is becoming a problem. It's expanding exponentially, because each collision generates in turn several thousand more fragments, which, although smaller, are no less dangerous than a large, abandoned satellite. NASA, which tracks 16,000 of these objects, can only monitor the largest ones (greater than 10 cm in diameter) – but at these incredible speeds even a simple paint chip can seriously damage a solar panel or the window on a shuttle.

### Questions 1–6

Complete the summary below.

Choose **NO MORE THAN TWO WORDS** from the passage for each answer.

**Floating debris**

Around the earth there is a **(1)** ........................................ of space rubbish consisting of disused satellites and rocket parts along with pieces of broken spacecraft of varying sizes, flying around earth at **(2)** ........................................ . NASA monitors a large number of the of bigger **(3)** ........................................ , as collision with one of them can destroy a **(4)** ........................................ , at huge cost. In addition, the impact can lead to the creation of many **(5)** ........................................ , which in turn makes the **(6)** ........................................ worse.

### Questions 7–10

Complete the flow chart below.

Choose **NO MORE THAN TWO WORDS** from the passage for each answer.

> **Tip**
>
> Find and mark the part of the text that relates to the flow chart. Always check the grammar of the text in the flow chart itself; it may be written in note form.

**Satellite cleanup**

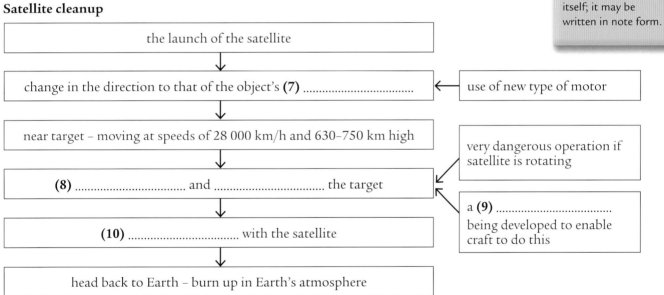

### Questions 11–14

Do the following statements agree with the information in the reading passage?

Write:

| **TRUE** | *if the statement agrees with the information* |
| **FALSE** | *if the statement contradicts the information* |
| **NOT GIVEN** | *if there is no information on this* |

**11** There will be only one type of clean-up satellite produced in future.

**12** The smaller particles of debris in space are moving faster than the bigger ones.

**13** Collisions between debris and working satellites are likely to become more common.

**14** It is possible for even the smallest pieces of debris created by collisions to cause problems in space.

# Language focus 2: Cause and effect verbs and nouns

**1** In the extract below from the reading passage, there are two causes and two effects. What are they?

> And the collision itself then generates thousands more fragments, further exacerbating the problem.

**2** Which two verbs below do not describe cause and effect?

> shape   cause   create   improve   affect   impact   produce
> lead to    result (in/from)   influence   link   show   change
> make something happen    transform

**3** Identify the causes and effects in the sentences below. Then rewrite the sentences using the words and phrases in brackets. Compare your answers with a partner.

  **1** The sharing of technology between the different companies resulted in considerable cost savings. (resulted from)

  **2** Early advances in science by people like Aristotle led to many discoveries we take for granted today. (were brought about by)

  **3** The scientific knowledge in many countries is developed by international collaboration. (shapes)

  **4** The choice of location for new science and engineering companies is often influenced by considerations such as the availability of skilled workers. (have an impact on)

  **5** The present world has been shaped enormously by the thinking and writing of many scientists such as Einstein and Stephen Hawking. (considerable influence over)

  **6** The establishment of new industries such as software companies can transform the economy for the better. (improve)

  **7** The building of a new science complex had a positive impact on the behaviour of young people in the community as employment increased. (made better)

  **8** It has been suggested that the internet is altering the way users think. (is being affected)

**4** Think about three recent events that have made your life better/easier.

buying a piece of technology, learning to use something, meeting someone

**5** Work in pairs. Take turns to describe the three events, giving reasons. Talk for a maximum of four minutes each.

www  Read more about cause and effect verbs and nouns in the online **Grammar Reference**.

## IELTS Writing Task 2

**1** Work in pairs. Think of one idea for each of the two views in the writing task below.

> *Some people think that it is wrong for humans to search for new worlds in space when we have so many problems on our own planet. Others believe such searches help mankind to develop.*

Discuss both views and give your own opinion.

**2** For each of your ideas, provide

  **1** a purpose or reason

  **2** an impact of the idea

**3** an example from your own country or part of the world

**4** a reservation you have about the idea

**5** a conclusion

## Tip

In Writing Task 2, use complex sentences to develop your ideas. Complex sentences are sentences that contain one or more ideas or clauses linked together, usually by linking devices such as *because, while, although.* Note that *complex* does not mean *complicated*.

**3** Work with another pair and compare your answers in exercise 2.

**4** Look at the underlined text in sentences 1–8. Decide whether it describes a result, a reason, a purpose, a concession or a condition. What words are used to do this?

**1** If new technologies are discovered while developing spacecraft, <u>life on earth can be improved</u>.

**2** <u>Although space research is valuable</u>, many problems such as famine and disease need to be addressed here on earth.

**3** Surely the human race needs to explore space <u>in order to learn more about our world and our past</u>.

**4** Climate change and natural disasters are affecting the planet enormously, <u>so that more money is needed to tackle these problems.</u>

**5** It is difficult to support funding for space research <u>because it appears unethical when there are large numbers of people dying from hunger in the world.</u>

**6** People tend to ignore the benefits of space research, <u>resulting in demands for it to cease.</u>

**7** <u>Provided problems such as overcrowding in cities and ignorance are dealt with</u>, research carried out in space is acceptable.

**8** <u>Unless scientists are allowed to continue with space research</u>, advances in technology will slow down.

1 result, 'If'

**5** Skim the sentences in exercise 4 and say which view in exercise 1 they relate to.

**6** Choose at least two sentences in exercise 4 and make them more specific by adding examples and reasons.

1 If new technologies such as new materials or medical applications that can be used in medical treatment are discovered while developing spacecraft, <u>life on earth can be improved</u>, because the quality of people's lives everywhere will be enhanced.

**7** Work in pairs. Note down ideas for each of the two views below very quickly. Then do the same for your own opinion.

You should spend about 40 minutes on this task.

Write about the following topic:

*Some people think that we should be more careful about sending satellites into space because they show where we are in the universe and we may attract the attention of dangerous aliens. Others believe that contact with other species may bring enormous benefits to humanity.*

Discuss both views and give your own opinion.

**8** Write an answer for Writing Task 2 in exercise 7.

**Writing bank: page 115**

### Tip

Write five paragraphs: an introduction, a body paragraph for view 1, a body paragraph for view 2, a paragraph for your own opinion and a conclusion.

### Useful language

Some people feel …

Others feel …

The former/latter view is more acceptable.

Personally, I feel/ believe …

# Review

## Vocabulary: Words related to space and place

**1** Work alone and name

**1** a system that you use every day.

**2** a place in the solar system that you would like to visit, if you could.

**3** a technology network that you use more now than in the past.

**4** an example of a type of infrastructure that will benefit from space research.

**5** a landscape in a science-fiction film that you liked or disliked.

**6** a location that is special, because it seems from another world.

**2** Write three questions you would like to answer about one of the answers in exercise 1.

**1** Why do you use this system? Do you think it is necessary in your life/in people's lives in general? How easy is it to use the system?

**3** Work in pairs. Take turns to ask and answer your questions from exercise 2.

## Language focus 1: Hypothesizing

**1** Complete the sentences so they are true for you.

**1** If I hadn't played ...

**2** Provided I work hard ...

**3** If I don't manage to ...

**4** Even if it takes me ...

**5** If I hadn't studied ...

**6** If I were to have the chance again, ...

**7** Unless something happens, ...

**8** Provided I find a job I ...

**1** If I hadn't played the violin in the local orchestra, I wouldn't have met Sally.

**2** Work in pairs and compare your sentences. Then ask each other questions about one or more of the sentences.

### IELTS Writing Task 1

**1** Draw a box or a circle to represent each item a–i on the map of Riverton, and label the items. You can also add your own items to the map. Then choose a date for the town, either 1990 or 2010.

**a** theatre

**b** houses

**c** woodland

**d** factories

**e** school

**f** fields

**g** hospital

**h** car park

**i** airport

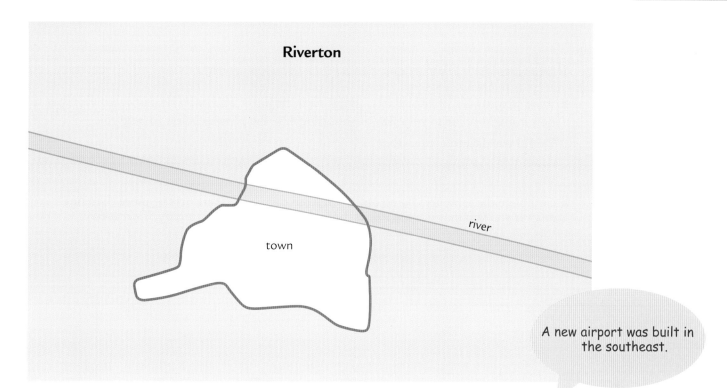

**Riverton**

river

town

A new airport was built in the southeast.

**2** Find a partner who chose a different date and compare the maps, describing the changes.

## Language focus 2: Cause and effect verbs and nouns

**1** How do A–D affect people's lives? Make a list.

**2** Work in pairs. Compare your lists and write several sentences about one of the photos.

Railways transform the economy because they speed up the movement of people and goods.

**For further practice, go to the Direct to IELTS website for downloadable worksheets.**

# Unit 7 A consumer society

## Vocabulary: Words related to *consumer*

**1** Work in groups and describe the photos A–E. Then choose one of the pictures and explain how it might relate to your way of shopping. Use the phrases below to help you.

**Useful words and expressions**

consumer    pay by    carry cash    use cards    afford    just look/don't buy    browse
impulse buying    compulsive buying    careful    go window shopping

**2** Complete the sentences using one word from each box. There may be more than one answer and you may use the words more than once. Use a dictionary, if necessary.

> **A**  household    government    consumer    basic    spending

> **B**  habits    boycott    expenditure    goods    necessities    confidence
> spending    behaviour    demand

**0** **Household expenditure** depends on the income of the various people in a dwelling.

**1** An increase in ................................... often boosts the economy.

**2** Shops and advertising companies are very sensitive to ................................... patterns.

**3** People sometimes do without ................................... to fund small luxuries.

**4** ................................... is driven by different factors and can easily fuel a country's economy.

**5** With globalization, the same ................................... such as the latest mobile phones are available everywhere.

**6** ................................... vary from person to person and community to community.

**7** ................................... is usually affected by financial news and the weather.

**8** A ................................... happens when people stop buying products made by a particular company or country.

**3** Work in pairs. Explain the meaning of the phrases you created in exercise 2.

Household expenditure is the amount of money that people living in a household spend in a particular period such as weekly, monthly or yearly.

**4** Check that you understand the phrases 1–7. Choose a phrase for your partner to talk about for one minute.

**1** doing window shopping

**2** browsing the internet

**3** earning and saving money

**4** cutting back personal spending

**5** understanding consumer preferences

**6** people's consumer habits

**7** consumer attitudes

**5** As a class, make a list of about 7 words and phrases that relate to one of the items 1–3. Then make sentences using the words and phrases.

**1** being a green consumer  pollute, avoid, ...

**2** spending money

**3** consumer spending

As green consumers are careful not to pollute the environment they avoid products and services that might cause pollution. They ...

## IELTS Listening Section 3

**1** Work in groups and discuss at least two of the questions 1–4.

    **1** What do you spend money on each day?

    **2** Do you prefer to buy things online or in a shop? What about your friends?

    **3** Is purchasing online becoming more common? Why do you think so?

    **4** What do you spend most of your money on?

**2** Which questions 1–10 relate to a) Angela, b) Adam, and c) possibly both of them?

**3**  **1.12** Listen and answer questions 1–10.

*Questions 1 and 2*

Choose the correct letter, **A**, **B** or **C**.

**1** What has Adam already done?

    **A** background reading and an introduction

    **B** background reading and the selection of his topic

    **C** the selection of his topic and an introduction

**2** Adam's topic is restricted to

    **A** a comparison of attitudes to online shopping in European countries.

    **B** the difference between attitudes in the UK and the USA to online shopping.

    **C** the attitude to online shopping among young people in the UK.

*Questions 3 and 4*

Choose **TWO** letters, **A–E**.

What **TWO** types of purchases is Adam going to focus on in his questionnaire?

**A** the food that teenagers consume

**B** the range of publications that teenagers read

**C** the music that teenagers purchase

**D** different electrical equipment that teenagers buy

**E** the travelling patterns of young people

*Questions 5 and 6*

Choose **TWO** letters, **A–E**.

What are the **TWO** main problems that Angela has encountered?

**A** starting to organize the working schedule

**B** deciding on the schools to carry out the study

**C** getting though the initial reading phase

**D** choosing the age group to focus on

**E** choosing the items she is going to ask about

*Questions 7–10*

Complete the table below.

Choose **NO MORE THAN THREE WORDS** for each answer.

| Points related to: | Advice | Reason |
|---|---|---|
| Permission letter | send the letter early | a reply could take a **(7)** _____ |
| Data | point out the data will be **(8)** _____ and for research purposes only | to make pupils feel **(9)** _____ about filling in the questionnaire |
| Questionnaire | use a clear and simple **(10)** _____ in the questionnaire | because of the age of the groups |

### Exam information

Listening Section 3 usually contains a conversation between two, three or four speakers. The conversation is usually about a subject of an academic nature. The speakers can be a tutor and students, or just students, talking about an essay or seminar. As you practise for the exam, listen to radio programmes where speakers are exchanging and developing ideas.

### Tip

When you have answered the questions for this section or any section of the IELTS listening exam, listen to the recording again and read the audioscript. Alternatively, read the script and then listen to help develop your listening skills.

## Language focus: Countable and uncountable nouns

**1** All of the nouns below from Listening Section 3 are uncountable. Can you use the phrases *a piece of/a type of* with all of the words?

footwear    clothing    accommodation    software    music    recreation    research

**2** Work in pairs. Decide which nouns below are countable, uncountable or both countable and uncountable. Give an example of a countable noun that relates to each of the countable and uncountable nouns below.

| | | |
|---|---|---|
| electronic equipment | medicine | change |
| cash | information | advice |
| music | job | entertainment |
| computer software | furniture | food |
| news | scenery | recreation |
| car | travel | |
| traffic | tree | |
| homework | work | |

electronic equipment: tablet, iPhone

**Tip**

When you talk about specific countable nouns you can use phrases such as *a/the piece/bit of*, e.g. *a/the piece of advice, electronic equipment*, or *a/the type/sort/kind of music*, etc.

**3** Decide on at least three of the goods or services in exercise 2 that you would like to *have, receive, use* or *do*. Work in pairs and explain why.

> The piece of electronic equipment I would like to have is an ebook reader because I think they are very convenient.

Read more about countable and uncountable nouns in the Grammar Reference.

### IELTS Speaking Parts 1 and 2

**Tip**

In Part 1, do not overdevelop your answers. Use one or two sentences for your answer.

**1** Work in pairs. Expand the notes to create questions.

  **0** what types/shops/popular/your country?
  **1** shops/markets/more popular/your country?
  **2** shopping malls/more popular/small shops/your country?
  **3** people prefer/use/cards/cash nowadays?
  **4** you/buy/books/music/online?
  **5** you/prefer/buy things/shops/online? Why?
  **6** you/spend/lot/money/media/books, films or music or electronic equipment?
  **7** you/think/cost of/certain electronic items/come down/future?
  **0** What types of shops are popular in your country?

**2** Choose at least three questions from exercise 1 and ask them to your partner.

**3** Match the words and phrases A–D to the relevant part of the Speaking Part 2 task card.

Describe a website (for shopping, information or entertainment) that you like using.

You should say:

 what the website is   D

 what the website provides

 how often you visit it

and explain why you like visiting the website.

**A**
daily/once a week/every other day/now and again/every other week/as often as I can

**B**
entertaining/fun/meet new friends/relaxing/love range of music/learn languages including English/save money/see wider range of goods/check and compare information/contacts/advice/social/shopping/entertainment/information/videos/music/film downloads

**C**
social networking/news/information/entertainment/shopping/advice

**D**
a social website called .../a music site called .../an entertainment site called .../a site providing news/information called ...

**4** Make notes for your answer to the task card in exercise 3. Use words and phrases from A–D to help you. Compare your notes in pairs.

**5** Work with a different partner and take turns to talk about the card. When you have finished, show your notes to your partner. Check how closely your partner followed his/her notes.

## IELTS Writing Task 1

**1** Work in pairs. Describe the contents of the charts and table extracts A–D. Then check your answers with another pair of students.

**A**

Buying or ordering goods or services over the Internet: EU comparison, 2009

Percentages

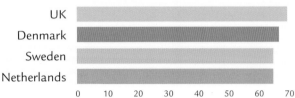

**B**

Selected activities performed in free time: by age, 2007/08

| England | 16–24 | 25–34 |
| --- | --- | --- |
| Watching television | 82 | 83 |
| Spending time with friends and family | 83 | 84 |
| Listening to music | 83 | 74 |
| Shopping | 69 | 67 |

**C**

Participation in voluntary activities: by age, 2009

England                    Percentages

| | At least once a month | |
| --- | --- | --- |
| | Informal Volunteering | Formal Volunteering |
| 16–25 | 40 | 25 |
| 26–34 | 34 | 22 |

**D**

Proportion of total amount given to charity: by cause, 2008/09, UK

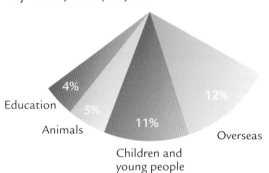

**2** Match 1–6 to the charts and table extracts A–D.

**1** Spending time with family and friends was almost equally important for 16–24- and 25–34-year-olds, 83 per cent and 84 per cent respectively.

**2** Forty percent of 16–25-year-olds are involved in informal voluntary activities compared to 25 per cent for formal activities.

**3** Listening to music was more significantly popular among 16–24-year-olds compared to those aged 25–34 (83 per cent against 74 per cent).

**4** Shopping was the least popular activity, 69 per cent for 16–24-year-olds and 67 per cent for 25–34-year-olds.

**5** At 12 per cent of the total, overseas donation accounted for more than any of the other areas.

**6** More people in the UK order or buy goods or services over the internet than in the other three countries.

**3** Paraphrase the statements in exercise 2 using these notes.

**1** spending time with family and friends/as important for/as/at 83 per cent compared to 84 per cent

**2** more 16–25-year-olds/participate/informal voluntary activities/formal activities

**3** greater proportion/those aged 25–34/listened to music

**4** Sixty-nine per cent/16–24-year-olds/67 per cent/25–34-year-olds/consider/shopping/less interesting/other activities

**5** exceed/other causes/with 12 per cent/compared to/respectively

**6** web/use/for ordering and purchasing/compared to

**1** Spending time with family and friends was as important for 16–24-year-olds as for 25–34-year-olds, at 83 per cent compared to 84 per cent.

4 Work in groups. Write one sentence about an aspect of each of the tables and charts A–D. Then give your sentences to another group to paraphrase.

5 Compare your sentences and the paraphrases with the whole class.

6 Write an answer for Writing Task 1 below.

You should spend about 20 minutes on this task.

*The table below shows the total consumer spending in the United Kingdom by method of payment.*

*Summarize the information by selecting and reporting the main features, and make comparisons where relevant.*

Write at least 150 words.

Total consumer spending: by method of payment
United Kingdom                                     Percentages

| | 2005 | 2006 | 2007 | 2008 |
|---|---|---|---|---|
| Debit cards | 29.5 | 33.6 | 34.6 | 36.3 |
| Credit, and charge cards | 19.4 | 19.8 | 20.1 | 19.7 |
| Cash | 33.1 | 31.2 | 30.4 | 29.2 |
| Cheques | 15.9 | 12.9 | 14.1 | 12.0 |
| Other | 2.1 | 2.6 | 0.8 | 2.8 |
| Total spending (= 100%) (£ billions) | 494.5 | 503.0 | 510.6 | 524.6 |

7 Compare your answer in pairs.

## IELTS Speaking Part 3

1 🎧 1.13 Listen and complete questions 1–6 in note form. Then make your notes into full sentences.

**Purchasing goods**

1 ........................................ purchasing the latest fashionable goods?
2 ........................................ do people purchase on the internet?
3 ........................................ purchasing goods on the internet? Are there any disadvantages?

**Influences on spending**

4 ........................................ on people's spending habits?
5 ........................................ makes people content? Why/Why not?
6 ........................................ to control people's spending habits?

*1*
*I think it depends on the age group, but, yes, young people are certainly very conscious of or even obsessed by the latest trends in consumer goods such as tablets and trainers.*

2 Work in groups of three. Check your answers and discuss what each question is asking you to talk about. Think of a suitable beginning to the answer and an example.

3 Take turns to ask and answer the questions in exercise 1. The third student should monitor the candidate's answer, giving prompts such as *because, for example (if), in order to* and *so* at appropriate places.

### IELTS Reading

**1** Work in groups and discuss at least two of the statements 1–4. Say whether you agree with them.

   **1** Changing fashion means many clothes are thrown away as waste.

   **2** People are too self-conscious to wear secondhand clothes nowadays.

   **3** Consumers are more conscious of throwing away materials nowadays compared to the past.

   **4** Charities provide a valuable service for society.

**2** Scan the text and find 1–5. Compare your answers in pairs.

   **1** a rise in sales despite hard times

   **2** how one charity is competing with shops selling inexpensive clothes

   **3** a reference to a criticism of fast fashion

   **4** a rejection of fast fashion

   **5** a reference to income decline

**3** Answer questions 1–13 about the reading passage.

*Charity shops are reporting rising sales thanks to the credit crunch. But it's not just about picking up a bargain – they're attracting shoppers looking for ethically sourced fashion. Sarah Butler reports*

**A** Last week, the House of Lords science committee criticised a culture of fast fashion for contributing to the growing amount of domestic waste in Britain. Textiles make up 3% of the 30m tonnes of waste collected from households by local authorities every year, and the committee accused retailers of encouraging consumers "to dispose of clothes which have only been worn a few times in favour of new, cheap garments which themselves will also go out of fashion and be discarded within a matter of months."

**B** But with the average household's disposable income down £2,500 in the past 12 months – the first drop for 11 years – it is unlikely that shoppers are about to swap regular purchases from the lower end of the high street for expensive well-made and ethically sourced fashion.

**C** However, in these lean times, another sector is experiencing a surge in sales: charity shops. It was revealed last week that sales at Oxfam stores across the country have risen 7% in a year. Indeed, *Charity Finance* magazine reports that profits across 72 charity shops are up 7.4% this year, and that sales have risen 5.7%. The British Heart Foundation, one of Britain's biggest chains of charity shops with 560 stores, says sales are up by as much as 6%. While many high street stores are pulling back on their expansion plans, the BHF plans 40 more stores this year. Age Concern is also bringing forward plans to open more stores after recording a 9% increase in sales last year.

**D** Fashion experts are also noting a shift in our approach to charity shopping. For a new breed of ethical and fashion-conscious consumers, secondhand purchases are not just driven by thrift. "I get a feeling that people are trying to become more individual at the moment, and buying secondhand clothes is a way to do that," says Jane Shepherdson, the former boss of Topshop who now heads the Whistles clothes chain. "There has been exposure of certain high street retailers who have not been as clean as they should be in their supply base, so if you want cheap clothes and a clean conscience then a charity shop is an obvious route."

**E** With the popularity of eBay and schemes such as the recent Visa Swap clothes exchanging event in London, fronted by Lindsay Lohan, there is less stigma than ever in wearing secondhand goods. "For shoppers who love the dig-and-delve experience of shops like TK Maxx, there is really not much difference in going to a charity shop – it is all about enjoying the experience of finding a bargain," says Lorna Hall, executive editor of fashion trade journal *Drapers*. "A certain section of consumers are turning their back on fast fashion and like the idea of recycling."

**F** For their part, charities have noted the increased competition from cheap clothing stores such as Primark and Peacocks and have stepped up their act. Oxfam has been particularly innovative, experimenting with specialist book, furniture and boutique clothing stores. The latter, which are being tried out in central London, sell a mix of fairtrade fashions, items made from recycled fabrics and vintage clothing picked to appeal to the fashion conscious. The charity is using Shepherdson as an adviser to get its stores right. As David McCullogh, deputy chief executive of Oxfam, says, "We are not in that place where charity shops used to be, where people come to us because they have no money and nowhere else to go. We think we are much more attractive as somewhere where you can find unusual, interesting and one-off pieces of clothing. Sales are driven by that and we have put a lot of work into getting better quality and interesting donations."

**G** As demand for secondhand clothes grows, a big issue is increasing competition in the hunt for quality donated goods, particularly from professional companies which collect secondhand clothing for sale overseas.

**H** The price of secondhand clothing on the international market has soared by more than 70% in the past two or three years. That increase in value has helped charities raise money; 50% of clothing donations unsuitable for sale in UK charity shops go on to be sold in developing countries, or are recycled into new products such as stuffing for mattresses. But it has also fuelled an increasing number of professional secondhand clothing traders, or "rag merchants".

## Questions 1–5

The reading passage has eight paragraphs, A–H. Which paragraph contains the following information?

**1** the rise of the fashion shopper with a conscience

**2** some uses for clothes not sold in charity shops

**3** the different types of goods on sale in Oxfam shops

**4** how many charity shopping outlets are owned by one organization

**5** the impact of retailers on the growth of clothes waste

## Questions 6–10

Choose **FIVE** letters, A–I.

**NB** Your answers may be given in any order.

Below are listed some common features of the latest charity shops.

Which **FIVE** of these features are reported by the writer of the text?

**A** They have become more profitable.

**B** They have started charging more for goods.

**C** They offer clothes for fashion-aware shoppers.

**D** Items on sale are cheaper than before.

**E** Shop assistants are paid more than before.

**F** The shopping experience is now similar to other shops.

**G** They only sell clothes made from recycled fabrics.

**H** They are no longer places for poor shoppers.

**I** They are places where shoppers might find unique items.

## Questions 11 and 12

Complete the sentences below.

Choose **NO MORE THAN TWO WORDS AND/OR A NUMBER** from the passage for each answer.

**11** The interest in secondhand clothes is driven in part by the collections by _____ which export the clothes.

**12** There has been a _____ increase in the value of secondhand clothes.

## Question 13

Choose the correct letter **A**, **B**, **C** or **D**.

Which alternative below is the best title for the reading passage?

**A** The importance of recycled clothing

**B** How charity shops made a profit

**C** The expansion of charity shops

**D** The rise of the ethical consumer

**Tip**

Make sure you take into account the following words as you analyse statements 1–5: 1 *rise*, 2 *reasons*, 3 *types*, 4 *how many*, 5 *impact*. The words help you understand the function or meaning of the part of the text the phrases 1–5 refer to.

**Tip**

When you try to locate the information in the reading passage for questions 1–5, learn to leave a question if you can't find the answer quickly. You may, for example, only answer questions 1 and 5 first time round. Then, try again and again until you find the answers to the other three. The danger is focusing on each question in turn. You should aim to finish questions 1–5 in seven and a half minutes.

## IELTS Writing Task 2

**1** Work in pairs. Read Writing Task 2 below, then discuss whether you agree with statements 1–7. Rank the statements from 1 (I totally agree) to 5 (I totally disagree).

> Write about the following topic:
>
> ***Advertising campaigns on TV that are targeted at children should be banned.***
> ***To what extent do you agree or disagree?***
>
> Give reasons for your answer and include any relevant examples from your own knowledge and experience.
>
> Write at least 250 words.

**1** TV advertisements targeted at children put pressure on parents.  1 2 3 4 5
**2** Banning TV advertisements targeted at children won't have any effect.  1 2 3 4 5
**3** Children are too young to understand manipulation by TV adverts.  1 2 3 4 5
**4** TV adverts aimed at children are unethical.  1 2 3 4 5
**5** Children don't notice the adverts on TV.  1 2 3 4 5
**6** Children should be protected from exposure to consumer advertising.  1 2 3 4 5
**7** Children have the right to be aware of consumer goods that are available.  1 2 3 4 5

**2** Answer questions a–e about statement 1 in exercise 1. Then compare your answers in groups.

   **a** Are TV adverts targeted at children acceptable? Why/Why not?
   **b** What example can you give relating to consumer goods such as toys?
   **c** What is the effect if parents don't buy the consumer goods?
   **d** Why is this the case?
   **e** What is the solution for the parents?

**3** Work in pairs. Underline the parts of the text that the words in bold refer to.

First of all, TV advertisements targeted at <u>children</u> are not acceptable because **they** put pressure on parents to buy items, such as the latest computer gadgets like a games console. If **this equipment** is not bought by parents, children may try to persuade **them** to buy it. **This** is partly because the adverts are repeated endlessly during children's programmes. **They** are shown at such times because **they** are the prime time for a young audience. The only option to tackle **this problem** is for parents to ban the programmes entirely. **This**, however, affects the children's development. Perhaps it's time for authorities to deal with **this situation**.

**4** Complete the text using the words in the box. There may be more than one answer.

| | | | | | |
|---|---|---|---|---|---|
| these products | those | this view | they | they | they |
| children | this | them | them | them | |

Some people, however, feel that young children between three and ten years of age don't notice the adverts **(1)** _____ see on TV during programmes such as cartoons or **(2)** _____ shows with special characters for children. **(3)** _____ argue that when there is a commercial break, **(4)** _____ stop watching and don't take any notice of the adverts aimed at **(5)** _____ . However, **(6)** _____ is surely mistaken. In TV adverts, toys like dolls or the latest computer gadgets or sweets are usually presented in such an attractive way to children that it makes **(7)** _____ want to have **(8)** _____ . Children, even at an early age, are sophisticated enough to watch adverts and know what **(9)** _____ want. Moreover, children have ways of letting their parents know **(10)** _____ and put enormous pressure on **(11)** _____ , as a walk around any supermarket or toy department will show.

**5** Write an answer for Writing Task 2 below.

> You should spend about 40 minutes on this task.
> Write about the following topic:
>
> ***Using celebrities to advertise consumer goods that are attractive to teenagers should be banned.***
>
> ***To what extent do you agree or disagree?***
>
> Give reasons for your answer and include any relevant examples from your own knowledge and experience.

Write at least 250 words.

**Additional material: page 108**

**Writing bank: page 118**

# Review

## Vocabulary: Words related to *consumer*

**1** Answer the questions 1–8.

  **1** What effect does consumer spending have on a nation's economy?
  **2** What types of things are included in household expenditure?
  **3** Why does business have to be sensitive to consumer behaviour patterns?
  **4** What kinds of consumer goods do you think you will buy in the next year?
  **5** Do you think your spending habits are the same as other people? Why/Why not?
  **6** What kinds of events affect consumer confidence?
  **7** Do consumer boycotts work?
  **8** Why do governments make spending cuts and what is the impact on services?

**2** Make a list of words that you associate with one of the following.

- browsing in department stores
- buying goods online
- finding a job you like
- earning lots of money
- surfing the internet

**3** Work in pairs. Talk about the item you chose in exercise 2, using as many of the words in the list you made as possible.

## Language focus: Countable and uncountable nouns

**1** Decide if the words below are countable, (C) uncountable (U) or both (U/C). Then add them to the correct list.

> ~~PC~~ (C)    slippers    accommodation    medicine    bedsit    vegetables    syrup
> jumper    fruit    electronic equipment    footwear

**(1)** ................... :    shoes, trainers, **(2)** ...................
clothing:    shirt, coat, **(3)** ...................
**(4)** ................... :    flat, **(5)** ................... , house
music:    jazz, pop, blues
**(6)** ................... :    **(7)** PC, laptop, tablet
**(8)** ................... :    tablets, **(9)** ................... , capsule
furniture:    chair, table, bed
food:    **(10)** ................... , **(11)** ................... , meat

**2** Prepare a brief description of no more than one minute about either a) the way you like to shop or b) how advertising influences your life. Work in pairs and take turns to talk about your chosen topic.

## IELTS Writing Task 2

**1** Work in groups and complete one of the texts 1–3 in your own words relating to IELTS Writing Task 2 in exercise 1 on page 86. You can adapt the outlines if you wish.

**1**

Banning TV advertisements won't have any effect on children. This is because
.......................................................... . For example, if ................................................
............................................... . So ..................................................................... .
Moreover, these advertisements .................................................................................. ,
which is why ........................................................................................... . Thus, TV
advertisements have little ....................................................................... .

**2**

TV adverts aimed at children are unethical because they are too young .............................................
......................................... . They know that they ................................................................. ,
but do not understand that their ....................................................................................... .
For example, if a child sees ........................................................ and it is very attractive, he/she is
likely.............................................................................. . So it is wrong to put pressure
............................................................................... through TV adverts. Therefore, they
................................................................ .

**3**

TV adverts should ................................................................ to protect children from exposure to
consumer advertising. The purpose of this kind of advertising is to
.............................................................. . As it is the duty of parents to protect their
children, they ................................................................ . For example, they can switch
............................................................ . They can also restrict
................................................................................................... .

**2** Work with a group who completed a different text. Take turns to ask each other questions about the text you completed and make notes about the answers.

**3** Work alone and complete the text you heard about in exercise 2. Compare your completed text with a student from the group you took the notes from.

**For further practice, go to the Direct to IELTS website for downloadable worksheets.**

## Vocabulary: Collocations with *culture*

**1** Work in groups and describe the pictures A–E. Discuss how they might relate to the exchange of ideas between countries in the modern world.

**2** Discuss questions 1–4 and check your answers with other groups.

1 What do you understand by 'culture'?

2 Is culture dynamic or static? What factors make it so?

3 What do you understand by the term 'business culture'?

4 What is the difference between traditional culture and workplace culture? Give an example to illustrate each.

**3** Complete the definitions with words from the box. Then check your answers in pairs.

| enterprise    modern    mainstream    football |

1 ................................. culture is the main or prevailing ideas and activities in a nation or society.

2 ................................. culture is to do with the beliefs, ideas and customs of fans and players of groups of the sport.

3 ................................. culture is the arts, literature and music of the world we live in today as opposed to traditional culture.

4 ................................. culture is the ethos or behaviour behind the making of money through the creation of new companies and businesses.

**4** Work in pairs. Explain at least two of the following terms in your own words. Use a dictionary if necessary.

celebrity culture    street culture    mass culture    contemporary culture

**5** Work in pairs. Change the position of two words in 1–7 to make the sense of the sentences clear.

0 <u>Mainstream</u> culture is vibrant and exciting and has an impact on <u>street</u> culture.

1 In the present age of diverse information, national cultures are being transformed gradually by instant influences.

2 Mainstream culture is affected by a host of factors and changes gradually over time. It is static, not dynamic.

3 Business culture can sometimes seem to be slow to embrace the changes that are occurring in the real world, especially the academic world.

4 Sadly, global culture is often eroded by local influences.

5 Young culture is an important influence on the media, yet it is often thought that it is the media that influences the youth of today.

6 Strong culture is a consumer force which drives the economy of many countries in today's world.

> 0 Street culture is vibrant and exciting and has an impact on mainstream culture.

**6** Categorize the meaning of the word 'culture' in the sentences in exercise 5. Decide whether it relates to a) the arts such as music, literature, etc.; or b) the ideas of a group of people or an organization.

**7** Think of three positive aspects of one of the topics below relating to your own experience or a country you know well.

contemporary culture    popular culture    celebrity culture    materialistic culture

**8** Find a student or students who chose the same topic and discuss your topic.

## IELTS Speaking Parts 1 and 2

**1** Work alone and make questions about your national culture using 1–4.

**1** the kinds of cultural activities/experiences a visitor to your country would expect to see (*What kind(s) of ... ?*)

**2** the frequency of celebrations and festivals (*How often ... ?*)

**3** the time of year of celebrations and festivals (*When/At what time of year ... ?*)

**4** whether you take part in them actively/passively (*Do you take part in ... ?*)

**2** Work in pairs and swap your questions. Take turns to ask and answer the questions. Then discuss the questions as a whole class.

**3** Work in pairs. Discuss the cultural activities 1–10 and assess their value. For example, are they valuable experiences for young people?

**1** going to the theatre/cinema

**2** doing artwork such as painting or drawing

**3** going to a museum/art gallery

**4** visiting a historical site

**5** visiting other countries

**6** learning another language

**7** watching a film with subtitles

**8** watching the news in another language

**9** going to a local, national or international festival

**10** going to a street market

Do you think going to the theatre or cinema is a valuable experience for young people?

Yes, I do because ...

**Tip**

For each of the notes that you make in exercise 4 to explain why you enjoyed or didn't enjoy the event or experience, think of a reason or purpose to help you develop your answer. Do not write the reason or purpose down.

**4** Make notes for the task card below. Compare your notes in pairs and explain what you are going to talk about. Make changes to your notes, if you wish.

> Describe a cultural experience or event you enjoyed or didn't enjoy attending.
>
> You should say:
>
>     when and where the event or experience took place
>
>     who you were with
>
>     what happened at the event or experience
>
> and explain why you enjoyed or didn't enjoy the event or experience.

You followed the notes logically. You glanced at the notes rather than trying to remember them.

**5** Work in different pairs and take turns to talk about the task card.
Give feedback about how well you think you partner followed his/her notes.

## IELTS Listening Section 4

**1** Work in pairs. Look at the picture and answer questions 1 and 2.

**1** Do you like art in the street such as street performances and 3D street art? Why/Why not?

**2** What criticisms do you think people might have of such street art?

**2** Look at the questions 1–10 below and decide what the talk is about.

**3** 1.14 Listen and answer questions 1–10.

### Questions 1–6

Complete the notes below.

Write **NO MORE THAN THREE WORDS AND/OR A NUMBER** for each answer.

Art lectures

art for therapeutic purposes

art classes to promote creativity in schools

various ways to promote participation in art in **(1)** ...........................................

Mainstream methods

- colouring books • TV programmes • school art classes
- trips to art galleries – running **(2)** ........................................... for various age groups

Non-mainstream methods

highlight art through **(3)** ........................................... with street art

street performers, e.g. jugglers, singers

astonishing form of street art – **(4)** ........................................... art

dramatic visual impact – stops people

shows vast holes in the ground with such **(5)** ...........................................

difficult to replicate in a gallery

past artists used similar effects

Problem: Pavement art is **(6)** ........................................... and disappears.

### Questions 7–10

Choose the correct letter, **A**, **B** or **C**.

**7** As regards the criticism of street art for not being mainstream, the speaker

  **A** agrees with it.

  **B** disagrees with it.

  **C** accepts it.

**8** To overcome reservations about street artists causing graffiti, it is suggested that

  **A** a monitoring system could be introduced.

  **B** a fine could be administered for damage.

  **C** a licence could be issued.

**9** Street art acts as a means to

  **A** make people's lives brighter.

  **B** provide employment for artists.

  **C** bring tourists to various areas.

**10** The speaker concludes that street art is

  **A** not yet mainstream art.

  **B** a misunderstood art form.

  **C** a legitimate form of art.

# Language focus: Defining and non-defining relative clauses

 Read more about defining and non-defining relative clauses in the online **Grammar Reference**.

**1** The three extracts from Listening Section 4 below contain relative clauses. Underline the clauses and answer questions 1–3.

**a** One non-mainstream way of drawing people's and especially children's attention to art, which is really intriguing, is random encounters with art in the street, so-called street art.

**b** Cities have always been full of street performers such as jugglers and singers, who add colour to otherwise drab environments, sometimes as part of festivals such as the Edinburgh Festival in Scotland.

**c** We've looked at ways that art can be used for therapeutic purposes with patients.

**1** Does the relative clause tell us essential information?

**2** Does the sentence still make sense if we remove the relative clause?

**3** Is there a comma before and after the clause?

**2** Complete the sentences 1–8 with the phrases a–h. There may be more than one answer. Add any necessary punctuation.

**1** The music concerts _____ are very colourful.

**2** Popular culture _____ is frowned upon by some people.

**3** Street art _____ is very exciting.

**4** Media _____ is invaluable.

**5** Any language _____ needs to be saved.

**6** Foreign language lessons _____ are not always taken seriously.

**7** Countries _____ often enjoy many economic benefits.

**8** The site for rock art _____ was just breathtaking.

**a** which is a relatively new form of art to me

**b** that helps spread an appreciation of art

**c** which is in danger of extinction

**d** which includes soap operas and light entertainment like musicals

**e** which are essential in any school curriculum

**f** which promote an enterprise culture

**g** I visited in the desert

**h** which are held in my home town in the spring

**3** Think about one of the following. Then work in pairs and take turns to talk about the item you chose.

A piece of contemporary or traditional art I like is ...

A TV programme I first saw as a child is ...

The book I like best is ...

## Grammar focus

Defining clauses

1 You can use defining relative clauses to provide information which cannot be left out as the information identifies who or what is being referred to. Such clauses do not have commas at the beginning and end of the clause.

*The artist who painted the pictures in this gallery has used very vibrant colours.*

2 You can omit the relative pronoun if it is the object of the clause, but only in defining clauses.

3 When speaking, some people use *that* instead of *who/whom*.

Non-defining clauses

1 You can use non-defining relative clauses to provide additional information which can be left out. Such clauses have commas at the beginning and the end.

2 You cannot leave out the relative pronoun in non-defining clauses when it is the object of the clause.

3 You cannot use the word *that* to introduce a non-defining clause.

• You use *which* with prepositions rather than *that*.

• You use *whose* to describe possession.

## IELTS Writing Task 1

**1** Work in groups. Discuss:

- whether reading is popular among your friends and family.
- what kinds of things the different people you know read.
- whether reading is valued in your country/country's educational system.
- whether the value of reading is declining and, if so, why.

**2** Look at Writing Task 1 below. Then discuss questions 1–7.

1 Does the chart show trends?
2 Can you call the bar chart a graph?
3 Are the patterns among boys and girls similar?
4 What is the most/least popular reading material among both boys and girls?
5 Who tends to read more, boys or girls?
6 In which categories does the proportion of boys exceed girls?
7 In how many categories does the proportion of girls exceed boys?

You should spend about 20 minutes on this task.

*The bar chart opposite shows the type of reading material read more than once a month by 9–14-year-olds outside of school in England in 2007.*

*Summarize the information by selecting and reporting the main features, and make comparisons where relevant.*

Write at least 150 words.

Type of reading material read[1] by children[2] outside of school 2007

England

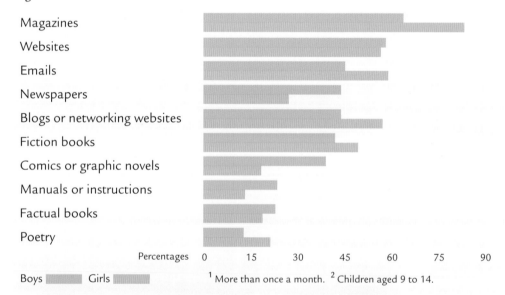

Boys ▢ Girls ▢    [1] More than once a month.  [2] Children aged 9 to 14.

**3** Work in pairs. In each pair of sentences 1–4, decide if b is a correct paraphrase of a. Correct any factual information in sentence b which is incorrect.

**1 a** The reading patterns for both genders differ significantly.

**b** There is a vast difference in the reading patterns for boys and girls.

**2 a** The most popular reading material among both boys and girls is magazines, approximately 65 per cent and 80 per cent respectively.

**b** Magazines are more popular among both genders than the other materials, with a greater proportion of girls than boys (approximately 80 per cent and 65 per cent respectively) reading such material.

**3 a** Almost as many girls as boys read websites, approximately 55 per cent and 58 per cent respectively.

**b** Not as many boys as girls read websites, approximately 58 per cent and 55 per cent respectively.

**4 a** The most noticeable difference between boys' and girls' reading habits is seen in magazines and newspapers.

**b** Magazines and newspapers stand out as the two types of reading materials in which the difference between boys and girl is striking.

**4** Write three sentences of your own about blogs or networking websites, fiction books or factual books in the chart, as in exercise 3. Then compare your sentences in pairs.

**5** Write an introduction and overview for the bar chart in exercise 2.

**6** Write an answer for Writing Task 1 below.

You should spend about 20 minutes on this task.

*The bar chart opposite shows selected types of television programmes viewed by sex in England in 2007/8.*

*Summarize the information by selecting and reporting the main features, and make comparisons where relevant.*

Write at least 150 words.

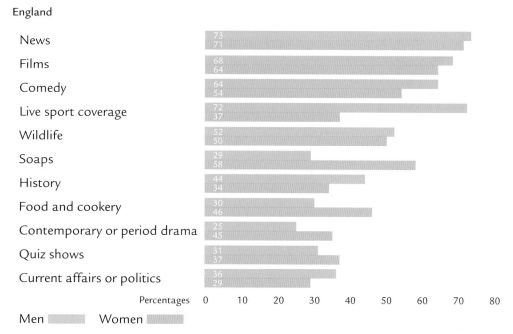

Selected types of television programmes viewed: by sex, 2007/2008

England

News 73 / 71
Films 68 / 64
Comedy 64 / 54
Live sport coverage 72 / 37
Wildlife 52 / 50
Soaps 29 / 58
History 44 / 34
Food and cookery 30 / 46
Contemporary or period drama 25 / 45
Quiz shows 31 / 37
Current affairs or politics 36 / 29

Percentages 0 10 20 30 40 50 60 70 80

Men    Women

**7** Compare your answers in pairs. Check how you have described/compared individual types of programmes.

**Additional material: page 108**

**Writing bank: page 113**

## IELTS Reading

**1** Work in groups. Decide whether you think the statements below are true.

    **1** Newspapers contain more positive than negative words.

    **2** The words used on Twitter are more positive than negative.

    **3** *Food* was considered a 'happier word' than *laughter* in happiness studies.

    **4** There is a universal human tendency to use positive words.

**2** Scan the text and find answers to the questions in exercise 1. Do they match your answers?

**3** Answer questions 1–13 about the reading passage.

### We May Be Less Happy, But Our Language Isn't
*News is bad news and the worst news gets the big story on the front page.*

So one might expect the *New York Times* to contain, on average, more negative and unhappy types of words – like "war," " funeral," "cancer," "murder" – than positive, happy ones – like "love," "peace" and "hero." Or take Twitter. A popular image of what people tweet about may contain a lot of complaints about bad days, worse coffee, busted relationships and lousy sitcoms. Again, it might be reasonable to guess that a giant bag containing all the words from the world's tweets – on average – would be more negative and unhappy than positive and happy. But new research shows just the opposite. "English, it turns out, is strongly biased toward being positive," said Peter Dodds, an applied mathematician at the University of Vermont.

This new study complements another study the same Vermont scientists presented previously on patterns of happiness and information in a global social network. That work attracted wide media attention showing that average global happiness, based on Twitter data, has been dropping for the past two years. Combined, the two studies show that short-term average happiness has dropped – against the backdrop of the long-term fundamental positivity of the English language.

In the new study, Dodds and his colleagues gathered billions of words from four sources: twenty years of the *New York Times*, the Google Books Project (with millions of titles going back to 1520), Twitter and a half-century of music lyrics. "The big surprise is that in each of these four sources it's the same," says Dodds. "We looked at the top 5,000 words in each, in terms of frequency, and in all of those words you see a preponderance of happier words." Or, as they write in their study, "a positivity bias is universal," both for very common words and less common ones and across sources as diverse as tweets, lyrics and British literature.

Why is this? "It's not to say that everything is fine and happy," Dodds says. "It's just that language is social." In contrast to traditional economic theory, which suggests people are inherently and rationally selfish, a wave of new social science and neuroscience data shows something quite different: that we are a pro-social storytelling species. As language emerged and evolved over the last million years, positive words, it seems, have been more widely and deeply engrained into our communications than negative ones. "If you want to remain in a social contract with other people, you can't be a...," well, Dodds here used a word that is rather too negative to be fit to print – which makes the point.

This new work adds depth to the Twitter study that the Vermont scientists published in December that attracted attention from different media outlets. "After that mild downer story, we can say, 'But wait – there's still happiness in the bank,'" Dodds notes. "On average, there's always a net happiness to language." Both studies drew on a service from Amazon called Mechanical Turk. On this website, the UVM researchers paid a group of volunteers to rate, from one to nine, their sense of the "happiness" – the emotional temperature – of the 10,222 most common words gathered from the four sources. Averaging their scores, the volunteers rated, for example, "laughter" at 8.50, "food" 7.44, "truck" 5.48, and "greed" 3.06.

The Vermont team then took these scores and applied them to the huge pools of words they collected. Unlike some other studies – with smaller samples or that elicited strong emotional words from volunteers – the new UVM study, based solely on frequency of use, found that "positive words strongly outnumber negative words overall."

This seems to lend support to the so-called Pollyanna Principle, put forth in 1969, that argues for a universal human tendency to use positive words more often, easily and in more ways than negative words. Of course, most people would rank some words, like "the," with the same score: a neutral 5. Other words, like "pregnancy," have a wide spread, with some people ranking it high and others low. "A lot of these words – the neutral words or ones that have big standard deviations – get washed out when we use them as a measure," Dodds notes. Instead, the trends he and his team have observed are driven by the bulk of English words tending to be happy.

If we think of words as atoms and sentences as molecules that combine to form a whole text, "we're looking at atoms," says Dodds. "A lot of news is bad," he says, and short-term happiness may rise and fall like the cycles of the economy, "but the atoms of the story – of language – are, overall, on the positive side."

### Questions 1–5

Do the following statements agree with the information given in the reading passage?

Write:

**YES**          *if the statement agrees with the claims of the writer*

**NO**           *if the statement contradicts the claims of the writer*

**NOT GIVEN** *if it is impossible to say what the writer thinks about this*

1  People might expect the *New York Times* and Twitter to have more positive than negative words.

2  According to Dodds, English people prefer using positive words.

3  Dodds' second study is linked to an earlier one.

4  Dodds' first study was mainly ignored by the media.

5  According to Dodds' studies, there has been a fall in the positivity of English along with a rise in short-term average happiness.

### Questions 6–9

Complete each sentence with the correct ending, **A–H**, below.

6  The source materials used in the second study were

7  According to traditional economic theory, people are

8  Using the Mechanical Turk, the most common words were

9  The new study focused on words that were

| | | |
|---|---|---|
| **A** essentially social. | **D** graded on a scale. | **G** similar to one another. |
| **B** used frequently. | **E** different from each other. | **H** basically self-centred. |
| **C** rarely spoken. | **F** emotional. | |

### Questions 10–13

Complete the summary using the list of words and phrases, **A–I**, below.

**The Pollyanna principle**

The work done by Dodds and his team seems to confirm **(10)** ............................... the Pollyanna Principle. This states that people generally use positive words more than negative words. **(11)** ............................... such as 'the' have a neutral ranking with others such as 'pregnancy' being ranked both high and low. However, **(12)** ............................... that have been noted are driven by the bulk of English words tending to be happy. Dodds compares words to atoms and sentences to molecules. While bad news affects short-term happiness (in effect the molecules), the atoms in the news item are **(13)** ............................... .

| | | |
|---|---|---|
| **A** generally positive | **B** the trend in | **C** doubts about |
| **D** the main trends | **E** partially negative | **F** the general ideas |
| **G** the existence of | **H** special terms | **I** common words |

## Reaction

4  **Work in groups. What is your reaction to the text? Do you agree with the contents? Do you find them surprising/funny?**

## IELTS Speaking Part 3

**1** Work in pairs. Match the notes a–c to the questions about world culture 1–3.

**World culture**

**1** Do you think it is important for schoolchildren to learn about other cultures in school? Why/Why not?

**2** In what ways can children be taught about culture?

**3** Do you think that one day there will be one world culture? Why/Why not?

    a  *enrich, improve, teach, stimulate*

    b  *impossible, unlikely, possible, feasible*

    c  *language, films, books, travel*

**2** Think of two words (either verbs or adjectives) you associate with each question 1–3 below. Write notes as in exercise 1.

**Cultural activities**

**1** Some people think that cultural activities should not be subsidized by the government. What is your opinion?

**2** What is the effect if the cost of cultural activities such as theatre or cinema visits is too high?

**3** What kind of cultural activities do you think will be popular in the future?

**3** Work in groups of three and take turns to discuss the questions in exercises 1 and 2 in pairs. The third student should give general feedback. Avoid looking at any notes.

## IELTS Writing Task 2

**1** Give at least one cause for each of the situations below.

**1** In some parts of the world traditional festivals and celebrations are disappearing.

**2** Film attendance in some counties is on the decline.

**3** Cultural activities such as theatre performances are becoming expensive to attend.

**4** Languages such as English are spreading while other local languages are dying out.

**5** Newspaper sales are declining.

**6** International travel is increasing with more people flying long distances than in the past.

**7** Young people are losing interest in traditional skills and crafts.

**8** The number of people working in traditional manufacturing jobs is declining.

**2** Work in groups and compare your answers to exercise 1. Then choose one of the statements and:

- state the cause and describe it from a national and/or international perspective.
- provide and explain the examples and effects.
- give at least one solution in each case.

1 In some parts of the world traditional festivals and celebrations have disappeared or are disappearing. From an international perspective, this is the direct result of globalization. For example ...

### Useful language

Talking about solutions:

should/could/a good idea is to/one solution/measure/ step/way/answer/ option is ...

**3** Select the three main causes of one of the problems 1–8 in exercise 1, and three measures that could be taken to reverse the problem.

| Causes | Measures |
|---|---|
| the adoption of a new (second/third) language | an economic boost to local/rural areas |
| globalization | cultural centres |
| travelling for leisure | more local museums |
| migration | schoolchildren participating in local festivals |
| the use of modern technology | education/school trips |
| young people's informed views | learning local languages |
| social change | inviting people into the school |

> **Tip**
>
> In exercise 5, think about: singular/plural, missing words, subject-verb agreement, articles, adjectives, spelling, prepositions, the form of words, and punctuation in relative clauses.

**4** Work in groups. Compare your answers to exercise 3 and discuss one of the causes and one of the measures in detail.

**5** Read Writing Task 2 below. Then find and correct the mistakes in paragraph 1, which is part of the answer to the task. Compare your answers in pairs.

---

You should spend about 40 minutes on this task. Write about the following topic:

***In some parts of the world traditional festivals and celebrations have disappeared or are disappearing. What do you think are the causes of this development and what measures could be taken to solve it?***

Give reasons for your answer and include any relevant examples from your own knowledge and experience. Write at least 250 words.

---

Paragraph 1

There are many cause of this situation, but perhaps the main is the migration of people away from rural areas to the cities, tends to occur mainly among young people. This process of urbanization is very damaging to local communities, as it means that only the older generations are left behind. With movement of people, there is a good chance that many of those who move away will loose contact with their home towns and tradition practices. They may also learn new languages and new customs, which may further erode the old customs and traditions. This may then make them feel their 'former culture' is old-fashioned and of less value than the new cultur they are experiencing. (7 mistakes )

---

**6** Work in pairs and find examples of the following in the answer in exercise 5.

**Paragraph 1**

**1** a topic sentence (see page 51)

**2** an evaluation of the situation

**3** a explanation of the evaluation

**4** a relative clause

**5** a second cause

**6** a conclusion

**7** Write an introduction for the essay in exercise 5.

**8** Write an answer for Writing Task 2 below.

---

You should spend about 40 minutes on this task. Write about the following topic:

***Interest in traditional skills and crafts among young people worldwide is declining. What do you think are the causes of this development and what measures could be taken to solve it?***

Give reasons for your answer and include any relevant examples from your own knowledge and experience. Write at least 250 words.

---

**9** Work in pairs. Use the lists of items in exercise 6 to help you analyse one or more of your paragraphs.

**Writing bank: page 119**

# Review

## Vocabulary: Collocations with *culture*

1 Provide an example of behaviour and activities for 1–4.

  **0** football culture
  **1** business culture
  **2** consumer culture
  **3** workplace culture
  **4** mainstream culture

  0 going to matches, wearing the colours of the football teams, going on trips to support teams

2 Provide an example of the arts relating to 1–5.

  **1** contemporary culture
  **2** traditional culture
  **3** popular culture
  **4** street culture
  **5** modern culture

3 Work in pairs and compare your answers.

## IELTS Writing Task 1 (Using defining and non-defining clauses)

1 Combine the pairs of sentences using a defining or non-defining relative clause.

  **0** The tickets for the ballet sold out overnight. They cost more than 100 euros each.
  **1** Concerts are very expensive. They don't attract students or poor people.
  **2** Culture is very important for all of us. It is often undervalued by the government.
  **3** Films often show a lot of violence. They should be banned.
  **4** Museums are centres of education. They should be free.
  **5** People read a lot of books and newspapers. They are often well informed.
  **6** The arts need to be subsidized. They reach a lot of people.

The tickets for the ballet, which cost more than 100 euros each, sold out overnight

2 Work in pairs. Read the extracts from the writing task on page 94. Which contains a defining relative clause and which a non-defining relative clause? How do you know?

  **1** The least common type of reading material among boys was poetry (approximately 10 per cent), which contrasted with manuals or instructions at around 12 per cent.
  **2** While the proportion of girls who read emails exceeded boys (about 60 per cent against 45 per cent), the reverse was the case regarding newspapers, with boys at just under 45 per cent and girls about 28 per cent.

3 Write two alternative sentences about three items in the chart opposite.

  **1** The main association that was made with the word 'culture' was arts, accounting for nearly 40 per cent of respondents.
  Arts, which accounted for nearly 40 per cent of respondents, was the main association made with the word 'culture'.

4 Compare your sentences with other students.

Associations made with the word 'culture', persons aged over 14 years, EU-27, 2007

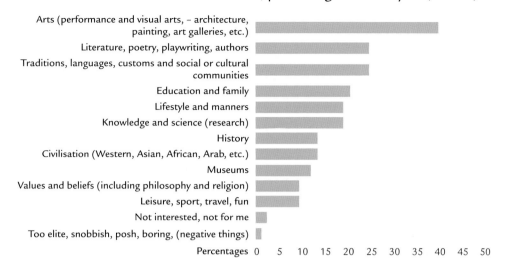

## IELTS Writing Task 2

**1** Work in pairs. Describe the graph below and make a list of factors that might influence the trend in cinema-going.

**Cinema admissions** United Kingdom

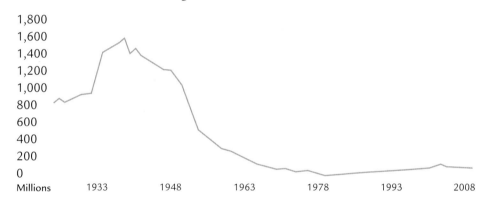

**2** Compare your answers with another pair of students.

**3** Read Writing Task 2 below. Then write a paragraph of about 80 words describing one or more cause.

You should spend about 40 minutes on this task.

Write about the following topic:

*Cinema attendance in some countries is on the decline.*

*What do you think are the causes of this development and what measures could be taken to solve it?*

Give reasons for your answer and include any relevant examples from your own knowledge and experience.

Write at least 250 words.

**4** Compare your paragraph with the whole class.

**For further practice, go to the Direct to IELTS website for downloadable worksheets.**

# Additional material

## Unit 1

### IELTS Speaking Parts 1 and 2  page 7

1 Make questions using the prompts 1–8.

0 enjoy/studying/English?

1 enjoy/living in a city?/Why/Why not?

2 how often/family/go/trips/away from home?

3 you/like/modern towns or cities?/Why/Why not?

4 kinds/places/you/visit/your country?

5 recommend/these places/tourists to visit? Why/Why not?

6 most modern/city/visited?

7 old buildings/important/your culture? Why/Why not?

8 prefer/modern buildings/old buildings?

0 Do you enjoy studying English?

2 Compare your questions in pairs. Then take turns to ask and answer the questions. Your answers should be no more than two or three sentences.

3 Work in groups and choose a task card, A or B. Make a list of at least five reasons why you might dislike a city or town, or reasons for liking a modern building.

A

Describe a city or town that you do not like.

You should say:

where the city or town is

when you first visited the city or town

what the city or town is like

and explain why you do not like the city or town.

B

Describe a modern building you like.

You should say:

where the modern building is

when you first saw the modern building

what the modern building is like

and explain why you like the modern building.

4 Work in pairs with a student who chose the same task card. Take turns to talk about the card. Compare your reasons and discuss which reasons were best.

### Vocabulary: Collocations with nouns  page 11

1 Think of a place that you know or are familiar with for at least three of 1–8.

1 a place that has/has not yet undergone enormous change

2 a place that has/has not yet undergone industrial change

3 a place where transport expansion has accelerated development

4 a place which has been/has not been improved by economic development

5 a place where a reduction in traffic jams has/has not been achieved

6 an area undergoing development in your country where you think more progress needs to be made

7 a place where you think economic development would help

8 an area of life where rapid advances in technology have taken/need to take place

**2** Work in pairs. Talk about three of the places in exercise 1 giving reasons, examples and purposes.

**3** Write 50–100 words about one of the places in exercise 1.

The area around the village where I come from has not undergone enormous change in the last 20 years. In fact, there has been very little economic or industrial development. The main reason for this is …

# Unit 2

## Vocabulary 1: Collocations – multiple combinations  page 18

**1** Answer the questions below. In some cases there may be more than one answer. Use words and phrases from page 18.

  1  What do you collect, examine, study as part of research?
  2  What do you keep, destroy or update in a business or your studies?
  3  What can governments conduct, fund or support in the field of science?
  4  What can the authorities conduct, pursue or lead if there has been a crime?
  5  What can you study if you are a student?
  6  What can you carry out, conduct or do for essays or dissertations?
  7  What can you make or perform if you have collected a lot of data?
  8  What can companies conduct to find out about their products?

**2** Compare your answers in pairs. Take turns to ask and answer the questions.

**3** Spend five minutes thinking about explanations for the statements below.

  1  It is important to carry out archaeological research.
  2  People keep personal records such as diaries.
  3  Studying history is as important as studying business or law.
  4  Scientific studies are essential even if they cost a lot of money.
  5  Customer surveys need to be carried out.

**4** Work in groups. Discuss one statement from exercise 3, giving reasons and examples. One member of the group then summarizes your discussion for the whole class in one minute.

## IELTS Writing Task 1  page 21

**1** Work in pairs. Study the pie charts below for two minutes. Close your books and write down as much information as you can about the charts.

Occupational structure of the employed population, by age group, EU, 2007 (%)

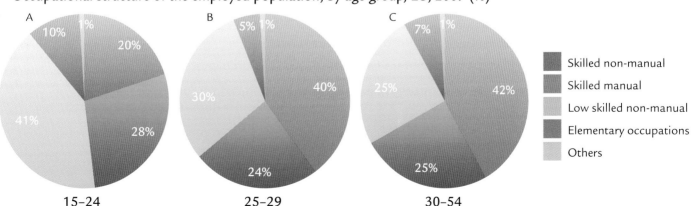

A — 15–24

B — 25–29

C — 30–54

Skilled non-manual
Skilled manual
Low skilled non-manual
Elementary occupations
Others

**Glossary:** Elementary occupations: light manual labour

103

**2** Compare your answers with another pair of students.

**3** As a whole class, collate the information on the board. When you have finished, look at the pie charts again and check if there is anything you want to add to the list on the board.

## Language focus: Using nouns to build ideas  page 26

**1** Work in pairs. Create a noun phrase for each set of words in italics. Write full sentences.

**0** There has been *dramatic fall cost travelling* in recent years.
**1** *dramatic increase new technology products* has made the choice for consumers difficult.
**2** *regeneration old parts towns* is needed to ensure *preservation important buildings historical interest*
**3** *impact study history young people's lives* must not be underestimated.
**4** *difference conducting research any subject university nowadays past* is enormous.
**5** *recent decline reading newspapers books paper form* has been attributed to *rise ebook readers*
**6** *range products available sale internet sites major stores* is increasing on a daily basis.
**7** *rise number tourists visiting national monuments temples country houses* is causing *considerable harm fabric buildings*
**8** *number TV programmes history* outnumbers programmes about other subjects.

**0** There has been a dramatic fall in the cost of travelling in recent years.

**2** Write a sentence about one of the following.

**1** a dramatic change in your life in recent years
**2** the impact of learning English on your life
**3** the number of electronic gadgets you possess
**4** the difference between life nowadays and previous generations in your country
**5** the cost of education now compared to the past

**3** Work in pairs and explain your sentence to your partner.

## Unit 3

## Language focus: Prepositions  page 33

**1** Use a preposition to continue the sentences in your own words.

**0** Overusing computers can result ...
**1** People often associate technology ...
**2** If someone wants to specialize ...
**3** The rise of the information age stems ...
**4** It's not always easy to comply ...
**5** My home town differs ...
**6** As far as libraries are concerned, we should insist ...

**0** Overusing computers can result in physical problems.

**2** Compare your answers in pairs. Prepare three questions for two of the statements you completed in exercise 1. Take turn to ask each other questions about the statements.

- Why does this happen?
- Are there any ways to combat this situation?
- Do you think the situation will become worse in the future?

**3** As a whole class, make a list of the main effects relating to sentence 3 in exercise 1. Discuss how the information age might develop in the future.

**1** Work in pairs. Look at photos A–D and say which type of process they represent: natural, manufacturing or both.

**2** Match the list of stages 1–4 to the pictures A–D.

**1** the planting of the tree, the care of the tree, the growth of the tree, the production of the fruit, the ripening of the fruit, the harvesting of the crop, the transportation to the factory, the grading and sorting of the fruit, the packaging, the shipping overseas, the storage, the sale

**2** the laying of the eggs, the hatching of the eggs, the emergence of the caterpillar, the growth of the caterpillar, the formation of the chrysalis, the emergence of the butterfly, the repetition of the cycle

**3** the construction of the windmill, the connection to the electricity grid by underground cables, the blowing of the wind, the turning of the blades, the production of energy

**4** the planting of a tree, the growth of the tree, the maturity of the tree, the chopping down of the tree, the selection of the wood, the cutting to size, the assembly of the pieces of wood, the attachment of the legs to the seat, the attachment of the back to the seat, the painting of the wood, the storage, the sale, the use

**3** Work in pairs. Choose one of the lists of stages in exercise 2 and, without preparation, describe to your partner the process or cycle. Use verbs, or a mixture of verbs and nouns.

*After the planting stage, the tree is taken care of …*

# Unit 4

## Vocabulary: Leisure and entertainment  page 43

**1** Make as many noun phrases as possible using the words below.

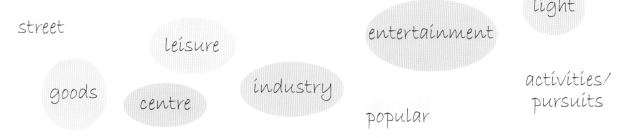

street    leisure    entertainment    light    goods    centre    industry    activities/pursuits    popular

street entertainment, leisure centre, …

**2** Decide what the purpose is of at least five of the items you made in exercise 1.

*The purpose of street entertainment is to bring pleasure to the public and also to earn money.*

**3** Work in pairs and explain your answers in exercise 2, giving reasons and examples.

# Unit 5

## IELTS Writing Task 2 page 59

1 Decide how you would evaluate 1–10. Use one or more of the adjectives in the box.

| highly desirable | prohibitive | essential | achievable | impossible | extravagant |
| invaluable | wasteful | sensible | uneconomical | effective | ineffective |

1 cutting the funding for healthcare
2 improving the healthcare of the country
3 ridding the world of disease
4 walking to work
5 joining a gym
6 employing more doctors
7 increasing the salaries of nurses
8 eating a healthy diet
9 investing in the best medical technology money can buy
10 making medication and operations free for all

2 Work in groups. Compare your answers and discuss your evaluations, giving reasons and examples.

3 The diagram below illustrates item 3 in exercise 1. In groups, complete the diagram with notes.

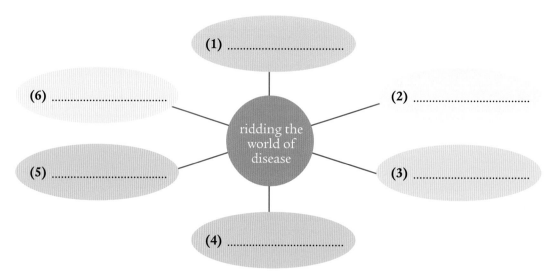

4 Compare your completed diagram with other groups and then the whole class.

5 Discuss and write the introduction and first paragraph of Writing Task 2 below.

> You should spend about 40 minutes on this task.
> Write about the following topic:
>
> *Some people think that ridding the world of disease should be the priority of healthcare systems.*
> *To what extent do you agree or disagree?*
>
> Give reasons for your answer and include any relevant examples from your own knowledge and experience.
> Write at least 250 words.

# Unit 6

## IELTS Writing Task 1   page 71

**Useful language**

Between 1985 and 2010,

... was constructed ...

By 2010, a ... had been constructed.

... had been lost

**1** Work in pairs, A and B. Student A: study the map for Tanton from 1985. Student B: study the map for Tanton from 2010. Do not look at each other's map.

**2** Student A: describe the map. Student B: each time Student A describes something that differs from your map, interrupt and describe the difference.

**Student A**

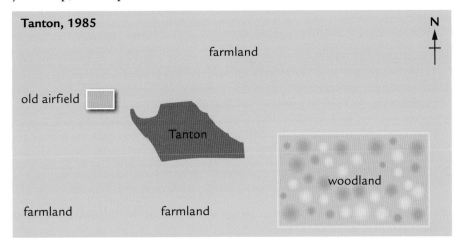

**Student B**

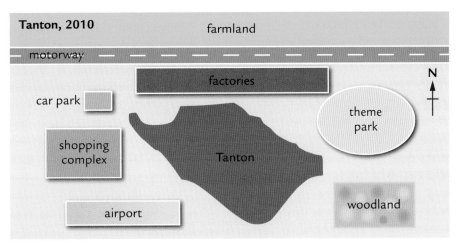

**3** Compare the two maps.

**4** Complete the text below describing the two maps. You can make changes to the words in the outline, if you wish.

The maps show the transformation **(1)** ......................................................................................... .
During this time, a number of developments occurred. By 2010, a **(2)** .........................................
.............................................. , preventing **(3)** ..........................................................................
.............. As the village spread **(4)** .......................................................................... , the
woodland **(5)** .......................................................... . West of the village, a
**(6)** ...................................................................... with the old airfield **(7)** ....................
............................................................ . Northeast of the village, farmland **(8)** ....................
.............................................................. . By 2010, north of the village close to the motorway,
more farmland had been lost as **(9)** .................................................................................. .
Overall, it is clear that the area around Tanton changed dramatically over the period with
**(10)** .............................................................. .

# Unit 7

## IELTS Writing Task 2  page 87

**1** Work in pairs. Rewrite sentences 1–5 so there is less repetition. Use *it*, *this*, *they* and *this* + a suitable noun. Compare your sentences other students.

**0** Children are exposed to a considerable number of adverts which are harmful from a very early age, so parents should be careful to protect children from adverts which are harmful.

**1** Browsing the internet can be fun, but browsing the internet also wastes a lot of time.

**2** People tend to be led by advertising when people shop, but advertising doesn't always affect people's shopping habits.

**3** TV adverts during children's programmes should be banned, but banning adverts during children's programmes is not going to stop the problem.

**4** Some people think that children don't notice the adverts on TV, but children do. So parents need to be aware of the fact that children notice adverts on TV.

**5** Companies such as supermarkets carry out surveys to gauge shoppers' preferences. Carrying out surveys to gauge shoppers' preferences is not the only practice that companies use to engage with shoppers.

**0** Children are exposed to a considerable number of adverts which are harmful from a very early age, so parents should be careful to protect them from this.

**2** Work in pairs and write three sentences about one of the following. Write on a large sheet of paper to display to the class.

- the time wasted by people of all ages playing on computers
- the time saved by using computers
- the best electronic gadget that I own
- the power of advertising

**3** Display your answers and check each other's work for repetition.

# Unit 8

## IELTS Writing Task 1  page 95

**1** Work in pairs. Write at least five questions about the bar chart below.

Participation rates in artistic activities, by age group, EU-27, 2007

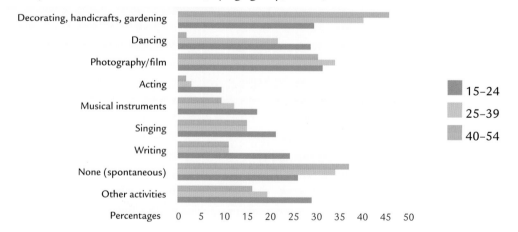

**2** Work with another partner. Take turns to ask and answer your questions from exercise 1.

**3** Write several sentences comparing the participation of the different age groups in one of the artistic activities.

## IELTS Writing Task 1

### Line graphs    Unit 1, page 10

> You should spend about 20 minutes on this task.
>
> *The graph below shows annual cinema admissions by age in the UK.*
>
> *Summarize the information by selecting and reporting the main features, and make comparisons where relevant.*
>
> Write at least 150 words.

Annual cinema admissions: by age  United Kingdom

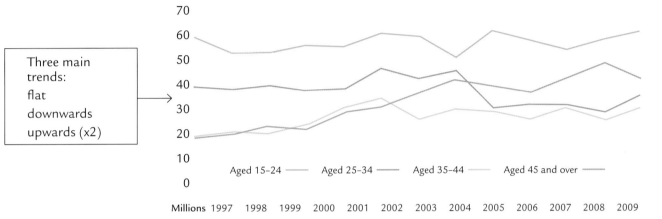

Three main trends:
flat
downwards
upwards (x2)

### Model answer

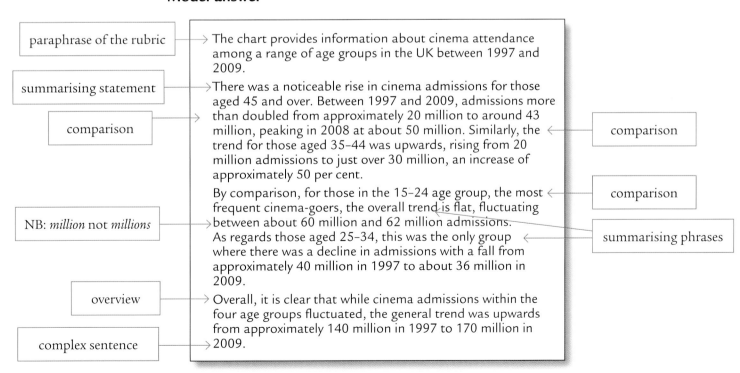

paraphrase of the rubric → The chart provides information about cinema attendance among a range of age groups in the UK between 1997 and 2009.

summarising statement → There was a noticeable rise in cinema admissions for those aged 45 and over. Between 1997 and 2009, admissions more than doubled from approximately 20 million to around 43 million, peaking in 2008 at about 50 million. Similarly, the trend for those aged 35–44 was upwards, rising from 20 million admissions to just over 30 million, an increase of approximately 50 per cent.

comparison

comparison

By comparison, for those in the 15–24 age group, the most frequent cinema-goers, the overall trend is flat, fluctuating between about 60 million and 62 million admissions.

comparison

NB: *million* not *millions*

As regards those aged 25–34, this was the only group where there was a decline in admissions with a fall from approximately 40 million in 1997 to about 36 million in 2009.

summarising phrases

overview → Overall, it is clear that while cinema admissions within the four age groups fluctuated, the general trend was upwards from approximately 140 million in 1997 to 170 million in 2009.

complex sentence

## Useful language for line graphs

Introduction

the graph shows/illustrates/provides/gives information about/provides/gives a breakdown of …

Trends

Verbs: rises/declines

Nouns: There is a (slight/moderate/dramatic) rise/decline in …

The trend in … is upward(s)/downward(s)/flat.

There is a(n) (upward/downward/flat) trend in …

Verbs

rise: go up, increase, soar, climb, leap, jump, improve, stage a recovery, grow

fall: decrease, decline, drop, plummet, plunge, dive, go down

remain flat: be steady/stable

fluctuate: be erratic, go up and down, experience some fluctuations

Comparisons

Nouns: More/fewer (people/teachers) … in … than in, as many … as …

Adjectives: experienced a bigger rise than …

Adverbs: (rose/fell) more slowly/quickly than …

Linking devices

Adverbs: by comparison, by contrast, in comparison

Conjunctions: while, whereas, although

Noun phrases

Those aged 15–24

Those in the 15–24 age group

25–24-year-olds

**Task**

You should spend about 20 minutes on this task.

*The graph below shows the number of full-time qualified teachers in state schools in the United Kingdom.*

*Summarize the information by selecting and reporting the main features, and make comparisons where relevant.*

Write at least 150 words.

Full-time teachers:[1] by sex and type of school          United Kingdom

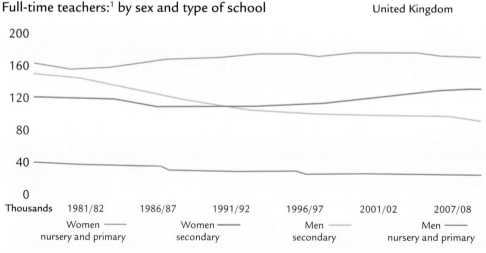

[1] Qualified teachers in public sector mainstream schools.

## Pie charts Unit 2, page 21

You should spend about 20 minutes on this task.

*The pie charts below show the expenditure of two technology companies of similar size in the UK in 2012.*

*Summarize the information by selecting and reporting the main features, and make comparisons where relevant.*

Write at least 150 words.

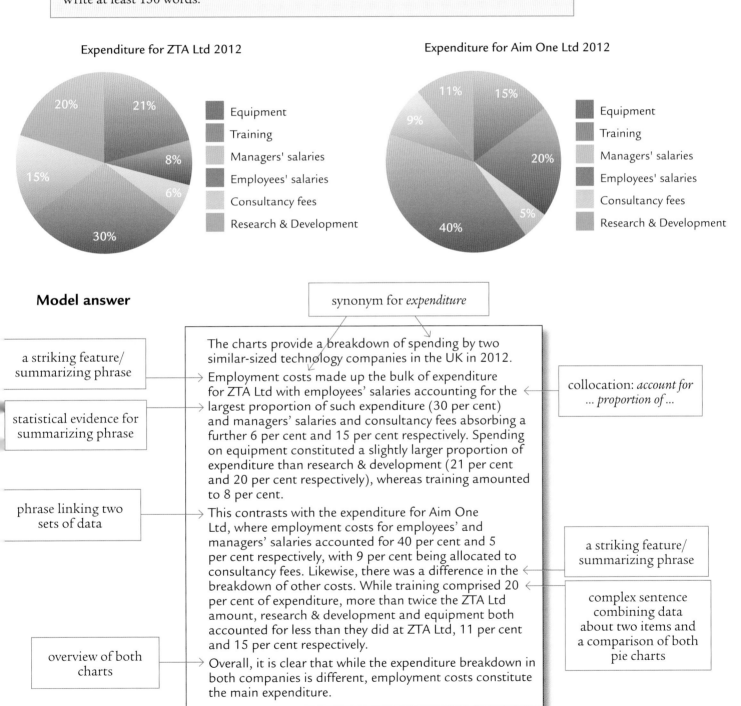

**Model answer**

synonym for *expenditure*

a striking feature/ summarizing phrase

statistical evidence for summarizing phrase

phrase linking two sets of data

overview of both charts

The charts provide a breakdown of spending by two similar-sized technology companies in the UK in 2012. Employment costs made up the bulk of expenditure for ZTA Ltd with employees' salaries accounting for the largest proportion of such expenditure (30 per cent) and managers' salaries and consultancy fees absorbing a further 6 per cent and 15 per cent respectively. Spending on equipment constituted a slightly larger proportion of expenditure than research & development (21 per cent and 20 per cent respectively), whereas training amounted to 8 per cent.

This contrasts with the expenditure for Aim One Ltd, where employment costs for employees' and managers' salaries accounted for 40 per cent and 5 per cent respectively, with 9 per cent being allocated to consultancy fees. Likewise, there was a difference in the breakdown of other costs. While training comprised 20 per cent of expenditure, more than twice the ZTA Ltd amount, research & development and equipment both accounted for less than they did at ZTA Ltd, 11 per cent and 15 per cent respectively.

Overall, it is clear that while the expenditure breakdown in both companies is different, employment costs constitute the main expenditure.

collocation: *account for ... proportion of ...*

a striking feature/ summarizing phrase

complex sentence combining data about two items and a comparison of both pie charts

## Useful language for pie charts

Verbs to use with proportion

account for, comprise, constitute, consist of, make up, form, total, represent

Other verbs

spend on, allocate, devote, apportion, amount to

Synonyms for *proportion*

amount, share

Phrases

The bulk of

The majority of

The main part of

A small/large/sizeable proportion of

Phrases connecting data

(This) contrasts (sharply) with (the expenditure for) ...

(This) compares/reflects/mirrors/correlates with/corresponds with/relates to ...

(This) is reflected in/mirrored in /related to ...

There is a similar/different pattern/trend in ...

A similar/(slightly/totally) different pattern is seen/witnessed in ...

### Task

You should spend about 20 minutes on this task.

*The pie charts below show the production of fruit and vegetables in the 27 countries of the European Union in 2009.*

*Summarize the information by selecting and reporting the main features, and make comparisons where relevant.*

Write at least 150 words.

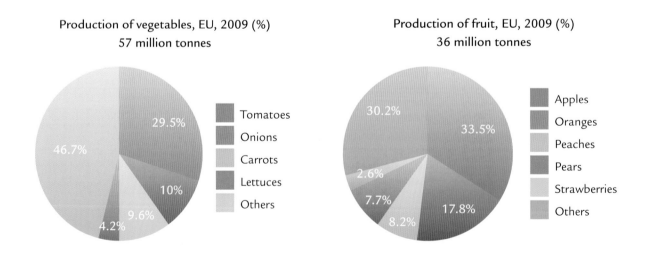

Production of vegetables, EU, 2009 (%)
57 million tonnes

Tomatoes 29.5%
Onions 10%
Carrots 9.6%
Lettuces 4.2%
Others 46.7%

Production of fruit, EU, 2009 (%)
36 million tonnes

Apples 33.5%
Oranges 17.8%
Peaches 8.2%
Pears 7.7%
Strawberries 2.6%
Others 30.2%

## Bar charts  Unit 5, page 63; Unit 8, page 95

You should spend about 20 minutes on this task.

*The bar chart below shows the minutes per day spent by different age groups in the United Kingdom on three media.*

*Summarize the information by selecting and reporting the main features, and make comparisons where relevant.*

Write at least 150 words.

Minutes per day using each medium: by age, 2009/10  United Kingdom

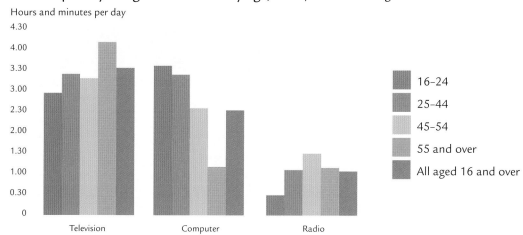

## Model answer

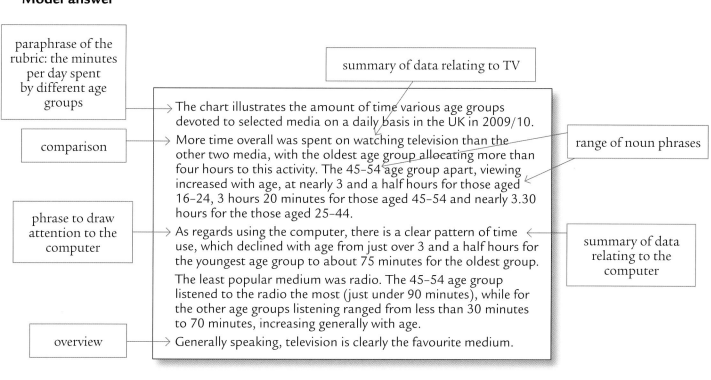

| paraphrase of the rubric: the minutes per day spent by different age groups | | summary of data relating to TV |

The chart illustrates the amount of time various age groups devoted to selected media on a daily basis in the UK in 2009/10.

**comparison** — More time overall was spent on watching television than the other two media, with the oldest age group allocating more than four hours to this activity. The 45–54 age group apart, viewing increased with age, at nearly 3 and a half hours for those aged 16–24, 3 hours 20 minutes for those aged 45–54 and nearly 3.30 hours for the those aged 25–44. — **range of noun phrases**

**phrase to draw attention to the computer** — As regards using the computer, there is a clear pattern of time use, which declined with age from just over 3 and a half hours for the youngest age group to about 75 minutes for the oldest group. — **summary of data relating to the computer**

The least popular medium was radio. The 45–54 age group listened to the radio the most (just under 90 minutes), while for the other age groups listening ranged from less than 30 minutes to 70 minutes, increasing generally with age.

**overview** — Generally speaking, television is clearly the favourite medium.

## Useful language

**Synonyms**

enjoy: like/take (considerable) pleasure in

do not enjoy: dislike/have no/do not have a liking for

**Describing attitudes**

what (people) think about ..., people's perception of/view on/position on/ thoughts about/views on

**Noun phrases**

those/children aged 8–16, boys/girls aged 8–16, boys/girls in the 8–16 age group, those who enjoy reading quite a lot/who take considerable pleasure in reading

**Referring to items on the chart**

as regards, regarding, with regard to, as for, when it comes to, turning to, as far as ... is concerned

**Ways of adding data**

With (+ noun) + verb in -*ing* form + object

*With the oldest age group ...*

*... with more girls than boys reading a lot, 28 per cent and 17 per cent respectively.*

## Task

You should spend about 20 minutes on this task.

*The bar chart below provides information about children's attitudes to reading in the United Kingdom in 2009.*

*Summarize the information by selecting and reporting the main features, and make comparisons where relevant.*

Write at least 150 words.

Children's[1] attitude towards reading, 2009

England

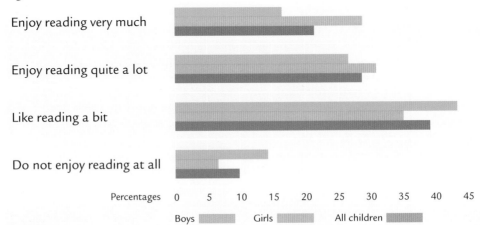

[1] Children aged 8 to 16

## IELTS Writing Task 2

**Discuss both these views and give your own opinion.**

**Unit 1, page 15; Unit 6, page 75**

You should spend about 40 minutes on this task.

Write about the following topic:

*Some people believe that education is the key to tackling hunger worldwide, while others feel that the answer lies in food aid.*

*Discuss both these views and give your own opinion.*

Give reasons for your answer and include any relevant examples from your own experience.

Write at least 250 words.

## Model answer

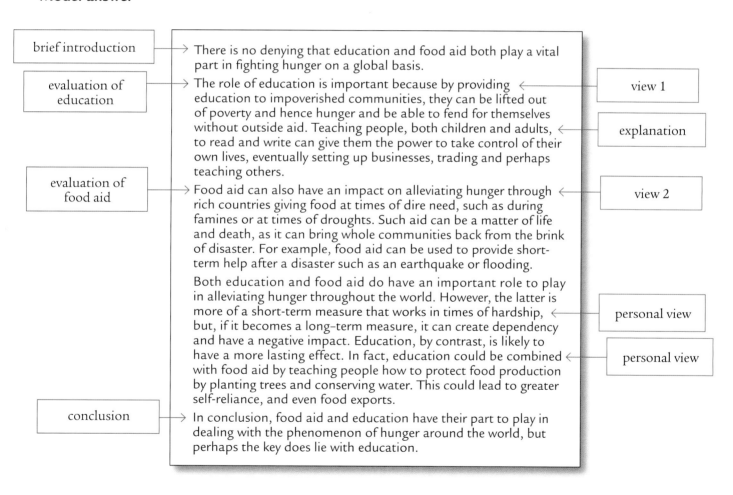

**brief introduction** → There is no denying that education and food aid both play a vital part in fighting hunger on a global basis.

**evaluation of education** → The role of education is important because by providing education to impoverished communities, they can be lifted out of poverty and hence hunger and be able to fend for themselves without outside aid. Teaching people, both children and adults, to read and write can give them the power to take control of their own lives, eventually setting up businesses, trading and perhaps teaching others. ← **view 1** ← **explanation**

**evaluation of food aid** → Food aid can also have an impact on alleviating hunger through rich countries giving food at times of dire need, such as during famines or at times of droughts. Such aid can be a matter of life and death, as it can bring whole communities back from the brink of disaster. For example, food aid can be used to provide short-term help after a disaster such as an earthquake or flooding. ← **view 2**

Both education and food aid do have an important role to play in alleviating hunger throughout the world. However, the latter is more of a short-term measure that works in times of hardship, but, if it becomes a long-term measure, it can create dependency and have a negative impact. Education, by contrast, is likely to have a more lasting effect. In fact, education could be combined with food aid by teaching people how to protect food production by planting trees and conserving water. This could lead to greater self-reliance, and even food exports. ← **personal view** ← **personal view**

**conclusion** → In conclusion, food aid and education have their part to play in dealing with the phenomenon of hunger around the world, but perhaps the key does lie with education.

## Useful language

**Stating a view**

The role of ... is important/crucial, vital etc, because ...

Some people think/argue/believe that ... is important because ...

Other people think that ... is important because ...

There is little doubt/no denying that ... is important because ...

**Introducing your own view**

Both ... play an important role/have an important role to play/are invaluable/ effective in, but ...

I feel, however, ...

I personally feel .../Personally, I feel ...

Having said this, however, I feel ...

Admittedly, both ...

... may both be important, I feel ...

Although both are ... , I feel ...

### Task

> You should spend about 40 minutes on this task. Write about the following topic:
>
> *Some people feel that young people should be made to work for a year before they go to university while others think that they should go straight to university from school.*
> *Discuss both these views and give your own opinion.*
>
> Give reasons for your answer and include any relevant examples from your own experience. Write at least 250 words.

### In what ways ... ? Has this become a positive or negative development?

### Unit 3, page 39

> You should spend about 40 minutes on this task. Write about the following topic:
>
> *Nowadays the way modern society is developing is being shaped by people's migration to large cities.*
> *In what ways is migration to large cities affecting society?*
> *Has this become a positive or negative development?*
>
> Give reasons for your answer and include any relevant examples from your own experience.
> Write at least 250 words.

## Model answer

| | | |
|---|---|---|
| general idea, or 'hook' | Cities have always been an engine of development worldwide, attracting people and resources, but nowadays the pace of change is increasing rapidly. As a result, modern society is now more urbanized than at any time in its history. | general impact |
| topic sentence | As part of this urbanization process, societies are experiencing both negative and positive changes. A possible negative development is the danger that through migration, society may generally become more selfish, using up resources in terms of energy, food and facilities at a faster rate than in the countryside. Moreover, once people lose contact with the values, traditions, and possibly languages of the communities they left behind, society undergoes further change. | negative impact |
| positive impact | The negative impact of urbanization on society generally cannot be ignored. However, migration benefits society. This is because large cities are dynamic and in a state of flux, offering people opportunities such as jobs and the chance to try out new ideas. The contribution of such ideas to the wealth of | reason |
| examples | any country can transform society enormously, funding more facilities in fields such as health and education. | examples |
| another positive impact | As well as transformation through new ideas, innovative ways of living, for example eco-houses and flexible working practices like partially working from home, can in turn affect the whole of society. The quality of life for city inhabitants can then be significantly improved, which, in turn, can stimulate growth and improvements in rural areas. | examples |
| | | results |
| evaluation/ conclusion | On balance, the contribution made by migration to society is positive. The transformation is not restricted to cities alone, but can stimulate developments beyond city boundaries, creating wealth, ideas, jobs and improvement in society at large. | |

## Useful language

Verbs

affect, effect, bring about, influence, cause, change, create, produce, lead to, play a role/part in, have an effect/impact on, have an influence over, shape, contribute to, result in, damage, destroy, benefit

Describing change

transform, develop, revolutionize, alter, adjust

Nouns

effect, influence, impact, changes, transformation, benefit

Other phrases

As a result,

As a consequence,

Consequently,

... is now ..., ... then ..., And so/So ..., Thus,

A/One negative/positive impact is ...

The main cause/effect/development (of this) is ...

Another/One cause/effect/development is ...

Giving reasons

.. because/as/since ...

This is because ...

The (main)/One reason for this is ...

## Task

You should spend about 40 minutes on this task. Write about the following topic:

*Nowadays the way that people of all ages interact with each other is being shaped by social media.*
*In what way is social media affecting the relationships that people make?*
*Has this become a positive or negative development?*

Give reasons for your answer and include any relevant examples from your own knowledge or experience. Write at least 250 words.

**To what extent do you agree or disagree? What other measures do you think might be effective?**

**Unit 4, page 51; Unit 5, page 59; Unit 7, page 87**

> You should spend about 40 minutes on this task.
>
> Write about the following topic:
>
> *Encouraging the development of creative industries such as the production of video games and computer software is the best way to reduce youth unemployment.*
>
> *To what extent do you agree or disagree?*
>
> *What other measures do you think might be effective?*
>
> Give reasons for your answer and include any relevant examples from your own experience.
>
> Write at least 250 words.

### Model answer

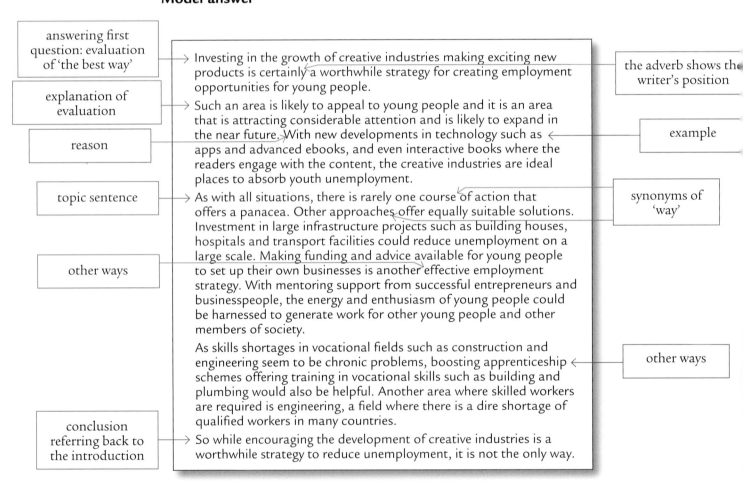

**answering first question: evaluation of 'the best way'** → Investing in the growth of creative industries making exciting new products is certainly a worthwhile strategy for creating employment opportunities for young people. *(the adverb shows the writer's position)*

**explanation of evaluation** → Such an area is likely to appeal to young people and it is an area that is attracting considerable attention and is likely to expand in the near future. **reason** → With new developments in technology such as apps and advanced ebooks, and even interactive books where the readers engage with the content, the creative industries are ideal places to absorb youth unemployment. *(example)*

**topic sentence** → As with all situations, there is rarely one course of action that offers a panacea. Other approaches offer equally suitable solutions. *(synonyms of 'way')* Investment in large infrastructure projects such as building houses, hospitals and transport facilities could reduce unemployment on a large scale. **other ways** → Making funding and advice available for young people to set up their own businesses is another effective employment strategy. With mentoring support from successful entrepreneurs and businesspeople, the energy and enthusiasm of young people could be harnessed to generate work for other young people and other members of society.

As skills shortages in vocational fields such as construction and engineering seem to be chronic problems, boosting apprenticeship schemes offering training in vocational skills such as building and plumbing would also be helpful. Another area where skilled workers are required is engineering, a field where there is a dire shortage of qualified workers in many countries. *(other ways)*

**conclusion referring back to the introduction** → So while encouraging the development of creative industries is a worthwhile strategy to reduce unemployment, it is not the only way.

## Useful language

Synonyms for *way/measure*

approach, step, strategy, course of action, method, means, scheme

Introducing measures

There are measures to ...

One measure is to ...

Another measure is to ... / ... is another measure.

It is possible to ...

... should/could/can

... is (also)/would (also) be possible.

Adjectives to evaluate

worthwhile, effective, sound, useful, helpful

Adverbs to evaluate

very, certainly, extremely

## Plan

1 Introduction

2 Evaluation

3 Explanation of evaluation

4 Other measures:

   1 (e.g. investment in large infrastructure projects)

   2 (e.g. making funding and advice available for young people to set up their own businesses)

   3 (e.g. boosting apprenticeship schemes)

5 Conclusion

## Task

You should spend about 40 minutes on this task.

Write about the following topic:

*Investing in major infrastructure projects such as motorways and other transport systems is the best way to reduce unemployment and boost economic development.*

*To what extent do you agree or disagree?*

*What other measures do you think might be effective?*

Give reasons for your answer and include any relevant examples from your own experience.

Write at least 250 words.

**What do you think are the causes of these problems and what measures could be taken to solve them?**

### Unit 8, page 99

You should spend about 40 minutes on this task.

Write about the following topic:

*In some countries, employers think young people nowadays lack verbal and non-verbal communication skills such as body language compared to the past.*

*What do you think are the causes of this problem and what measures could be taken to solve it?*

Give reasons for your answer and include any relevant examples from your own experience.

Write at least 250 words.

## Model answer

| | |
|---|---|
| introduction with restatement of the problem | Given the vitality of youth culture, it seems strange that there should be shortcomings as regards young people's verbal and non-verbal communication skills. However, there is no doubt that they do exist. There are <u>various</u> factors behind this and, of course, a number of approaches exist to tackle the situation. |
| nouns indicating the organization of the essay | |
| a synonym for *factor/ cause*, linking the paragraph to the introduction and the writing task | One major reason is the nature of many leisure pursuits in which young people take part nowadays. Take video games, for instance. Although more than one participant can take part in these simultaneously, they are played mainly by solitary individuals, especially young men. Moreover, by spending up to four hours or more per day on computers – communicating by email and on social networking sites – the ability to interact verbally and non-verbally through body language is being lost. This shows up clearly when some young people go for job interviews or when they are in a job and start interacting with other people. |

example followed by explanation as evidence

| | |
|---|---|
| solutions from two angles | The situation can be dealt with from different angles. At home, parents can be encouraged to talk to their children more. This, however, may prove difficult in all circumstances if parents are working. Schools and employers then need to play a key role. Schools, for example, could introduce communication classes or better still ensure that schoolchildren interact with people and organizations outside the classroom. |

example

| | |
|---|---|
| more solutions | Older students can also go on visits to employers and do work placements. Employers could also have their own in-work communication training sessions using actors and actresses to simulate real-life scenarios. |

more solutions

| | |
|---|---|
| conclusion with a comment on the future | The problem of a lack of communication skills does exist and may even become a greater problem in the future, but it can be managed if the right strategies are used. |

## Useful language

**Stating causes**

Synonyms for *cause of*: (underlying/contributing) factor, reason (for/behind)

Phrases: play(s) a part/role in, contribute(s) to, is/are the result of, result(s) from, happen(s)/occur(s), because, come(s)/arise(s) from, is/are responsible for

**Stating solutions**

The solution/key/answer/to the problem/ situation is …

can/could/should

It is possible to …

Another way/measure is to …/… is another way/ measure.

… can be solved/resolved by …

can be dealt with/tackled by …

## Task

You should spend about 40 minutes on this task.

Write about the following topic:

*All countries throughout the world are facing health issues related to modern lifestyles.*
*What do you think are the causes of these problems and what measures could be taken to solve them?*

Give reasons for your answer and include any relevant examples from your own experience.
Write at least 250 words.

## 1 A very modern world

### IELTS Speaking Parts 1 and 2, Exercise 3

 **1.1**

The view that I'd like to describe is one which is etched on my memory and that is ... mmm ... the view of the Acropolis in Athens at night, which I saw for the first time ... when I was staying there with my grandmother. I was only fourteen years old at the time. The hotel we stayed in had a ... mmm ... roof terrace like many buildings in the area and we watched the sun setting on the Acropolis. It was really magical and ... mmm ... certainly worth visiting Athens to see. I wasn't very keen on going there, because ... mmm ... I thought it, would be really boring, but I will always remember ... sitting there, watching the city darken and the Acropolis shining out. I enjoyed looking at the view, because the remains of the ancient buildings were very ... striking at night when everything was lit up. One thing I regret not ... mmm ... doing is taking photographs on that first evening as the sun was setting, but I managed to get ... mmm ... a few photographs later in the evening. I love this view because every time I think of it or see it, it reminds me of my first trip abroad, ... mmm ... and my grandmother. I keep thinking about the view, as it reminds me that some things can stay the same in a changing world.

### IELTS Listening Section 1, Exercise 4

 **1.2**

(W = woman; M = man)

**W:** Hello. Can I help you?

**M:** Yes, ... mmm ... Hi, I got your telephone number from your newsletter for the Skyline Club. Are you the secretary, Mary Lloyd?

**W:** Yes, I am. How can I help you?

**M:** Hi, my name's Paul. I'm enquiring about the walking club and I'd like some more details.

**W:** Well, we meet once a month throughout the year, weather permitting, and the walks are usually either Tuesday evening or Saturday morning.

**M:** Oh, OK. Both those days suit me.

**W:** Well, we've tried arranging other days and times and those are the two that suit the lifestyles of nearly everyone in the group.

**M:** I see. And who leads the walks? Is it you?

**W:** Oh, no. We don't have the same guide each time. And if we can't get someone, one of our members is usually able to do it.

**M:** OK. It says in the newsletter that the walks are generally at least two hours long and that you have a wide range of different walks with different themes.

**W:** Well, yes, it depends on ... who we can get, but the theme is usually historical. Most of the walkers in the club are interested in the changing cityscape of London in one form or another and we like to photograph the skyline of different areas being transformed.

**M:** It sounds really quite exciting.

**W:** Yes, we think so.

**M:** And how many people do you get going on the walks?

**W:** Anything up to twenty. After that, it's too large.

**M:** And do you pay the guides?

**W:** We pay leaders of the walks out of the newsletter subscription and sometimes people give the walk leaders tips, but that's really up to the individual.

**M:** How much is the newsletter subscription?

**W:** It's twenty-five pounds a year. We produce the newsletter twice yearly with the dates and the themes of the walks and we have a new website.

**M:** OK.

**W:** And for the twenty-five pounds a year, we normally manage to send out the newsletter by email twice yearly. And at the moment, there are ninety members on the newsletter list.

**M:** Do you send the newsletter by post?

**W:** No, it's all electronic. We don't send out paper copies.

**M:** How do I join?

**W:** Well, if you come to one of our walks, you can pay by cash or cheque. We don't have the facilities to accept payment in any other way at the moment.

**M:** When is the next walk and what is it?

**W:** It's on the fourteenth of May.

**M:** Next Saturday.

**W:** Yes. It's worth coming on that one. It's a ... river walk along the south side of the River Thames from London Bridge, looking at the enormous changes that have taken place there in recent years.

**M:** That sounds really interesting. I'll aim to come to that. Where are you meeting?

**W:** We are meeting at a place called Hays Galleria by the old telephone boxes at 9.30 am. Do you want to give me your email address?

**M:** Yeah, it's p.trimble765g@thomas.com.

**W:** Is that all lower case?

**M:** Mmm.

**W:** And is that T-R-I-M-B-L-E?

**M:** Yes, that's right. And I'll give you my mobile number. It's 07899875543.

**W:** We can text you walk dates.

**M:** See you on Saturday.

## 2 The past – public and private

### IELTS Listening Section 2, Exercise 3

 **1.3**

Good morning and welcome to White Bay Coastal Park, which has just celebrated its first anniversary. The park covers a huge area along the coast, spreading over approximately 1000 hectares, so there are lots of things to see; in fact, it is unlikely that you'll see everything on one visit alone. The opening of the park has led to increased interest in local historical issues among children and adults alike, and also in our research, with visitors arriving daily from all over the world, including academics coming to see the work being done. The park is essentially divided into two parts: the area where all the research and excavations are taking place at the moment and the open parkland, which includes the beach and the coastal area.

You can see here on the plasma screen that we are in the foyer of the educational centre. When you leave this centre through this door over here you will go south past the souvenir shop, where you can also sit down and have light refreshments. Immediately after this building is ... the minibus stop. The minibuses leave from here every ten to fifteen minutes, if you don't feel like walking through the first part of the park and wish to go straight to the coastal area to explore the beach and the rocks. You can see here on the screen that after the minibus stop, the path goes east, parallel to the coast. The first place you come to on the north side of the path is the remains of an ancient marketplace. East of that and still on the north side of the path is a very good example of an open-air theatre.

If you follow the path along here on the south side you can see the remains of a harbour, which is in very good condition considering how old it is. And the next area is the ruins of an ancient village, which the path goes through. After this the path goes south again and stops just west of a row of preserved fishermen's cottages.

As you walk around, please do follow the signs and don't remove any plants or artefacts from the site, even stones, as this might affect the analysis being carried out by researchers. The oldest objects discovered till now by the researchers in the archaeological digs are small rings and necklaces dating from the 7th century AD. So if you remove even the smallest piece of material you might be removing valuable historical evidence, which will affect the historical records. On the route, you will come across areas which are being prepared for excavation, or where surveys are going on. These areas are restricted to protect them, as they are very fragile. Some ruins of old buildings are dangerous because they are unstable and so, I'm afraid, there is no access to protect the buildings. All areas which are dangerous or where research is going on are also protected by electronic barriers which will sound an alarm if you cross beyond the signs.

When you leave the preservation area you will reach the beach in less than five minutes, even if you walk slowly. The beach is well known for its white sand and rocks, which on a day like today will be dazzling. There is a refreshment area just before the beach, with a café and some souvenir shops, which are housed in the renovated fishermen's cottages. Apart from the usual souvenirs, you can buy books on the local area and on the work we do at the park, as well as pictures painted by artists living in the area.

And one last thing: remember your entrance ticket to the site is not just valid once. It allows you to come back again any time within the next twelve months, so make sure you do not throw it away or lose it.

## IELTS Speaking Parts 2 and 3 & Vocabulary 2: Adjectives of evaluation, Exercise 2

 1.4

I'm going to describe a museum that I visited in the neighbourhood where I live. My first visit took place six months ago, ... mmm ... even though I have been living in the area for the past two years. The museum contains exhibits and displays about the local history. There is also a large exhibition of early black and white photographs ... mmm ... showing how the buildings have changed over the years, along with examples of clothes and rooms from people's houses of different periods. The photos were fascinating as they showed old forms of transport like horses and carts, ... mmm ... and there were no cars on the roads and houses didn't have television aerials or satellite dishes. There were also rooms with displays of objects that have been found on construction sites, like old pots and vases and some jewellery. These displays all contained minor objects but they were very effective. I've been back to the museum several times because it is very old-fashioned and doesn't have a lot of interactive exhibits. ... mmm ... I don't really like interactive exhibits. Although the displays and exhibits are very simple and straightforward, I found them very effective and ... mmm ... quite compelling. The simplicity of the way people lived in the past in this area was very moving when you compare it to the stress of today. Also, as few people visit the museum in the afternoon, it is a good place to relax.

## 3 The age of information

## IELTS Listening Section 3, Exercise 4

 1.5

(D = David; M = Martha)

**D:** Hi, Martha. You've found a quiet place.

**M:** Hi, David. Yes, but I think it's just because we're early.

**D:** Have you done much on collecting material yet for your long essay?

**M:** Mmm, yeah. I've done quite a lot of research. I planned to have it all finished by today. And I think I've just about succeeded in doing so.

**D:** Mmm. I'm not there yet. I'd like to get the research time down considerably.

**M:** It's difficult making yourself do it on time. But now I'm so used to putting notes and materials into order as I do it. Everything's stored electronically and ... I also print out and annotate a paper copy of journals, and everything.

**D:** You're always so organized.

**M:** Not always. When I was in my first couple of years as an undergraduate, I used to accumulate so much information I became overwhelmed by it.

**D:** I still do that! I don't know when to stop. I wish I knew how to be so organized.

**M:** It's not that difficult. I think it's possible to do it quicker than I have. The next time round, I'm planning to get the searching down to about a couple of weeks initially.

**D:** I'm not sure I could do that.

**M:** Well, I think we all can. When you start off, it's about analysing the essay title thoroughly and collecting ideas. Then keep the title in mind as you search for evidence and have particular targets to aim for. So let's say you're using the internet to do a journal search. Rather than searching at random, stick to a narrow range of key terms to search for. Maybe just one or two, and if necessary then broaden the search by adding more.

**D:** I think that's my trouble: I go straight in and download everything I can find even vaguely related to the subject and don't know when to stop.

**M:** Maybe, as well as narrowing down your search initially, you could restrict yourself to examining a certain number of sources.

**D:** Wouldn't that be artificial? And what happens if I miss something?

**M:** No, just aim for it and then if you don't find what you want then set more targets and maybe change your search words.

**D:** OK. It might make the process a bit more organized than it has been.

**M:** And then you might want to throw in a bit of random searching. But just like targets, give yourself a time limit and try to stick to it and also review what you are doing as you collect the information.

**D:** It all sounds a lot less haphazard than what I've been doing.

**M:** There're obviously loads of different ways to help keep yourself focused and find interesting material, but also don't forget to look at the bibliography accompanying each article when you're searching, and also who has quoted the articles.

**D:** I do that but I tend to do it after I should've finished searching, and then start another search.

**M:** Remember, the search goes on all the way through the writing process of the essay as new things come up. But the aim is to organize yourself, and cut down on wasting time and overloading yourself with information.

**D:** I do some of this, but I'm nowhere near as organized as you are, generally.

**M:** But you get good grades for your essays.

**D:** Yes, but getting there is not always easy. I think I create extra work for myself and often seem to be struggling with the essay when everyone else has finished.

**M:** Yes, but you're good at constructing an argument within an essay. When you state something, your supporting evidence is normally not only clear but also compelling. The strength of your arguments is ...

**D:** Maybe, yes. I find it easy to integrate information and present ideas. I get

really absorbed in it and before I know it I've finished, but it's getting to that point that is difficult.

## 4 Leisure and the environment

### IELTS Speaking Part 2, Exercise 2

 1.6

I'd like to describe a day that I didn't go to work a few months ago ... ahh ... when my flatmate and I took a day off work. We decided to make good use of the time and go somewhere we normally wouldn't go. We borrowed bicycles from friends who live nearby and headed off on a cycling trip along the canal, which runs for miles through the city into the countryside. When we got tired, we, ... ahh ... stopped for a while and watched the canal boats go by. As the first part of the canal was built up, we were able to stop for lunch before going on and it was much more peaceful than the city ... ahh ... as we watched people passing by slowly on their boats and taking their time doing things. When we reached the countryside, we locked up the bicycles in a safe place and ... ahh ... walked for a while along the canal. I remember the day well, because ... ahh ... I really enjoyed the day out, and because it was ... mmm ... so relaxing to be outdoors rather than being stuck in a shop in the middle of the city. We saw loads of wild animals and birds and watched birds catching insects on the water. The people on the boats were friendlier than the people in the city and waved to us. The journey back was tiring, but it didn't matter as we had such a great day out.

### IELTS Listening Section 4, Exercise 3

 1.7

Good morning, my name is Dr Hammer from the Business Department at the university and welcome to all of you who have come to this lunchtime lecture on *Leisure and entertainment: A rosy future*. Before I look at a few predictions for the leisure and entertainment industry worldwide in the next few decades, I'm going to talk briefly about past predictions that were wrong and some statistics comparing the situation in the UK and the USA.

So, first of all let us look at some general past predictions, which some of you may already be familiar with, mainly to show you how forecasting in any field is notoriously difficult. The past is littered with strange predictions relating to all fields, from the railways to the motorcar and the electric light. Many of these seem outlandish to us now. More recent predictions about devices such as television and the home computer, for example, may surprise you. If we look at this first slide we can see a quote from Darryl Zanuck, a film producer at 20th Century Fox, from 1946. He said that television wouldn't be able to hold on to any market it captures after the first six months. People will soon get tired of staring at a plywood box. Next we have this quote by Thomas Watson, chairman of IBM, in 1943, who said: 'I think there is a world market for maybe five computers.' And then much later, in 1977, according to Ken Olson, the president, chairman and founder of Digital Equipment Corporation (DEC), there was no reason anyone would want a computer in their home.

If we look at predictions regarding the telephone we find similar scepticism as to its practicality. A news item in a New York newspaper in 1868 reported that:

'A man has been arrested in New York for attempting to extort funds from ignorant and superstitious people by exhibiting a device which he says will convey the human voice any distance over metallic wires so that it will be heard by the listener at the other end. He calls this instrument a telephone. Well-informed people know that it is impossible.'

A brief comparison of statistics relating to media in the United Kingdom and the United States will show how wrong these predictions have been. We can see from the chart on this next slide that according to the World Development indicators database for 2002, in the United Kingdom alone there were 84.49 mobile phones per 100 people. By comparison, in the USA, for the same year, the corresponding figure was much less at 48.81. It has recently been reported that there are now more mobile phones on the planet than human beings. If we look at television ownership, the figures for both countries were very similar. The United Kingdom, ranked 15th in the world in 2001, had 97.5 per cent ownership. The USA, ranked 11th, had 98.2 per cent.

As regards personal computers, the gap between the UK and the USA is more striking, with 599.8 per one thousand people in the UK owning a PC, ranked 12th in 2004; with the corresponding figure for the USA (ranked 4th place) being 762.2 per one thousand people. This was 27 per cent more than in the United Kingdom.

So, it is with some timidity that I come to my predictions for the future of the leisure industry. My first prediction is in the area of home entertainment. I forecast that the area where the most noticeable developments in the leisure and entertainment industries will be is in home entertainment. With high definition or HD television, 3D TVs and more sophisticated sound systems becoming more widely available, home entertainment will become cheaper and more attractive to families. As with predictions about the demise of the cinema when videos and DVDs came on the market, I do not think that this will lead to a downturn in cinema-going. In fact, I think the opposite will occur with ever more sophisticated films being released.

My second prediction is linked with mobile technology. I predict that the mobile will replace credit cards, travel cards and tablets with the end of the personal computer in the long term. I predict that this will come about in the next decade.

My third prediction relates to the internet and …

## 5 A healthy world

### IELTS Listening Section 1, Exercise 3

🎧 1.8

(M = man; W = woman)

**M:** Good afternoon, Dover House. Cliff speaking. How can I help you?

**W:** Oh, hi. My name's Sharon Diaz.

**M:** Hi.

**W:** Mmm, I'm phoning about the advert for volunteers to work with elderly people who are living on their own.

**M:** Oh, yes. Was that in the local paper yesterday or was it the online advert for volunteers on our website noticeboard?

**W:** I saw it in the local paper. Actually, a friend pointed it out to me, as

I've been looking into doing some volunteer work.

**M:** OK, the local … paper. We just keep a record of where potential volunteers saw information about the organization. It helps with advertising.

**W:** Mmm.

**M:** OK. Is there anything in particular you'd like to ask about?

**W:** Mmm, … basically I'd like to know what's involved in the volunteering programme for the elderly.

**M:** Well, we are looking for volunteers for different things. We have three different schemes. First, there's volunteer work here in the office helping with maintaining our database of members.

**W:** Do you need any special skills for that?

**M:** Well, you need to be familiar with using a computer and completing record sheets.

**W:** Mmm … That's not really the sort of thing I was looking for.

**M:** OK. Then there's the second volunteer scheme which involves raising money, running events and sending out letters.

**W:** Is there anything that involves working with people?

**M:** Well, there's … mmm … the third scheme where you make friends with an old person who lives on their own and you help them with various things.

**W:** Mmm. That's more appealing. What sort of things would I be expected to do?

**M:** Nothing very difficult. If elderly people can't get out of the house for one reason or another, volunteers can do the shopping for them.

**W:** Mmm …

**M:** … or accompany them when they have a hospital appointment.

**W:** Yes, that's the sort of thing I've been looking for, but I won't have to deal with medication or anything like that, will I?

**M:** Oh, no. That's for qualified health visitors. We don't get involved in anyone's medication. Is there anything else?

**W:** So how can I become a volunteer?

**M:** You'll need to send in a very brief application form along with a copy of your CV and … give the names of two referees and then once that has been processed, … you have a … brief induction course which lasts a morning.

**W:** OK.

**M:** You can complete and submit the application online.

**W:** OK, I'll do it online. What's the website address?

**M:** It's www.doverhouse.co.uk.

**W:** I'll do that right away … And how much time do you expect people to volunteer for?

**M:** At least two hours a week.

**W:** Oh, that's fine. I've got plenty of time at the moment. I'm available every weekday except Wednesday morning and Friday afternoon, and I can't do weekends.

**M:** That sounds fine.

### Language focus: Degrees of certainty & IELTS Speaking Part 3, Exercise 1

🎧 1.9

(E = examiner; C = candidate)

**E:** Do you think the world will be free of disease in the future?

**C:** I'm not sure really. It is possible in the distant future, but it's unlikely in the near future. Mmm, for example, in order to have a world free of disease we need to get rid of poverty and educate people as well as finding cures for illnesses.

**E:** And in the distant future?

**C:** Mmm, in one hundred years' time, it's likely that there will be no more illness.

## 6 Shaping the world and beyond

### Vocabulary: Words related to space and place, Exercise 5

🎧 1.10

(E = examiner; C = candidate)

**E:** Do you think we rely too much on systems such as satellites?

**C:** Yes, I think there is a tendency to do so. Mmm, for example if the GPS navigation systems on cars or a communication satellite broke down for a long time, it would have a huge impact on social order. It would result not only in financial costs for businesses, but it could also lead to loss of life and social chaos. In fact I think it would be chaotic.

**E:** In what way?

**C:** Well, mmm, while GPS systems are not used that much in my country, phone networks would be affected and maybe other communications, so supermarkets might not be able to order food, which could lead to huge problems, and people in remote areas might be cut off. I think we should always …

## IELTS Listening Section 2, Exercise 2

 **1.11**

Welcome everybody, good morning and thanks for coming. The reason for arranging the meeting is to make sure that we are all up-to-date about the progress for the preparation for the college's anniversary in two months' time, which is focusing this year on our scientific achievements over the past year, especially the Young Rocket Scientist Team of the Year Award. As you all know, we've been having individual meetings, but now that everything is firming up I thought it would be wise to have a meeting and make sure that everyone knows where we all are. I think if we hadn't had the individual meetings up to now, things wouldn't have gone so smoothly.

First of all, just a few general details. The sponsorship that we were hoping for from the various sources has now been confirmed and with the support from former pupils, I can now confirm that we have raised all of the costs of the anniversary celebration plus 50 per cent to spare. So we don't need to worry on the money front! We have a number of special guests coming to the event. In fact, we have the Mayor, Doris Jackson, along with several famous footballers and actors and TV stars. I'll reveal the names when we have the invitations printed.

As for the invitations, we are sending out five thousand, but expect to have about two thousand guests on the day. If more were to turn up, that'd be great. We can cater for up to six thousand with the marquee, but we agreed to limit it to about two thousand.

There are just a few things that need to be pointed out. The first one is the organization of the various events. These are now all in hand. The refreshments will be in the sports block because we can attach a large tent to the side doors in the café there. We can't use the sports halls for any of the stalls as people walking around them would mark the newly laid floors, so they'll be out of bounds on the big day. The stalls will be in the science and arts blocks. In the arts block, there'll be publishers' exhibits and exhibits from local businesses and sponsors. In the science block will be the stalls for students' work, with posters about the visit to the Space Research Centre, the meeting with astronauts and of course the award presentation, plus work items from all subjects along with displays on the history of the college. The organization of this is all well advanced. The pupils will help set things up, as will the maintenance staff. If anyone has any questions about this, they'll be able to see me afterwards.

As always, there are still a few things that need to be finalized. They are not serious, but I have provisional dates for them and would like the various teams to come back to me by the end of the week with confirmation. First is John's team, which is dealing with catering and refreshments for the whole day – a big and important job, I might say. We need to check that all catering arrangements are finalized by the twenty-ninth of May. As regards the history display of the college, that's, mmm, Mary's team, and this needs to be done by the tenth of next month. The student displays, that's Angus's team, have to be finished by the end of this week, that's the seventeenth of May. The date for choosing the design of the invitations is tomorrow, the fourteenth. And that's Sara's team. We would like to send them out early next week so people can have the date in their diaries.

We have a busy time ahead, but we've got so far without too many hiccoughs. Let's hope it continues that way.

## 7 A consumer society

## IELTS Listening Section 3, Exercise 3

 **1.12**

(T = tutor; Ad = Adam; An = Angela)

**T:** OK, shall we start now that you're both here? Who wants to go first? Angela? Adam?

**Ad:** I'm happy to start.

**An:** Yeah. That's fine by me.

**T:** So, Adam. How far have you got with everything?

**Ad:** I'd say I'm further along than I thought. I've done a lot of background reading and I've decided on a topic for my research project.

**T:** Mmm.

**Ad:** Yeah. I've read … closely … about twenty articles so far and about ten marketing books on the general booklist and those three articles you suggested on digital expenditure. I've decided to do my research project on online shopping, specifically young consumer's perceptions about such shopping in the UK.

**An:** It sounds interesting. I'm relieved it's so different from mine.

**T:** Have you decided to narrow it down to a particular place and age group?

**Ad:** I'm thinking of … teenagers, late teens, say eighteen- to nineteen-year-olds.

**T:** OK. That's probably a good group to work on. Have you thought of the products you're going to ask about?

**Ad:** I've selected twelve items and I've got five questions. I've been looking at spending in various areas such as music … and films, clothing and sports goods, holiday accommodation, publications like books, magazines and journals, and tickets for events and electronic equipment, computer hardware and software … and food. But in my questionnaire I think I'm going to just concentrate on what music teenagers buy online and their spending on computers, mobiles and the like on the internet and their perceptions about purchasing items there compared to, say, in a shop.

**T:** And your questions?

**Ad:** They're fairly straightforward ... I think. Three are about amount with a scale from one to five, with one being the least frequent and five being the most. I've got them here if you want to see them.

**T:** These look fine.

**An:** Yes, I like them.

**T:** You seem to have been working hard, with the preparation you've done already.

**Ad:** Thanks.

**T:** And Angela, how far have you got?

**An:** Mmm, I think I'm at about the same stage really.

**T:** That's good.

**An:** I'm looking at children's expenditure in the UK on selected items, that is children aged eleven to fifteen at secondary school, provided that is that they get pocket money. I'm going to ask about spending on recreation and culture, and things like snacks, clothing and footwear, communication and transport.

**T:** What would you say the challenges have been for you so far?

**An:** Mmm, there've been many. I initially thought I'd never finish reading around the subject. There seemed to be so much to read, but perhaps the two biggest that I have faced have been narrowing down the items to ask about and ... I suppose picking the schools to approach to conduct the study.

**Ad:** And it's been the same for me.

**T:** There are a couple of points that you need to be aware of when you're conducting the surveys.

**Ad:** OK.

**An:** All right.

**T:** First, you need to get permission from the schools where you are going to do the research project.

**Ad:** We've both got our letters ready if you want to look at them. But can you say how long it's going to take to get permission?

**T:** That's the point. It's difficult to say. You need to get them out as early as possible. You might get a reply by return of post or you might wait a couple of weeks. If you don't hear

anything after a couple of weeks, I'd contact the headmaster's secretary.

**Ad:** OK.

**T:** Secondly, you need to make sure that everyone, including the children, realize that the data is anonymous and that it will not be used for any other purposes than your research. This will make the pupils feel comfortable about completing the questionnaire. Make sure that you are very polite and don't interfere in any way with the data collection.

**An:** I think we are going to be all right on all of this because we both have the questionnaires ready to go out.

**T:** And finally make sure the questionnaire layout is clear and simple, given the age groups you're both aiming at. If it's too long it'll be off-putting.

**An:** We can give them to you now as we've finished them.

## IELTS Speaking Part 3, Exercise 1

 1.13

1  Do people attach too much value to purchasing the latest fashionable goods?

2  What kinds of goods or services do people purchase on the internet?

3  What are the advantages of purchasing goods on the internet? Are there any disadvantages?

4  What kind of influence does advertising have on people's spending habits?

5  Do you think having lots of money to spend makes people content? Why/Why not?

6  How important would you say it is for governments to control people's spending habits?

## 8  Culture on the move

## IELTS Listening Section 4, Exercise 3

 1.14

Good morning everyone, and welcome to the third in the continuing series of lectures on using art to raise people's cultural awareness. We've looked at ways that art can be used for therapeutic

purposes with patients, and how art classes can help promote creativity in other classes in schools. This week we're going to look at different ways to encourage people of all ages to become involved in art in all its forms.

It's never too soon to introduce children to art, especially drawing. There are many mainstream methods that are effective in attracting young children to art early on in life, such as using colouring books at home, watching TV programmes, going to art classes at school and even going on visits to art galleries, which these days have educational programmes for children at both secondary and primary level. However, some children never have opportunities like this, even if they are living in big cities.

One non-mainstream way of drawing people's and especially children's attention to art, which is really intriguing, is random encounters with art in the street, so-called street art. Cities have always been full of street performers such as jugglers and singers, who add colour to otherwise drab environments, sometimes as part of festivals such as the Edinburgh Festival in Scotland.

A form of street art that is literally breathtaking is 3D pavement art, which has a dramatic visual impact, so much so that it is almost impossible to stop oneself from interacting with it. When people first encounter it, they stop short on the pavement. Some 3D pavement art shows vast holes in the ground with such realistic perspective that it almost dares you to walk across it. It would be difficult to replicate this effect on a canvas in an art gallery, which is perhaps why it is so suited to the street. However, many of the great artists of the past employed similar techniques in architectural paintings, as have interior decorators in large houses, creating paintings to look like doors or creating doors that look like bookcases. But, apart from some modern statues in public places, few have the ability to startle you and bring you up short even when you know it is a pavement. These works of art on pavements are temporary and disappear, unless they are done on canvasses that are spread out over the pavement, which is not really the same.

Such art comes in for a lot of criticism, as it is not seen as part of mainstream culture, which I think is unjustified. Another complaint is that street art, like 3D art, encourages graffiti and damage to property. Damage to property cannot be condoned in any way, but if artists restrict themselves to pavements, what is the harm? In fact they are brightening up public spaces. If necessary, street artists can be given a licence by local authorities to paint in the street and be encouraged to do so rather than discouraged. Some local utilities like rubbish bins might benefit from decoration by street artists, as might derelict buildings – just like the frescoes by the great artists of the past.

In fact, instead of thinking of the negative aspects of street art and thus street culture, it would perhaps be better to think of the positive. Street art is an important part of street culture. It brightens up people's lives. It also has the potential to encourage people of all ages, but especially young people, to engage with art. It might change people's attitudes and show them that art in galleries and museums is not just for rich people, but for everyone. If street art breaks this barrier, even for a small number of people, and inspires one future great artist, it is worthwhile.

So I think street art is an important form of street culture which is a valid art form that can bring art to the people, and has the potential to influence people's lives.

## Unit 1 A very modern world

### IELTS Speaking Parts 1 and 2

**1/2**

Student's own answers

**3**

1 memory  2 no synonym  3 at night
4 no synonym  5 magical  6 no synonym
7 wasn't very keen  8 remember  9 regret
10 no synonym  11 keep

**4**

1 yes  2 yes  3/4 Student's own answers

**5/6**

Student's own answers

### Language focus: Verbs followed by *-ing* and/or infinitive

**1**

1 both – with the *-ing* form the emphasis
is on the process of the sun setting,
with the infinitive without *to*, the
emphasis is on the point at which the
sun sets.
2 both – with the *-ing* form the emphasis
is on the period of time that the person
spent sitting. You could not use *to sit*
here, but you can say *I remembered to
buy some milk* where the emphasis is on
the act of buying.
3 *-ing*  4 infinitive  5 both – see 1

**2**

*-ing*:       enjoy, dislike, miss, mind
infinitive: afford, help, fail, appear
both:       love, like, continue, seem, hate
             remember, forget, stop, start

**3**

1 studying, to leave  2 going, to visit
3 working, to pay  4 to reduce, rising
5 to take up, doing  6 (to) overcome,
meeting  7 studying, to wait
8 to be, staying  9 sightseeing, to see

**4**

1 ✓  2 avoid buying  3 ✓ (can be either
*like to work* or *like working*)  4 afford not to
adjust  5 ~~to~~ updating  6 helps to find
7 ✓  8 stop to think

**5**

Student's own answers

### IELTS Listening Section 1

**1**

A walking club

**2/3**

Student's own answers

**4**

1 C  2 B  3 A  4/5/6 B, D, E  7 14th May
8 9.30  9 p.trimble765g  10 07899875543

**5/6**

Student's own answers

### IELTS Writing Task 1

**1**

Student's own answers

**2**

1 b  2 f  3 e  4 c  5 a  6 d

**Combined text as model answer**

The graph shows the proportion of the
population in the 27 European countries
along with selected countries who have
never used the internet between 2005 and
2010.

Overall, there is a clear downward trend
in the proportion of those who have never
accessed the internet with the European
average of 27 countries almost halving
(from approximately 45 per cent to 25 per
cent). As regards Denmark and the UK,
which had the two lowest rates of non-
usage of the internet, there was a marked
fall from approximately 15 per cent to just
under 10 per cent and from about 30 per
cent to around 12 per cent respectively.
Germany followed a similar pattern to the
United Kingdom with a drop from about
30 per cent to 15 per cent, while France
experienced a more marked decline from
approximately 48 per cent in 2006 to
about 18 per cent in 2010.

Likewise, Spain, the only country above
the European Union average, mirrored
the decline of the latter falling to
approximately 32 per cent from around
50 per cent.

**3**

Student's own answers

**4**

**Model answer**

The chart shows the proportion of those
using the internet who download and use
a range of entertainment media in various
European countries compared to the
European Union average.

Overall, there is a clear upward trend in
downloads across Europe, although at
varying degrees. For example, in Bulgaria,
the country with the highest proportion
of downloads among internet users,
there was only a small increase over the
period from about 50 per cent to 52 per
cent with a peak of about 58 per cent in
2009. By contrast, France experienced
the most striking increase from about 20
per cent to 35 per cent between 2006 and
2011. In Germany, likewise, the rise in the
proportion of downloads was gradual,
from approximately 24 per cent in 2004 to
just about the same level as France in 2011.

Although internet users in the UK did
not follow exactly the same pattern as
the European Union average, fluctuating
around the 40 per cent level, the
proportion of downloads among the
former was the same as the latter in 2011,
at about 40 per cent.

### Vocabulary: Collocation with nouns

**1**

enormous:        huge/substantial/
                 considerable
have taken place: have occurred/
                 happened

**2**

**Model answers**

1 Unfortunately, very limited
progress is being made in preparing
schoolchildren for the modern world.
2 Enormous change is taking place in
people's lifestyles at the moment.
3 The introduction of high-speed rail
links between cities will promote
the economic development of the
continent.
4 A substantial reduction in traffic can
only be achieved if and when the focus
of transport moves away from the
private car.
5 As cities develop, the gradual evolution
of new ways of living and working will
follow.
6 Huge advances in design technology
have improved the world we live in.

**3**

**Model answers**

1 Unfortunately, progress is being made
slowly in preparing schoolchildren for
the modern world. /Unfortunately,
the preparation of schoolchildren for
the modern world is being made/is
occurring/happening slowly.
2 People's lifestyles are changing
enormously at the moment.
3 The introduction of high-speed rail
links between cities will develop the
continent economically./The continent
will develop economically as a result
of/because of/with the introduction of
high-speed rail links between cities.
4 The traffic can only be reduced
substantially if and when the focus of
transport moves away from the private
car.
5 As cities develop, new ways of living
and working will then evolve gradually.
6 As design technology has advanced
hugely, it has improved the world we
live in.

**4–6**

Student's own answers

## IELTS Reading

**1**

**Model answers**

1 This is a large proportion of young people and the numbers are likely to increase.
2 I can't say I am always happy but it is interesting to be online for a while, but after an hour or so it is boring.
3 This can be true but if you have a lot of friends online it takes away time from developing face-to-face friendships, which are more important.
4 I'd agree with this. We are used to using different media simultaneously, because we have grown up with them.

**2**
Young people in the modern technological age.

**3**
Student's own answers

**4**
1 D  2 F  3 A  4 G  5 C  6 B  7 C  8 A
9 C  10 A  11 reach and connectivity
12 face-to-face communication
13 hybrid (lives)

**5**
Student's own answers

## IELTS Writing Task 2

**1**
1 d  2 c  3 e  4 f  5 b  6 a

**2**
2 c  3 b  4 a  5 a  6 c  7 c  8 c

**3/4**
Student's own answers

**5**
1 This phenomenon is happening as a result of
2 enable people to change working practices
3 Good examples of this are
4 are able to access their main place of work
5 The consequence of this is that
6 airports

**6**

**Model answer**
A reduction in, and perhaps the elimination of, world poverty is a highly desirable aim. While some feel that the key is a shift in the perception of other countries, others feel that the most crucial impact is made through trade.

If nations around the world build better relationships, this can have a positive effect on world poverty. Countries can, for example, have cultural exchanges such as art exhibitions or plays. At an educational level, young people from Australia or the UK can also go on visits to places like Kenya to learn about the language and the culture. This can increase contact between countries and bring about better understanding and development with jobs in poorer regions of the world, including those in rich countries.

Trade is also certainly a crucial factor in poverty reduction worldwide, because just like improving relationships with other nations, trade can also help to break down barriers. Through trade, different countries can learn to trust each other and build working relationships that lead to jobs. Rich countries, for example, can import agricultural goods from north and east Africa, thus leading to job creation and a reduction in poverty.

In my opinion, both the factors described above are important, but perhaps, another element is also crucial, namely a trade in skills and know-how. If poorer countries are always at a disadvantage through a lack of skills such as technological expertise, the imbalance between rich and poor will continue and poverty levels will remain the same.

As we have seen, building relationships and trade are both equally important, but the latter needs to include skills as well as goods.

**Review**

**Language focus: Verbs followed by -ing and/or infinitive**

1 altering  2 to save  3 to save  4 keeping
5 looking  6 to protect  7 constructing
8 living  9 working

**Vocabulary: Collocations with nouns**

1 Fortunately, substantial progress has been made in educating young people about the demands of the 21st century.
2 ✓
3 The evolution of transport has occurred steadily over the past hundred years.
4 Changes that take place gradually tend to achieve more than abrupt transformations.
5 A substantial reduction in ignorance can only be achieved through education.
6 The enormous advances in medicine in recent years are improving the lives of everyone.
7 Too much control of the way children behave and think can hinder the development of creativity.
8 ✓

## IELTS Reading: Understanding noun phrases

**1**

1 the effect of a university education on the earning potential of graduates
2 the development of different types of vocational courses for young people
3 the progress made by young people in the field of education in recent years
4 suggestions about how to promote the growth of creative industries
5 an awareness of the impact of technology on improving the way that people work
6 a reduction in the amount of time spent studying for a university degree
7 an explanation of the relative importance of knowledge and experience

**2**

1 The text or paragraph describes what effects or impact having a university education has on graduates' earnings in the future when they start working.
2 The text or paragraph describes how the different types of vocational courses for young people are created and then how they grow; or just how the courses grow.
3 The text or paragraph plots the progress that young people have made in education generally in the recent past.
4 The text or paragraph describes two or more ways that will encourage creative industries to grow.
5 The text or paragraph talks about an understanding of what effect technology has on making people's working methods better.
6 The text or paragraph talks about how the time devoted to studying at university is reduced or cut.
7 The text or paragraph compares the importance of knowledge with that of experience.

## IELTS Writing Task 2: The negative viewpoint

**1**

1

**2**

The development (2 of home working) may be attractive to employees, but to some people the idea that such working practices give people freedom is an illusion. They quote the negative aspect of these practices (5 to the workers), namely the social impact of people working alone and the increased costs of having to pay for heating, lighting and equipment. (**3** In latter case, the costs can be considerable in both hot and cold climates, and if essentials such as computers or telephones break down.) This (**1** situation) benefits companies, because less office space is needed (**4**, thus reducing costs for employers).

## Unit 2 The past – public and private

### Vocabulary 1: Collocations - multiple combinations

**1**
Student's own answers
**2**
1 A  2 B/D  3 B/D  4 A/C  5 A/C
**3**

| do | verb |
| carry out | verb |
| into | preposition |
| search for | verb |
| take part in | verb |
| undertake | verb |
| historical | adjective |
| groundbreaking | adjective |
| market | noun/verb |
| compelling | adjective |

**4**

| carry out | 2, 4, 5, 6, 7 |
| into | 4, 5, 7 |
| search for: | 1, 3, 5, 6, 7, 8 |
| take part in | 4, 5, 6, 7 |
| undertake | 2, 4, 5, 6, 7 |
| historical | 1, 2, 3, 4, 5, 6, 7 |
| groundbreaking | 1, 2, 4, 5, 7 |
| market | 2, 5 |
| compelling | 1, 4, 5, 7, 8 |

**5**
1  fund; studies/research
2  carrying out/conducting/doing/pursuing
3  undertaking/doing/conducting/carrying out; research
4  research surveys
5  evidence
6  analysis/study
**6**
Student's own answers

### IELTS Listening Section 2

**1**
Possible answers: research, walk, coastal area, ruins, route of walk, merchandise in shop, features of the beach
**2**
Student's own answers

**3**
1 A  2 minibus stop  3 harbour
4 village  5 C  6 A  7 A  8 A  9 B  10 C
**4**
Student's own answers

### IELTS Writing Task 1

**1**
account for, consist of, comprise, constitute
**2**
1 b  2 d  3 a  4 g  5 c  6 f  7 e
**3**
1  Archaeology represents 15 per cent of the total student body in 2000.
2  Social history made up a smaller proportion of students in 2000 compared to 2010, 5 per cent and 20 per cent respectively.
3  History of warfare constituted 10 per cent of the student body in the history department in 2000.
4  Ancient history comprised a smaller proportion of the student body in 2010 compared to 2000, 10 per cent and 25 per cent respectively.
5  The proportion/students studying archaeology was equal to that of the history of warfare in 2010, 10 per cent in each case.
**4**
Student's own answers
**5**
1 changed  2 a reliance on small individual gifts  3 accounted for
4 constituting  5 came from  6 the largest proportion of the total  7 20 per cent and 20 per cent respectively  8 15 per cent  9 a much smaller proportion  10 a doubling in the proportion contributed to total income  11 20 per cent
**6**
**Model answer**
The charts provide information about how much money was received by different museums in a European country in two separate years.

Overall, it is clear that half of the museums experienced a rise in their funding and half a decline. While for the Museum of the Ancient World the amount of money fell from 20 per cent of the total budget to 15 per cent, a 25 per cent drop, the Museum of Medieval Art was given a 25 per cent increase in funding from 20 per cent to 25 per cent of the total. The proportion of funding allocated to both the Natural History Museum and the Transport Museum also went up from 10 per cent to 15 per cent and 5 per cent to 10 per cent, respectively.

By contrast, the funding for the Technology Museum accounted for 15 per cent in 2000 against 10 per cent in 2010, a fall of one-third, whereas the National Museum saw only a reduction of one-sixth of its funding as this decreased from 30 per cent to 25 per cent.

### IELTS Speaking Parts 2 and 3 & Vocabulary 2: Adjectives of evaluation

**1**
Student's own answers
**2**
1  local history
2  black and white photographs
3  old forms of transport
4  on construction sites
5  it is very old-fashioned
6  very simple and straightforward
**3**
3  The photos were <u>fascinating</u> as they showed old forms of transport like horses and carts.
5  it is very <u>old-fashioned</u>
6  <u>very simple and straightforward</u> / very <u>effective</u> and quite <u>compelling</u>
**4**
1 ineffective  2 reasonable
3 appropriate  4 impractical  5 minor
6 crucial  7 unimportant  8 significant
9 straightforward
**5**
1  The changes that took place in my home town were unimportant to the people.
2  Taking part in a survey isn't pointless./It isn't pointless to take part in a survey. It's a confidence-building experience.
3  Studying history is irrelevant to the modern world.
4  It isn't sensible to ignore the experience of the past.
5  Some people think that it is impractical to rely solely on sponsorship for the arts.
6  Innovation in industry has been effective in developing new products.
7  Do you think qualifications are more worthwhile nowadays compared the past?
8  The evidence from the study was unconvincing.
**6**
Student's own answers
**7/8**
**Model answers**
**A**
**1**
a  people travel, have busy lives/more important in the past, especially as it

was difficult to communicate quickly/ people lived long distances apart
b  Yes, it's crucial, because …
c  business/studying requires the internet, people expect more instant contact

**2**

a  use of mobiles, videophones, Skype, videoconferencing, text messages, emails all are commonplace and fast
b  Even compared to a decade ago, it is very efficient and convenient.
c  it is possible to contact anyone anywhere very quickly; send data easily

**3**

a  head offices and production in different parts of the world; people can chat by videoconferencing – there is less need to travel
b  Definitely, the speed of communication between businesses anywhere is the world is now almost instant.
c  Car manufacturers can send prototypes to other parts of the world to be produced; products can be made more quickly as the different stages are faster.

**B**

**1**

a  access to more information, views, ideas compared to the past; in many ways more mature at an earlier age
b  I think it depends, but many seem to be more confident.
c  young people travel more, e.g. going abroad to study and work; they set up businesses; use the internet to communicate

**2**

a  meeting people, studying abroad, learning through working
b  Yes, if possible, but it is not always easy.
c  work in a cafe, work as an au pair, brings the language to life as have to solve problems instantly

**3**

a  internet/technology affecting young people's social skills; necessary in the modern world as job market is very competitive; need to be articulate to get on
b  Nowadays, yes, I think that that is definitely the case.
c  job interviews self-expression very important; most jobs not for life – short-term so easy to get rid of workers – need to be able to promote oneself

## IELTS Reading

**1**

b

**2**

Student's own answers

**3**

1 v  2 iii  3 vii  4 i  5 vi  6 Yes  7 No
8 Not Given  9 No (the frames were made of different materials)  10 Yes  11 glare
12 image  13 rays

## Language focus: Using nouns to build ideas

**1**

1 a  2 c  3 b  4 c  5 c  6 b

**2**

The history of sunglasses
the effect of the sun's glare
The very first actual recorded evidence of the use of sunglasses
any expressions in their eyes
the end of each trial
flat panes of quartz
prescription glasses for the public
A Blessing to the Aged
The longest noun phrase: The (very first actual recorded) evidence of the use of sunglasses

**3**

1  various reasons for climate changes in the past/various reasons for past changes in the climate
2  the range of consumer products on sale
3  the most dynamic period in the country's history
4  the answer to the problem of overcrowding in cities
5  a brief description of different types of ancient buildings
6  the impact of war on people's lives

**4**

2  This refers to different consumer products that are being sold.
3  This refers to the fact that there was a period in history that was more dynamic than other periods.
4  This refers to the solution to a problem that exists in cities, namely to overcrowding.
5  This refers to the fact that there are different types of ancient buildings and they are being described.
6  This refers to the effect war has on people's lives.

**5**

1  There was a dramatic increase in the population of the world in the latter half of the 20th century.
2  The advent of new technologies such as CDs DVD, iPads and tablets has led to a decline in the popularity of the radio./There has a been a decline in the popularity of the radio with the advent of new technologies such as CDs DVD, iPads and tablets.
3  There was a huge difference between the Medieval and Renaissance periods in European history.
4  The pace of development of TV technology in the past decade has been considerable./The development of TV technology has occurred at a considerable pace in the past decade.
5  The Industrial Revolution had a significant effect on the economic development of the whole world.
6  Extreme interest was shown in the launch of the latest ultra-thin laptop./ There was extreme interest in the launch of the latest ultra-thin laptop.
7  The rise in the establishment of cities was due to developments in agriculture./Developments in agriculture gave rise to the establishment of cities.
8  Analysis of the data from the site was then carried out by the archaeologists.

**6**

Student's own answers

## IELTS Writing Task 2

**1**

Student's own answers

**2**

1 B  2 A  3 C  4 C  5 B  6 C  7 A  8 B

**3**

A

**4**

When any school subject is made a **(8)** mandatory part of the school curriculum, it does not necessarily mean that it will increase enough interest in the subject for students to go on to study it at university. In fact, sometimes it might have the opposite effect.

Compulsion regarding history will certainly bring **(5)** the attention of these subjects to pupils, many of whom might not have considered it **(6)** a worthwhile subject to study. Admittedly, this would in some cases encourage interest in the subject, but on its own as **(7)** a means of encouragement it is not enough. For history, there are many strategies that can be implemented to encourage its uptake at university.

History could be made compulsory for the first few years of secondary school. During this time lessons could be made interesting and absorbing for students by **(1)** visits not just to museums, **(2)** but to historical sites of local and national interest. **(3)** Visits to museums such as the transport museum in London are a good way to encourage even primary schoolchildren, because many exhibits are interactive, and engage the students. **(4)** Modern facilities such as the internet and computers can be used to bring history to life by carrying out simple research into local history or conducting social surveys.

**5**

**Model answer**

**C** In many parts of the world, a university education is now becoming out of reach financially for many students. Many factors have contributed to this situation, but there are steps that can be taken to address the problem.

The main factor is the increased cost of living worldwide. As student numbers have increased in recent years, accommodation and construction costs along with salaries have risen for universities, especially in large cities like London. Many governments have also reduced their expenditure in areas such as education, which has meant the burden of funding further education at university level has been transferred from the taxpayer to students.

More sponsorship of university students would go some way to addressing the problem. Many of the larger universities in the USA and the UK, such as Harvard and Oxford and Cambridge, attract large sums of money to their endowment funds to help students facing hardship. Such funding can be sought from large companies and philanthropists, as well as former university students. To encourage such donations, the government could increase tax breaks for donors.

Another possible step is the use of distance learning. With modern technology, especially through the use of videoconferencing (via telephone lines and over the internet), webinars, and tutorials using Skype, university costs can be reduced. Students can be further helped by making courses more intensive, thus reducing accommodation costs. Alternatively, courses could be made more modular and spread over a longer period of time, allowing students to finish the courses when they can afford to do so.

In conclusion, while the rising cost of university education is making it too expensive for many prospective students, much can be done to offer help.

**Review**

**Vocabulary 1**

1 b  2 a  3 h  4 d  5 f  6 c  7 g  8 e

**IELTS Speaking Parts 2 and 3 & Vocabulary 2: Adjectives of evaluation**

**1**

1 sensible  2 practical  3 trivial
4 important, not immaterial  5 simple
6 most significant  7 definitely worthless
8 effective

**2**

Students' own answers

**Language focus: Using nouns to build ideas**

1 Various important factors contributed to the fall of the Roman Empire.
2 The effect of studying history on young people's critical skills must not be underestimated.
3 An analysis of world history can help us in the development of a better understanding of modern life.
4 The improvement in the infrastructure of the city played a major role in economic development.
5 There is a clear link between an awareness of history and being able to function in the modern world./A clear link exists between an awareness of history and being able to function in the modern world.
6 A general knowledge of many different subjects is better than a detailed knowledge of one field.
7 Extensive research has been done into the relationship between education and happiness.

**IELTS Writing Task 2**

**1**

Student's own answers

**2**

True:    2, 4, 5, 6
False:   1, 3, 7
1 The study of history plays an important role in the education process of all young people.
2 While there may be some discussion as to its main purpose in the education system, to impart knowledge or skills for life,
3 I personally feel that the latter is its main function, but that the former is also relevant.
The study of history could not be more relevant nowadays to young people's lives.
4 and 5 because the modern workplace demands that employees understand the processes of life and skills that studying history teaches them. Take for example …
5 This process can teach young people of the effect of consequences of change and developments, which they can

then personalize by relating them to developments in their own lives.
6 At the same time, factual information like dates, names and places can be learnt to help put the developments into context and also to personalize the process. While important, this aspect of learning about history is of secondary importance.
7 While there may be some discussion as to its main purpose in the education system, to impart knowledge or skills for life,

**3**

**Model answer**

An introduction and first paragraph supporting the teaching of historical facts:

The study of history plays an important role in the education process of all young people. There may be some discussion as to its main purpose in the education system, whether to impart knowledge or skills for life, but I personally feel that the former is its main function, but that the latter is also relevant.

The study of historical information could not be more relevant nowadays to young people's lives, as it gives young people an awareness of their past and of the world

Such awareness can also help workers as they solve work problems and problems in their personal lives, because knowledge of the past can help people avoid mistakes

Another reason for studying historical facts is that it helps to enrich people's lives by making them aware of their environment, both physical and social.

## Unit 3 The age of information

**IELTS Listening Section 3**

**1**

1 A  2 D  3 B  4 C

**2**

Students' own answers

**3**

The listening section is about students discussing how to do research.
1 research habits –Question 1
2 flow chart – Questions 5–7
3 journal article search – heading in Questions 5–7
4 a detailed analysis of the essay title – first item in Questions 5–7
5 specific targets – second item in Questions 5–7
6 Organize, reduce time wasting and don't overwhelm yourself with information. – last item in Questions 5–7

7 struggling with the essay after everyone else has finished – after Question 8

**4**

1 B   2 B   3 A   4 C   5 key terms   6 time limit   7 bibliography   8 good grades   9 an argument   10 supporting evidence

**5/6**

Students' own answers

## IELTS Speaking Part 3 & Language focus: Prepositions

**1**

1 in   2 into (also *in*)   3 to   4 for   5 with

**2**

1 specialize in   2 associate with   3 benefit from   4 result in/from   5 stem from   6 elaborate on   7 coincide with   8 insist on   9 concern with   10 argue with   11 arise from   12 comply with   13 suffer from   14 depend on   15 distinguish from

**3**

1 result   2 succeed   3 is associated   4 benefit   5 differs   6 be distinguished   7 arise/stem   8 comply/struggle   9 insisted   10 depend

**4**

Students' own answers

**5**

**Model answer**

7 Many social and related problems stem from illiteracy and innumeracy. For example, if young people are unable to read or write properly or do basic mathematics, they may find it difficult to find a job. They may not even get past the first hurdle in a job application, which involves form-filling or writing a CV.

**6**

**Model answers**

1 I think it differs enormously from the past, because …

2 First of all, I think they will benefit from even more advanced systems where they can locate information instantly, just like the way we switch on a light.

3 I partially agree. Universities are often associated with learning factual knowledge, and work and the real world require the use of skills and experience, but the situation is changing …

4 Mmm, they have I think resulted in students accessing knowledge much faster than the generation before and in making it easier to 'carry' knowledge around with them.

5 Yes, they are suffering from having so much knowledge to learn that there isn't time to focus on one particular area. It's a superficial age.

6 Definitely and the overload mainly stems from technology and the number of books published each year.

7 I actually don't think it differs that much from the past, except perhaps that students may not need to learn so much by heart if they know where to find information quickly.

**7**

Students' own answers

## IELTS Writing Task 1

**1**

**Model answers**

1 a new car: an idea for a new car is conceived; the idea is developed; the car is designed; a prototype is made; the prototype is tested

2 a mobile phone app: see answers for Exercise 3

3 a documentary: a topic/area is chosen, the people involved are selected, the camera crew are prepared, the story board is written, the location(s) is/are selected, the filming is done, the editing is carried out and the documentary is shown

**2**

1 conception   2 submission   3 approval   4 design   5 production   6 testing   7 refining   8 uploading

**3**

The idea of the app is conceived.
The proposal is submitted.
The proposal is approved.
The prototype is designed.
The prototype is produced.
The prototype is tested.
The prototype is refined.
The app is uploaded.

**4**

Students' own answers

**5**

**Model answer**

1 the idea is conceived/the concept is discussed/discussion of a concept/the concept is approved/the app is created/it is checked, proofread, reviewed/the prototype is tested/ the design is finalized/the app is uploaded onto the web/it is downloaded/it is used

**6**

Students' own answers

**7**

1 f   2 e   3 i   4 c   5 b   6 d   7 g   8 a   9 h

**8**

**Model answer**

The illustration outlines the steps in the production of newspapers. It is clear that this process involves two main phases, one where paper is produced from wood and the other from recycled newspapers.

First of all, when the pine trees in the plantation are cut down, the logs are taken to a plant where the removal of the bark occurs. At the next stage, the logs are turned into chips of wood, which are put into a thermomechanical refiner, where the wood chippings are refined and the moisture is extracted. Then the refined wood chippings are fed into a machine which turns them into paper.

Once the newspaper has been printed and read, it is left outside for recycling collection. The newspapers are taken to a recycling plant where they are processed. The ink is removed from the paper and subsequently it is cleaned and checked. The blending of the pulp from the thermomechanical refiner and the recycled pulp takes place next and the mixture is fed into the paper-making machine. The recycling process is then repeated.

## IELTS Reading

**1**

**Model answer**

The modern information age has made studying considerably easier in one way by providing lots of information electronically. On the downside, there is now so much available it is difficult to choose what to read.

Slow reading has helped me to look at information carefully in my studies, as sometimes I tend to look at things too quickly and cannot take in all the information.

Nowadays it's important to be able to read fast when studying, working and even for leisure as there is so much information around us. But sometimes it becomes overwhelming.

It's easy to get lost on the internet as one surfs from one page to another. I often forget what I started off looking for and waste a lot of time.

**2**

Students' own answers

**3**

1 D   2 G   3 B   4 J   5 J   6 A   7 C   8 B   9 D   10 C   11 bewilderment   12 valid opinions   13 creative process

## Vocabulary: Verbs related to connections

**1**

1 a   2 b

**2**

a) change/transformation: translate, transform, develop

b) a cause/effect relationship: affect, develop, interfere with, create

c) a connection without any relationship indicated: link, connect, associate, correlate, liaise, involve, correspond, belong to, conflict with, match, combine

**3**

link, translation, connection, association, transformation, effect, development, correlation, liaison, involvement, correspondence, belonging, conflict, match, combination, interference, creation

**4**

1 c, d, e  2 c, d, e, f  3 a, b  4 b
5 b, c, d, f  6 e

**5/6**

Students' own answers

**IELTS Writing Task 2**

**1**

**Similarities:** same subject, similar ideas can be used – advantages and disadvantages can be expressed as ways and vice versa, ways can be positive and negative

**Differences:** different focus/topic, B asks for an evaluation of the development whereas A doesn't. Students need to write a paragraph to express this and then give evidence to support the evaluation. Some students tend to state the evaluation in one sentence or using a phrase or word without supporting it.

**2**

They relate to both A and B.

**3**

B

**4**

**Introduction:** Recent years have seen increasing volumes of knowledge coming into the public domain. While such a flood of information has an impact on people's lives in various ways, both positive and negative, the trend, I feel, is harmful.

**Conclusion:** In conclusion, despite the obvious positive effects of the availability of large amounts of information nowadays, the impact of increasing volumes of knowledge is harmful to everyone.

**5**

**Model answers**

1  Having access to information on the internet outside library hours makes life convenient for students.

2  The availability of knowledge in electronic form nowadays results in a less stressful life for students.

3  Studying is often associated with stress.

4  Students and workers alike can suffer from stress due to the overwhelming amount of information.

5  Studying and writing essays at university depend on having access to the relevant information.

6  Information overload stems from not being able to select, control and organize information.

7  If anyone is faced with too much information, it usually means that they cannot read and examine the information closely.

8  The way information is packaged in software such as apps is transforming our lives.

9  Many libraries and museums around the world are linked to the internet.

**6**

2  1, 2, 5, 8, 9
3 and 4  4, 6, 7

**7**

**Model answer**

Recent years have seen increasing volumes of knowledge being made available in the public domain. Such a flood of information has had a huge impact on people's lives, both positively and negatively, but, on balance, I think the trend is harmful.

There is no doubt that having access to large amounts of information is beneficial. Take students studying outside library hours, for example. Having access to the internet makes life easier for them, as they can research journals and articles 24 hours a day. The availability of such knowledge nowadays also results in a reduction in travelling to libraries and saves students and researchers lots of time. So the benefits are enormous.

Being overwhelmed by information, however, is a major negative consequence. It is difficult for everyone, including shoppers, students and researchers, for example, to find the right information, as there is now too much available. For example, a shopper looking for a fridge or clothes may be hindered by the amount of choice available. Likewise, not being able to examine the information closely is also a problem. Students, for example, may not have time to read details they come across on the internet, or indeed in paper journals, carefully enough to examine whether they are correct.

There are some positive aspects of having access to large amounts of information, but it is largely a dangerous trend. Apart from the negative impact mentioned above, it is easy for people to waste time searching through large volumes of information. In addition, the information load is increasing daily both in paper form and electronically, so the problem is due to worsen.

In conclusion, despite the obvious positive effects of the availabilty of large amounts of information nowadays, the impact of increasing volumes of knowledge is harmul to everyone.

**Review**

**Language focus: Prepositions**

**1**

1 from  2 in  3 from  4 in  5 from  6 on
7 with  8 from  9 on  10 about

**2**

Students' own answers

**IELTS Writing Task 1**

**1**

1  Once the concept is arrived at, it is discussed with interested parties and a proposal is submitted to the publishing company involved in developing the app. After that, the proposal undergoes a process where it is approved both conceptually and financially.

2  Once the concept is arrived at

3  The illustration shows the process of producing a language app for mobile phones and tablets.

4  Before being tested, the contents of the app are checked, edited and reviewed.

5  A prototype is then produced, which is tested and refined.

6  The next stage is the writing of the app itself.

7  The illustration shows the process of producing a language app for a mobile phone and tablets. Before being tested,

8  The illustration shows the process of producing a language app for mobile phones and tablets.

9  Generally speaking, the production process involves three main phases: the creation of the concept of the app and its development, the production of a prototype and the launching of the app on the web.

10 The illustration shows the process of producing a language app for mobile phones and tablets.

**2**

1  select, design, include, write, add

2  select, include, write, add

3  select, design, include, write, add, apply, monitor

4  select, design, include, add, monitor

5  design, include, add (monitor)
Sample noun phrases for 1: the selection of the information; the

writing of the leaflet; the design of the leaflet; the inclusion of statistics; the adding of illustrations

**3**

**Model answer**

the dumping of the computer, the transportation of the computer, the removal of reusable components, the crushing of the plastic, the recycling of the plastic, the reusing/reuse of components such as metal, the renovation, repair, resale, donation, reuse of the computer

**4**

Sample verbs for writing a newspaper article: select, research, check, write, include, add, edit, publish

Sample stages: the selection of the news item subject, research for the news item/subject, the checking of details, the writing of the article, the inclusion of quotes and illustrations/images, the addition of any relevant information, the editing of the article, the publication of the article

**5**

Student's own answers

## Vocabulary: Verbs related to connections

**1**

1 a  2 c  3 a  4 b  5 a  6 b  7 b

**2/3**

**Model answers**

1 Reliable information is associated with/means better choice.
2 Footballers are associated with huge salaries.
3 Happiness can result in good health.
4 Money transforms people's lives.
5 Water shortages stem from human activities.
6 The way we read has been transformed by technology.
7 Rote learning is linked to good memory.

## Unit 4 Leisure and the environment

### Vocabulary: Leisure and entertainment

**1**

Students' own answers

**2**

Students' own answers

C and E potentially yes – harming the environment, also A – use of electricity/energy

**3**

1 entertainment venue  2 leisure activities/pursuits  3 leisure centre  4 entertainment industry  5 street entertainment  6 light entertainment  7 leisure goods  8 popular entertainment

**4**

b 6  c 1  d 3  e 5  f 4  g 2  h 8

**5**

Students' own answers

**6**

**Model answers**

1 Leisure pursuits such as surfing the internet and going on to networking sites are really relaxing. All ages can spend hours on the internet each day.
2 The cinema especially now with all the specials effects including 3D brings enjoyment to a lot of people.
3 Leisure activities such as going to the gym increase people's general well-being by making them healthy and boosting their immune system.

**7**

Student's own answers

### IELTS Speaking Part 2

**1**

Students' own answers

**2**

1 who live nearby and headed off on a cycling trip along the canal which runs for miles through the city into the countryside.
2 we, … mmm … stopped for a while and watched the canal boats go by.
3 much more peaceful than the city … mmm … as we watched people passing by slowly on their boats and taking their time doing things.
4 I really enjoyed the day out
5 it was so relaxing to be outdoors rather than being stuck in a shop in the middle of the city.
6 loads of wild animals and birds and watched birds catching insects on the water. The people on the boats were friendlier than the people in the city and waved to us.

**3** six hesitations

**4**

Students' own answers

### Language focus: Comparative and superlative adjectives

**1**

Both use the comparative. *Peaceful* has two syllables and requires the words *more* or *less* to form the comparative adjective. The comparative adjective of *friendly* can be formed with *more* or *less* and can also be formed by changing the *y* to *i* and adding -*er*.

**2**

1 easier/the easiest  2 hotter/the hottest
3 more/less effective, the most/least effective  4 more/less expensive, the most/least expensive  5 poorer/the poorest
6 quieter/the quietest  7 worse/the worst

8 more common/commoner, the most common/commonest

**3/4**

1 difficult, more/less difficult, the most/least difficult  2 cold, colder, the coldest
3 useless/ineffective, more/less useless/ineffective, the most/least useless/ineffective  4 cheap, cheaper, the cheapest
5 rich, richer, the richest  6 loud, louder, the loudest  7 good, better, the best  8 rare, rarer, the rarest

**5**

Refer to the online Grammar Reference for further information about comparative and superlative adjectives.

**6**

**Model answers**

1 Cities are less friendly than the countryside.
2 Chess is more interesting than video games.
3 Days out are much more exciting than long breaks.
4 Leisure pursuits such as team sports are the most thrilling activity of all.
5 Outdoor sports such as football and rugby are much more rewarding to play than those in leisure centres.
6 The most entertaining film ever is ….
7 Reading books is not the most boring leisure activity.
8 Computer skills are one of the most crucial skills to possess nowadays.
9 Video games are more harmful to young people than films.
10 Active leisure pursuits are more beneficial for physical well-being than passive activities.

**7**

Students' own answers

### IELTS Speaking Part 3

**1**

**Model answers**

**Leisure time**

Do you think it's good to have days off during the week? Why/why not?
example: a half or whole day off in the middle of the week
reason: important for mental and physical health not to work all the time
purpose: to help them recharge their batteries

In terms of relaxation, is it better to have long or short breaks from work?
example: short breaks e.g. for a weekend up to 4 days
reason: can have more breaks/less difficult coming back to work
purpose: to make it easier to come back to work/for more variety

What are the benefits of going away for long breaks?

example: complete relaxation/escape
reason: forget work completely
purpose: to replenish energy and to clear the mind

**Time and work**
Which should be more important for people: earning money or having time to spend with friends and family?
example: time is more valuable – spending time with friends and family or alone
reason: healthier attitude to life
purpose: to relax/be creative
People seem to spend longer hours at work than in the past. Why do you think this is?
example: young professionals, long hours
reason: life more expensive/need more money for basics
purpose: to earn more
How can work affect people's leisure time?
example: young professionals don't stop/ no leisure time
reason: becomes automatic
purpose: to keep pace with modern life/ colleagues

**2**
Students' own answers

**IELTS Listening Section 4**

**1**
Students' own answers
Leisure and Entertainment

**2**
1 (adverb) adjective  2 noun  3 noun
4 number probably with a decimal point
5 number probably with a decimal point
6 number probably with a decimal point
7 number  8 noun/noun phrase  9 noun
10 noun phrase/abbreviation

**3**
1 notoriously difficult  2 television
3 home  4 84.49  5 48.81  6 599.8
7 4th/fourth  8 home (entertainment)
9 downturn  10 personal computer/PC

**IELTS Writing Task 1**

**1**
Students' own answers

**2**
3 There is a chance that leisure pursuits such as outdoor skiing will have disappeared by the middle of the century. (This can be changed to: *There is a chance that leisure pursuits such as outdoor skiing will disappear by the middle of the century.* The future perfect emphasizes the completion of the action.)
5 The characters in video games are projected to become almost lifelike in the very near future. (This can be changed to: *It is projected that the characters in video games will become almost lifelike in the very near future.* There is no difference in meaning.)

7 The world will have changed dramatically by the end of the century. (This can be changed to: *The world will change dramatically by the end of the century.* The future perfect emphasizes the completion of the action.)

**3**

**Model answers**
1 According to the UN, the global population is expected to rise to between 7.8 and 10.5 billion people in 2050.
2 Egypt's population and the populations of Ethiopia, Sudan and the remaining countries of the Nile basin are projected to double by 2050.
3 The UK population will rise to around 73 million in 2050, according to the Office for National Statistics.
4 As urban areas, particularly smaller towns and cities, continue to grow in size, about 5 billion people are expected to live in cities by 2030.

**4**
1 6,051, residential  2 2030, industrial and commercial, 3,021  3 industrial and commercial, residential  4 2025, residential, industrial and commercial
5 residential  6 974

**5**
1 5
2 3
3 expected, estimated; others: predicted/anticipated/envisaged/set to
4 simple present (*is expected to*), simple future (*will be required*), future perfect (*will have risen*, sentence 4 – to emphasize that the fact that the rise will have happened by that time)
5 (3) future industrial and commercial and residential construction on land that is already in use between 2011 and 2030.
6 1, 2, 5
7 2

**6**

**Model answer**
The data illustrates how much undeveloped land in hectares will be needed for a range of uses in England up to 2030.

As regards industrial and commercial purposes, it is estimated that there will be a dramatic rise in demand between 2011 and 2015 from 330 to 702 hectares, followed by a decline to 549 hectares in 2030. By contrast, the demand for undeveloped land for residential purposes, although considerably greater than that for industrial and commercial, is expected to decline, falling to 2,030 hectares in 2030, after a peak of 2,373 in 2015.

While it is projected that the need for undeveloped land for both transport & utilities will be greater than that for community services, the demand for the former is expected to rise only marginally in 2030 to 916 hectares after hitting a high of 1,084 in 2015. The demand for land for community services is anticipated to fluctuate, falling to 452 hectares compared to 485 in 2011.

Overall, it is clear that the demand for undeveloped land is projected to increase marginally over the period with the highest demand expected in 2015 in all four areas.

**IELTS Reading**

**1**
It's about leisure activities related to snow and the effect these have on the environment.

**2**
1 plant life/vegetation may be destroyed, animals may be driven away or become extinct, people might take plants, etc. as souvenirs and destroy the environment, rubbish left by people might pollute the environment, if certain areas are overused, they will be destroyed, noisy machines for building or carrying people around will drive off wildlife

**3**
Usually towards the end, because the problem/cause and effect need to be discussed first.

**4**
1 A  2 B  3 D  4 C  5 C  6 natural water flows  7 animals/wildlife/(local) fauna
8 biodiversity, habitat  9 B  10 E  11 H
12 F  13 A

**5**
Students' own answers

**IELTS Writing Task 2**

**1**
To maintain tour business revenue and viability

**2**

**Model answers**
1 to compete against others/to win/ to engage with other people/to learn strategies
2 to relax and to obtain information
3 to relax/to enjoy oneself
4 to learn cooperative and team skills/to meet people
5 to enjoy oneself/to relax
6 to build up stamina/to relax/to see the sights and views
7 to relax/to build up knowledge
8 to meet other people
9 to relax

**3**

1   <u>so that</u> people will be encouraged to adopt a more active lifestyle.
3   <u>To</u> bring performances such as plays and musical concerts to a wider public,
4   <u>in order</u> to help promote fitness and reduce health costs.
5   <u>so as to</u> attract people to such facilities.
8   <u>to</u> have a break and relax.
9   <u>to</u> discourage overuse of air travel.
10  <u>in order to</u> meet new friends as well as <u>to</u> learn something.

**4**

**Model answers**

1   to encourage people to use the facilities
2   to reduce health costs by keeping people fit mentally and physically/ to improve people's lives/to entertain people/to improve well-being
3   very beneficial – see the purposes / reasons in 2; it can keep elderly/young people fit/promote an awareness of the environment/promote responsible behaviour, etc
4   by taking money away from other vital areas such as health to pay for theatres/ concerts/leisure facilities
5   education/teaching at school when young/TV advertising/promotions/free vouchers
6   only rich can afford/increase in obesity, etc
7   No – good value for money and cost-effective
8   agree with a few reservations – people do not always appreciate things which they do not see the full value of in monetary terms

**5**

**Model answer**

Some people believe that supporting activities such as entertainment and leisure pursuits using public money is wasteful. However, while I accept that financial help can lead to a lack of appreciation of the facilities provided, there are clearly many benefits to be gained from financial subsidies.
Topic sentences:
1 There is no denying that some people think that entertainment and leisure pursuits should not be subsidized.
2 However, financial subsidies of art exhibitions and public leisure complexes through sponsorship or grants can help encourage people to use the facilities.
3 Subsidies also provide access for people such as students to entertainment and leisure.

**6**

**Model answer**

2
However, financial subsidies of art exhibitions and public leisure complexes through sponsorship or grants can help encourage people to use the facilities. Such support has added benefits such as reducing health costs by keeping people fit mentally and physically and improving people's lives generally. For example, if people are happier they are less likely to be stressed and a drain on public health resources. Moreover, ...

**7**

**Model answer**

There is little doubt that modern technology such as the latest televisions and other modern gadgets are affecting people, mainly the younger generation, but, at the same time, the benefits cannot be ignored.

Modern entertainment devices, such as TVs and the internet, can affect people physically because they can make people lazy, leading to obesity-related problems, or worse. For example, if young people spend hours each day using the computer for playing games, studying or watching TV, they are missing out on valuable exercise. Even worse, long periods of time sitting using the computer or watching TV can have serious consequences for your health. Other consequences, which are harmful for young people, are a reduction in social interaction and isolation.

Despite such negative impacts, modern TVs and other modern technology can enhance people's lives enormously because they provide valuable information, and also entertainment. Take the latest TVs. Not only do they have 3D technology, but they can be connected to computer screens and even be used to connect users directly to the internet. As a result, a wide range of entertainment and information sources such as news websites can be made available in the home.

A further positive impact is the convenience of technology like tablets. These devices are very useful, especially for students, because they are so compact that they can be easily carried around. Further, they can function not just as computers, but as ebook readers and data stores for information, photographs, music and study materials. So they are ideal for the modern youth in education.

As we have seen, there may be negative consequences arising from the use of modern entertainment and communication devices, but still the beneficial impact cannot be overlooked.

**8**

Students' own answers

**Review**

**Vocabulary: Leisure and entertainment**

**1/2**

Students' own answers

**Language focus: Comparative and superlative adjectives**

**1/2**

Students' own answers

**IELTS Speaking Part 3**

**1**

**Model answer**

1   Do you think leisure activities have a positive effect on people's health? If so, how?
    In terms of health, do you think leisure activities have a positive effect?
    How do leisure activities affect people's health?

**2**

Students' own answers

**IELTS Writing Task 1**

**1**

**Model answers**

The 15–29 age group is projected to increase in number from 12.471 million to 13.543 million.
There is expected to be an increase in the number of those in the 30–44 age group from 12.725 million to 13.644 million over the period.
It is forecast that numbers in the 45–59 age group will rise less than the younger age groups, from 12.126 million to 12.986 million.
The 60–74 age group is set to grow in number from 9.163 million to 11.981 million.
It is estimated that the number of those 75 and over will almost double over the period from approximately 4.9 million to 8.9 million.
Overall, it is forecast that there will be a substantial increase in the population of the UK.

**2**

Students' own answers

## Unit 5 A healthy world

**Vocabulary: Collocations related to health**

**1**

A   physical exercise improves health/ prevents illness/improves mental well-being

B a motorcycle medic can get to an accident more quickly than an ambulance in the city

C healthy eating – the benefit of fruit and vegetables

D physical activity – the benefit of starting at an early age

**2**

Students' own answers

**3**

service: noun/verb   care: noun/verb
financed: past participle   eating: noun
(gerund)   way: noun   education: noun
lifestyle: noun   economic: adjective
expenditure: noun   public: adjective

1 eating, way   2 education   3 lifestyle
4 care   5 service   6 economic   7 financed
8 expenditure   9 Public

**4/5**

Students' own answers

## IELTS Speaking Part 2

**1**

1, 3 and 8 are probably the healthiest, if done properly

**2**

**Model answers**

All are good for mental and physical fitness.

1 good for fitness, gets individuals out of the house, meeting people, helps fight obesity, etc.
2 good for all-round fitness, relaxing
3 good for general fitness, meeting people
4 meeting people, gets one out of the house, may involve walking or doing general physical exercise
5 general fitness, losing weight, meeting people
6 physical exercise at home, don't need a gym
7 meeting people, general fitness
8 very good exercise, weight loss

**3/4**

Students' own answers

## IELTS Listening Section 1

**1**

1 It's a dialogue between someone making an enquiry about volunteering of some kind, and a receptionist.
2 Yes, there are references to volunteering in questions 1–6 and 8 and 10.
3 Where did you see the advert?
4 The receptionist
5 Students' own answers, but probably C or A

**2**

**Model answers**

4 What words go with the word *raise*?

5 What activities can you suggest?/Can you make a list of possible activities?
6 Can you make a few suggestions about things that volunteers shouldn't help people with?

**3**

1 B   2 A   3 C   4 money   5 (their)
shopping   6 medication/medicine
7 two/2 referees   8 morning   9 online
10 two/2 (hours)

**4**

Students' own answers

## Language focus: Degrees of certainty & IELTS Speaking Part 3

**1**

1 Do you think the world will be free of disease in the future?
2 No. He says 'but it's unlikely in the near future' and 'I'm not sure really. It is possible in the distant future.'
3 And in the distant future?
4 Yes. He says 'in one hundred years' time, it's likely that there will be no more illness.'

**2**

1 probability   2 possibility   3 necessity
4 probability   5 (weak) possibility
6 certainty   7 impossibility   8 lack of
necessity   9 probability

**3**

**Model answers**

1 It is possible that children will be encouraged to do more exercise at school in future.
2 It's possible that too many adverts about food on TV are harmful to people's health.
3 no rewrite possible
4 It's probable/likely that in 50 years' time, food shortages will be a thing of the past.
5 It's possible that in future, the world will be more worried about the lack of clean water than oil.
6 It's certain that cities will be more overcrowded than now.
7 no rewrite possible
8 In the distant future, it won't be necessary for people to work.
9 It's possible that working less (can) reduce(s) stress and make people happier.

**4**

**Model answers**

1 It's extremely likely that robots will look after children and old people in 100 years' time.
2 It's impossible for machines to replace doctors and nurses in the near future.

3 It's certain that all medicines will be free in 20 years' time.
4 It's likely that people will no longer work in 50 years' time.
5 I think we should all be living in a stress-free world in four or five decades' time.
6 People are likely to live twice as long as today in the distant future.
7 In about 30 years' time, I think machines may repair people's bodies in their homes.

**5/6**

**Model answer**

Diet and exercise
Do you think people worry too much about diet and exercise nowadays? Why/Why not?
Yes, because people are bombarded by programmes and health warnings every day.

## IELTS Writing Task 2

**1**

1 A   2 C   3 B

**2**

Positive: 2, 3, 5, 8
Negative: 1, 4, 6, 7

**3**

**Model answers**

0 essential/valid/crucial/achievable
1 extremely
2 basic human right, not just for the rich
3 just like food and water
4 to make the population healthy and productive
5 no
6 it is essential whatever the cost

**4**

Students' own answers

**5**

**Model answers**

3 so   4 like/such as/for instance/take
(for example)   5 as a consequence/so
6 although/though   7 nevertheless

**6/7**

Students' own answers

**8**

**Model answer**

There is no doubt that both advertising and family and friends have an enormous impact on young people's eating habits, but I think that the former has a much more powerful effect than the latter.

The effect that family and friends have on young people's diet is not inconsiderable, because young people spend a lot of time with both groups. So the possibility of being influenced by them is great. The former group can be beneficial as well as harmful, depending on the diet that the family has. For example, if junk food like hamburgers instead of healthy food such as vegetables and fruit is commonly eaten within the family, the chances of any young person doing anything different are small. Inside and outside school, in order to fit in, young people are likely to follow the eating patterns of their friends.

Advertising for unhealthy food such as junk food is difficult for everyone, especially young people, to avoid. For example, adverts for junk food, which are found on TV programmes, in cinemas, and on street billboards, are often designed to attract young people. The adverts are often very alluring, making the junk food highly desirable. As such, the adverts are very effective. Take cinemas, for example. The food that is offered for sale is often made up of sugary drinks, sweets, hamburgers and popcorn. It is difficult to resist the temptation of these, especially when they are advertised on screen as well before a film starts.

The convenience and the cheapness of the food such as fizzy drinks and junk food are also highlighted by advertisements, as is its trendiness. For example, the actors are young and attractive. So they appeal to a young audience, which is crucial for advertisers, but dangerous for young people.

So as we can see, despite the influence of family and friends on young people's diets, advertisements exert much greater influence.

**9**
Students' own answers

**IELTS Reading**

**1**
Students' own answers

**2**
1 gadgets   2 around   3 integrating
4 components   5 liable   6 track

**3**
1 J   2 H   3 C   4 E   5 A   6 D   7 B   8 A
9 C   10 B   11 False   12 True   13 Not Given

**4**
Students' own answers

**IELTS Writing Task 1**

**1**

**Model answers**
1 generally more girls than boys eat/ate fruit in both periods
2 the order/pattern is the same in both years for both boys and girls
3 consumption decreases with age
4 boys: roughly the same; girls: upwards slightly

5 approximately 45 per cent for 11-year-old girls in 2005/06; approximately 38 per cent for 11-year-old boys in the same period

**2**
Students' own answers

**3**
1 e   2 d   3 a   4 b   5 c

**4**

**Model answer**
c  The highest consumption of fruit among girls was in those aged 11 in 2005–06 and in the same year among boys of the same age group, approximately 45 per cent and 38 per cent respectively.

**5**
The chart provides information about the proportion of children by age group and gender who consume fruit in two specific periods.

**6/7**

**Model answer**
The chart provides information about the number of doctors per capita in various countries in the European Union and the European average, together with the proportional increase in the ratio between 2000 and 2008.

While Germany, Denmark and Estonia had the highest doctor numbers per capita, exceeding the European average of 3.3 in 2008 with 3.6, 3.4 and 3.4 respectively, the pattern of change between 2000 and 2008 was very different across the three countries, comprising 1.1 per cent, 2.3 per cent and 0.3 per cent

By comparison, whereas France matched the per capita average for the EU in 2008, the ratio rose by a smaller proportion, amounting to 0.2 per cent, compared to the EU average of 1.5 per cent. Physician numbers in the Irish population were only slightly lower than the EU average, but the increase in the ratio between 2000 and 2008 constituted 4.8 per cent, by far the largest increase.

Generally speaking, while the numbers of physicians per capita are generally similar among the selected countries, the rate of increase in the ratio varies considerably.

**Review**

**Vocabulary: Collocations related to health**

**1**

**Model answers**
1  In order to promote a healthy lifestyle among people of all ages, health education should be started at school.

2  The best way to keep health costs down is to invest money in preventive medicine.
3  It is likely that healthcare in the future will be very different from today.
4  Health professionals such as doctors and nurses should be paid more than footballers and similar celebrities.
5  Healthcare should be financed by the taxpayer.
6  Running a health service requires a lot of talent and resources.
7  The economic health of any country depends on many factors, including the health of the population.
8  Health expenditure in my country is increasing year by year.

**2**
Students' own answers

**Language focus: Degrees of certainty**

**1**
1  It is possible that I will study medicine at university.
2  It's unlikely that people will have a lot of personal space.
3  In the future, it is likely that the world will be a better place to live in.
4  It will be unnecessary for people to work long hours each week.
5  In my home country, it is probable that the next generation of young people will have a better standard of living.
6  It will be impossible for people to live in the countryside.
7  It is possible that finding a good job will become very difficult in coming years.

**2**
Student's own answers

**3**

**Model answers**
1  It is possible that healthcare will become more expensive.
2  It's unlikely that transport will become cheaper.
3  Education should become much more technologically driven.

**4**
Students' own answers

**IELTS Writing Task 2**

**1**
Students' own answers

**2**
They favour prevention.

**3**

**Model answers**
Focus on prevention: effective, less expensive, saves money
Focus on cure: costly, not worthwhile, not all diseases can be prevented, quicker

**4**

**Model answer**

Paragraph supporting prevention.
Prevention of diseases is clearly better
than focusing resources on cures. For
example, if people are encouraged to
take responsibility for their own health,
through health education in schools
and TV adverts, then many illnesses
such as diabetes, heart disease and joint
problems will be prevented. This will save
considerable sums of money in health
budgets as doctors will not have to resort
to expensive medicines and operations.

## Unit 6 Shaping the world and beyond

### Vocabulary 1: Words related to space and place

**1**

**Model answers**

A  Satellites help humans connect with
each other.
B  example of control and shaping
of the physical working and living
environment
C  shaping of the environment to control
food production
D  preparing a space shuttle to explore the
world beyond us

**2**

1 place   2 a gap   3 gap   4 setting
5 spaces   6 systems   7 organization
8 organizations

**3**

**Model answer**

5  No, as they are crowded and not always
pleasant. Take a city like London. There
are too many people and the transport
system will soon not be able to cope
with everyone.

**4**

roomy, spacious, distant, environmental,
spaced, located, local, orderly, organized,
organizational, systematic, chaotic,
disorderly

**5**

1 too much on systems   2 GPS navigation
systems   3 social chaos   4 chaotic
5 phone networks   6 huge problems
7 remote areas

**6**

**Model answers**

a telephone system
the transport system
my home town
The coast where I was brought up in ...
Leptis Magna in Libya

### IELTS Speaking Parts 1 and 2

**1/2**

**Model answers**

1  What's your name?
2  Do you have any hobbies/interests?
What are they?
3  Have there been changes to places in
your home town recently? Like what?
4  Have there been any positive or
negative developments in the town?
5  Is there any space for future
development(s)?
6  Is there any room for facilities for
young people in your home town?
7  What kind of systems/infrastructure
are needed most?
8  Are the surroundings in your home
town/neighbourhood in recent years
pleasant? In what way?

**3**

**Model answers**

Space scientists spend most of their time
out of the public eye, but they have a huge
impact on people's lives as the technology
they develop finds its way into fields such
as medicine and satellite technology.
Computer software designers impact
on our lives enormously, providing for
example games for entertainment and the
technology we use on our computers.
Research scientists help improve our lives
through new developments in all fields
such as food production and preservation,
transport and medicine, especially in
finding new medicines and cures for
disease.
People often think of engineers in the
traditional sense of building bridges,
but engineers now work in all fields,
from building bridges to technology
for sportswear such as sports shoes and
computing.

**4**

**Model answers**

1  sports (e.g. football), work,
volunteering
2  meeting people, learning new skills,
socializing, spending time usefully

3  the social aspect, meeting new people,
becoming involved in new situations

**5/6**

Students' own answers

### IELTS Listening Section 2

**1**

a  See the stem in question 1.
b  See the stem in question 1.
c  See the stem in question 3.
d  See questions 4–6.
e  See the first column of the table in
questions 7–10.

f  See the second column of the table in
questions 7–10.
g  See the last column of the table in
questions 7–10.

**2**

1 A   2 B   3 C   4 B   5 C   6 A   7 catering
8 Mary's   9 17th (of)   10 invitations

### Language focus 1: Hypothesizing

**1**

1 third   2 second   3 first

**2**

a 6   b 1   c 4   d 3   e 5   f 2

**3**

**Model answers**

1  Provided international scientists
pool their resources, more and more
breakthroughs will occur.
2  Unless primary schoolchildren are
taught basic scientific processes
through projects such as learning
about space travel, they will be at a
disadvantage later on in life.
3  If there were fewer rules and regulations,
more young people would set up their
own businesses.
4  Even if we managed to explore the
moon and other planets in the near
future, it would not be possible to
exploit them easily.
5  If international governments
cooperated on standardizing electronic
products, many scientific goods such as
computer hardware would be cheaper.

**4**

**Model answers**
**Working in teams**

1 to give some criteria, factors,
characteristics   2 to give some criteria,
factors, characteristics   3 compare several
items or ideas   4 evaluate something
5 evaluate something   6 evaluate something

**5**

3

**6/7**

Students' own answers

### IELTS Writing Task 1

**1**

1 space centre larger, with admin offices
2 school inside town replaced with space
museum   3 lake almost surrounded by
town   4 bridge built   5 forest shrunk
6 new sports complex   7 town expanded
8 most of farmland gone   9 science
academy built on farmland   10 hospital
converted to space theme park   11 science
laboratories built on farmland

**2**

Mistakes in bold: 1 southeast   2 south
3 Most   6 mostly

**3**

Transitive:
was turned into, made way for, was built, linking, surrounded, was given over to
Intransitive:
increased, disappearing, vanished, remained, changed
Both: increased, changed (elsewhere)

**4**

**Model answers**

1 The maps show the transformation of the area around Welton between 1995 and 2012.
2 The school was replaced with a space museum.
3 The forest shrank considerably as trees were chopped down to make way for a science academy and the sports complex.
4 Welton space centre expanded, with additional admin offices.

**5**

**Model answer**

1 park replaced with science park and museum   2 school replaced with hotel and spa   3 shops built   4 most of wood gone   5 hospital replaced with hi-tech centre   6 size of town increased
7 farmhouse and farmland made way for science academy and science laboratories

**6**

**Model answer**

The maps illustrate the developments that occurred around Tumbledown between 1995 and 2010.

Generally speaking, it is clear that the area saw significant changes over the period with old buildings being transformed and new ones being constructed. For example, the park in the northwest became a science park and museum with the school to the east of the park being turned into a hotel and spa. Near the hotel, along the north bank of the river, running from the west to the northeast, shops were built.

South of the river some noticeable changes took place. The town itself expanded in size and the hospital east of the town disappeared. Another addition to the area east of the town was the construction of a hi-tech centre, for which a large part of the wood was chopped down. The farmland south of the town was replaced with science laboratories with the farmhouse being converted into a science academy.

As a result of these changes, the area is less green and less open.

**7**

Students' own answers

## IELTS Reading

**1/2**

Students' own answers

**3**

| | |
|---|---|
| debris | rubbish/waste |
| fragments | bits/pieces |
| dangerous | risky/hazardous |

**4**

1 growing crowd   2 breathtaking speeds
3 objects   4 satellite/spacecraft   5 more fragments   6 problem   7 orbital plane
8 grab, stabilize   9 gripping mechanism
10 coupled   11 False   12 Not Given
13 True   14 True

## Language focus 2: Cause and effect verbs and nouns

**1**

| | |
|---|---|
| Cause: | And the collision itself then generates |
| Effect: | thousands more fragments, |
| Cause: | thousands more fragments, |
| Effect: | further exacerbating the problem. |

**2**

*link* and *show*

**3**

1 The sharing of technology between the different companies (cause) resulted in considerable cost savings. (effect)
2 Early advances in science by people like Aristotle (cause) led to many discoveries we take for granted today. (effect)
3 The scientific knowledge in many countries (effect) is developed by international collaboration. (cause)
4 The choice of location for new science and engineering companies (effect) is often influenced by considerations such as the availability of skilled workers. (cause)
5 The present world has been shaped enormously (effect) by the thinking and writing of many scientists such as Einstein and Stephen Hawking. (cause)
6 The establishment of new industries such as software companies (cause) can transform the economy for the better. (effect)
7 The building of a new science complex (cause) had a positive impact on the behaviour of young people in the community as employment increased. (effect)
8 It has been suggested that the internet (cause) is altering the way users think. (effect)

## Rewrite

1 Considerable cost savings have resulted from the sharing of technology between the different companies.

2 Many discoveries we take for granted today were brought about by early advances in science by people like Aristotle.
3 International collaboration shapes the scientific knowledge in many countries.
4 Considerations such as the availability of skilled workers have an impact on the choice of location for new science and engineering companies.
5 The thinking and writing of many scientists such as Einstein and Stephen Hawking have had considerable influence over the present world.
6 The establishment of new industries such as software companies can improve the economy.
7 The behaviour of young people in the community was made better by the building of a new science complex as employment increased.
8 It has been suggested that the way users think is being affected by the internet.

**4/5**

Students' own answers

## IELTS Writing Task 2

**1/2/3**

Students' own answers

**4**

1 a result (If)   2 a concession (Although)
3 a purpose (in order to)   4 a result (so that)   5 a reason (because)   6 a result (resulting in)   7 a condition (Provided)
8 a condition (Unless)

**5**

View 1:   2, 4, 5
View 2:   1, 3, 6, 7, 8

**6**

**Model answers**

2 Although space research such as going by spacecraft to other planets is valuable, many problems such as famine and disease need to be addressed here on earth. This is because human life is too precious to waste.
3 Surely the human race needs to explore space such as the moon and the planets in our solar system in order to learn more about our world and our past.

**7**

**Model answers**

| | |
|---|---|
| View 1: | aliens/destructive, want our resources |
| View 2: | new technologies, help with diseases |
| Own opinion: | |
| | many reservations because of the dangers, but curious to find if anyone is out there |

**8**

**Model answer**

In recent decades, the human race has been launching satellites into space for various purposes, including communication and exploration.

While there is a fear that we may attract unwelcome visitors from many planets, other species may not be as bad as people often imagine.

People are sometimes afraid that they might draw the attention of other species, because they are perhaps afraid of the unknown and they then give such species negative human qualities. Take, for example, science-fiction films. In most cases alien worlds and creatures are portrayed in a negative light, as beings who want to destroy or control the earth.

Very rarely are they depicted positively. Even when this does happen, as in the film *ET*, some human beings are shown as antagonistic.

Yet, if there are other beings in other worlds they may not be as terrifying as some people imagine. They may be very similar to ourselves and even if they aren't they may have the same fears as some human beings. We may be able to exchange ideas and technology with them and trade with them just as different nations have done over the millennia on earth. They may have very advanced knowledge that could benefit human beings enormously.

Some people may think that it is naive to believe that aliens from another world will be harmful to the human race, but I agree that we may have much to offer each other. They may be able to give us the means to remove disease and poverty from our own planet.

In conclusion, there may be monsters out there in space which have the potential to cause us harm, but there may also be other creatures that can be of benefit to us.

**Review**

**Vocabulary 1: Words related to space and place**

**1**

**Model answers**

1 a system that you use every day: telephone.
2 a place in the solar system that you would like to visit, if you could: the moon.
3 a technology network that you use more now than in the past: the internet.

4 an example of a type of infrastructure that will benefit from space research: the health system.
5 a landscape in a science-fiction film that you liked or disliked: a planet in *Dune* – liked.
6 a location that is special, because it seems from another world; the Giant's Causeway in Northern Ireland.

**2/3**

Students' own answers

**Language focus 1: Hypothesizing**

**1**

**Model answers**

2 Provided I work hard, I'll be able to go to university.
3 If I don't manage to manage to pass my exams, I'll look for a job.
4 Even if it takes me several attempts, I'll pass the IELTS.
5 If I hadn't studied English when I was younger, I wouldn't be here now.
6 If I were to have the chance again, I'd study science as well as languages, if I could.
7 Unless something happens, I'll be going to the countryside at the weekend.
8 Provided I find a job I'll be able to travel around Europe later.

**2**

Students' own answers

**IELTS Writing Task 1**

**1/2**

Students' own answers

**Language focus 2: Cause and effect verbs and nouns**

**1**

A helps people to travel and visit people; develops the economy   B helps people relax; makes cities less threatening and hostile   C makes people stressed; makes them feel lonely   D helps people to relax, clear their minds

**2**

**Model answer**

Parks in cities are important for a number of reasons. They not only make the concrete environments of cities less threatening, but provide places for workers and people living there to relax.

**Unit 7 A consumer society**

**Vocabulary: Words related to *consumer***

**1**

Students' own answers

**2**

**Model answers**

1 consumer spending/government spending   2 consumer behaviour/consumer spending   3 basic necessities   4 Consumer demand/Consumer confidence/Consumer spending/Government spending/Government expenditure   5 consumer goods   6 Spending habits/Basic necessities   7 Consumer confidence/Consumer spending   8 consumer boycott

**3**

**Model answers**

1 Consumer spending is the money that consumers spend when they shop, government spending is the money raised by taxes or borrowing that the government spends.
2 Consumer behaviour is the way that consumers or shoppers behave when they buy things such as clothes items or new technology.
3 Basic necessities are items such as food and water.
4 Consumer demand is what consumers want to buy. Consumer confidence is to do with how well consumers feel, which is then related to how much they spend. If they are confident, they spend more. Government expenditure is the same as government spending in 1.
5 Consumer goods are items which consumers buy, such as TVs, clothes, etc.
6 Spending habits are the habits people have when they spend, whether they buy the same items or new items and where they shop.
7 Consumer confidence/Consumer spending as in 4 and 1.
8 A consumer boycott is to do with avoiding the purchase of certain items for particular reasons, such as political reasons.

**4**

**Model answer**

1 Window shopping is an enjoyable pastime for many people. Sometimes, shoppers or consumers do it before they buy something. They just look to see what is available. It is in fact a good way of getting exercise, if you can bear the crowds of people in the streets. Window shopping may not suit everyone's personality, as some people prefer to go into the shop and look at items that they want to buy immediately. They may consider the seeming aimlessness of window shopping a complete waste of time. Perhaps the main advantage of window shopping is that it is cheap if

you don't get seduced into the shop.

**5**

**Model answer**

1 pollute, avoid, products, services, habits, careful, carbon footprint

As green consumers are careful not to pollute the environment they avoid products and services that might cause pollution. They will change their habits and are careful with things like their carbon footprint.

**IELTS Listening Section 3**

**1**

Students' own answers

**2**

a questions 5 and 6   b questions 1–4
c questions 7–10

**3**

1 B   2 C   3/4 C, D   5/6 B, E   7 couple of weeks   8 anonymous   9 comfortable
10 layout

**Language focus: Countable and uncountable nouns**

**1**

No: *accommodation* and *recreation* only go with *a type of*

**2**

electronic equipment (U)
cash (U)   music (U)   computer software (U)   news (U)   car (C)   traffic (U)   homework (U)   medicine (C/U)   information (U)   job (C)   furniture (U)   scenery (U)   travel (U)   tree (C)   work (C/U)   change (C/U)   advice (U)   entertainment (U)   food (C/U)   recreation (U)
Examples:
cash: coins, paper money   music: jazz, pop   computer software: video/computer games   news: sport, political   car: convertible, electric   traffic: cars, lorries, vans   homework: essays, tasks   medicine: tablets, capsules, syrup   information: data in charts, knowledge in books   job: role, position   furniture: chair, table   scenery: mountain, woodland   travel: by air, car, boat   tree: oak, ash   work: in an office, school, outside, paintings   change: developments such as new infrastructure, bridges, etc.   advice: verbal, written   entertainment: TV, concerts, shows   food: vegetables, meat, fish   recreation: games, TV, sport

**3**

**Model answers**

1 For entertainment, I'd like to receive tickets for a live TV show, because I have always wanted to be part of a TV audience.

2 I'd like to walk through a very pleasant woodland area, because such places are very relaxing and far away from the stresses of life.

3 Like many other people, the piece of equipment I'd like to receive is the latest tablet with touch screen technology, because you can do many things with them such as draw and store notes and photographs easily.

**IELTS Speaking Parts 1 and 2**

**1**

**Model answers**

1 Are shops or markets more popular in your country?

2 Are shopping malls more popular than small shops in your country?

3 Do people prefer to use cards or cash nowadays?

4 Do you buy books and music online?

5 Do you prefer to buy things in shops or online? Why?

6 Do you spend a lot of money on media such as books, films or music, or on electronic equipment?

7 Do you think the cost of certain electronic items will come down in future?

**2**

Students' own answers

**3**

| | |
|---|---|
| what the website is | D |
| what the website provides | C |
| how often you visit it | A |
| and explain why you like visiting the website | B |

**4/5**

Students' own answers

**IELTS Writing Task 1**

**1**

**Model answers**

A This chart shows the percentage of people ordering goods over the internet. The extract only gives four countries. It's clear that the UK exceeds the other countries, at around 70 per cent, although there is little difference seen between the four countries.

B The table shows four types of activities that people of different age groups in England do in their spare time in 2007/08. Apart from the third item, listening to music, where the younger age group listen more, the proportions of people doing the activities are very similar.

C The table is about the participation in percentage terms of different age groups in different types of voluntary activities (formal and informal) in England in 2009. The rates vary considerably.

D The pie chart extract shows the amount given to different charitable causes in the UK in 2008/09. The amount given to overseas causes is largest proportion in the extract, with children and young people coming second.

**2**

1 B   2 C   3 B   4 B   5 D   6 A

**3**

**Model answers**

2 More 16-25-year-olds (40 per cent) participated in informal voluntary activities than formal activities (25 per cent).

3 A greater proportion of 16-24-year-olds (83 per cent) than those aged 25-34 (74 per cent) listened to music.

4 Sixty-nine percent of 16-24-year-olds and 67 per cent of 25-34-year-olds considered shopping less interesting than the other activities.

5 Donations to overseas charities exceeded other causes with 12 per cent compared to 11 per cent for charities dealing with children and young people, 5 per cent for animal charities, and 4 per cent for educational charities respectively.

6 The worldwide web is used for ordering and purchasing goods more in the United Kingdom compared to the other three countries.

**4**

**Model answers**

A The proportion of people ordering or buying items online is remarkably similar (at around 63 per cent) with the United Kingdom being marginally higher at about 65 per cent.
Paraphrase: Fewer goods were acquired online by people in Denmark, Sweden and the Netherlands compared to the United Kingdom (approximately 63 per cent on average and 65 per cent respectively).

B The proportions of people in both age groups spending time with friends and family were very similar (83 per cent for the younger group and 84 per cent for the older).
Paraphrase: A slightly larger proportion of people (84 per cent) in the 25–34 age group than the younger (83 per cent) spent time with their family and friends.

3 Forty percent of those aged 16–25 were engaged in informal voluntary activities compared to 25 per cent for formal activities.
Paraphrase: Informal voluntary activities seemed to be more popular than formal activities in the 16–25 age group, 40 per cent and 25 per cent respectively.

4 Education attracted less support than

the other three causes.
Paraphrase: The support for education was lower than the other three causes.

**5**
Students' own answers

**6/7**

**Model answer**
The data provides a breakdown of the expenditure by consumers in the United Kingdom according to different ways of paying between 2005 and 2008.

Debit card payment was the top method of payment in 2008, increasing fairly gradually from 29.5 per cent to 36.3 per cent, to capture just over a third of the market, while that for credit and charge cards barely changed over the period, rising to 19.7 per cent in 2008 from 19.4 per cent in 2005. By contrast, there was a decline in payments by both cash and cheques with the former dropping from 33.1 per cent to 29.2 per cent and the latter falling proportionally more from 15.9 per cent to just 12 per cent, a fall of almost 25 per cent overall.

Other payment methods, while much lower than the other means of payment, amounted to 2.1 per cent in 2005 compared to 2.8 per cent in 2008 with a low of 0.8 per cent in 2007.

It is clear that while overall expenditure increased gradually over the period (from £494.5 billion to £524.6 billion), the methods for making payment changed, with cash and cheques becoming less popular.

**IELTS Speaking Part 3**

**1**
1 Do people attach too much value to
2 What kinds of goods or services
3 What are the advantages of
4 What kind of influence does advertising have
5 Do you think having lots of money to spend
6 How important would you say it is for governments

**2**

**Model answers**
2 Beginning: These days people buy everything from food to cars to collectible items. (The question is about 'what', not primarily about evaluation, but it is good to give reasons and examples.)
3 Beginning: The main advantages are that they are often cheaper ... (Again the question is about 'what', not primarily about evaluation, but it is good to give reasons and examples.)
4 Beginning: Advertising can affect

consumer habits in different ways. (This question is about what and how and requires a cause and effect development not just listing ideas and then giving reasons and examples. However, reasons and examples are also needed.)
5 Beginning: I don't think it's always necessarily the case. (This question is asking for an evaluation – does it make people content or not? Supporting evidence for the student's evaluation is required as in an argument essay.)
6 It is crucial, because ... (This question, like 5, is asking for an evaluation.)

**3**
Students' own answers

**IELTS Reading**

**1**
Students' own answers

**2**
1 paragraph C   2 paragraph F
3 paragraph A   4 paragraph E
5 paragraph B

**3**
1 D   2 F   3 F   4 C   5 A   6–10 A, C, F, H, I
11 professional companies   12 70 per cent /%   13 D

**IELTS Writing Task 2**

**1/2**
Students' own answers

**3**
this equipment = the latest computer gadgets like a games console
them = parents
it = the latest computer gadgets like a games console
This = children may try to persuade them to buy it
They = adverts
they = during children's programmes
this problem = the fact that the adverts are shown at the prime time for a young audience
This = ban the programmes entirely
this situation = TV advertisements targeted at children are not acceptable in the first line (and then the supporting evidence in the rest of the paragraph)

**4**
1 they   2 those   3 They   4 children
5 them   6 this view   7 them   8 these products   9 they   10 this   11 them

**5**

**Model answer**
Celebrities such as sports stars and TV personalities are used to advertise all kinds of consumer products to people of all ages. The need for a ban on such advertising directed at young people in their teens is an idea that I agree with to a certain extent, but I have reservations

about a total ban.

Adverts where sports stars advertise particular sportswear or clothes is one area which can cause problems for young teenagers especially, and their parents. Footwear such as trainers is a good example. If a sports star advertises a pair of trainers, they can become highly desirable among young teenagers. This can then lead to the youngsters putting pressure on their parents to buy them, especially if friends have them. In a family with more than one teenager this can cause friction and financial problems for the family.

Young adults in their late teens may be under similar pressure. Even if they are working and have their own money to spend, they may feel compelled to keep up with the latest trends in clothes and accessories like expensive watches advertised by famous personalities. Being trapped into keeping up with the latest gadgets can then lead to debt.

Yet, celebrity endorsement of consumer goods in adverts is not all harmful, because stars can act as role models, promoting a healthy lifestyle. If buying the latest trainers advertised by a football star encourages teenagers to be more active, then that is beneficial. Likewise, consumer products such as healthy food and drinks can lead to a greater awareness of health issues.

In conclusion, when considering a ban on celebrities advertising products, we also need to bear in mind the benefits in certain cases and consider whether a total ban might not be harmful.

**Review**

**Vocabulary: Words related to *consumer***

**1**

**Model answer**
1 It helps to boost the economy. As people spend, businesses increase their profits and the government can raise taxes/revenue/money from the spending and businesses.

**2/3**
Students' own answers

**Language focus: Countable and uncountable nouns**

**1**
1 footwear (U)   2 slippers (C)   3 jumper (C)   4 accommodation (U)   5 bedsit (C)
6 electronic equipment (U)   7 PC (C)
8 medicine (C/U)   9 syrup (U)
10 vegetables (C)   11 fruit (C/U)

**2**
Students' own answers

**IELTS Writing Task 2**

**1/2/3**
**Model answers**

**1**
Banning TV advertisements won't have any effect on children. This is because children are not sophisticated enough to distinguish between what is a commercial and what is part of the programme. For example, if a toy which is a character from a TV programme is advertised during a commercial break, then it will probably seem like part of the programme. So they will not notice any difference. Moreover, these advertisements are often very good entertainment, which is why parents do not need to worry about them. Thus, TV advertisements have little negative impact on children.

**2**
TV adverts aimed at children are unethical because they are too young to appreciate what the purpose of the adverts is. They know that they can possibly obtain the products though, but do not understand that their parents will have to buy them and that they are not free. For example, if a child sees a toy like a doll or a train and it is very attractive, he/she is likely to want it and put pressure on his/her parents to buy the item, especially whilst in shops. So it is wrong to put pressure on children, and hence families, through TV adverts. Therefore, they should be carefully monitored or even banned.

**3**
TV adverts should be carefully checked by parents to protect children from exposure to consumer advertising. The purpose of this kind of advertising is to sell products such as toys and sweets to a largely unsophisticated audience. As it is the duty of parents to protect their children, they need to monitor all adverts during the TV programmes their children watch. For example, they can switch off adverts when they come on during programmes. They can also restrict the amount of TV programmes their children watch.

## Unit 8 Culture on the move

### Vocabulary: Collocations with *culture*

**1**
Students' own answers

**2**
**Model answers**
1 culture in an organization and culture vis-a-vis the arts
2 dynamic: technology, travel, communication, advertising, media, cultural exchanges

3 what happens inside a business – the behaviour, ideas, etc.
4 traditional culture is to do with the crafts and festivals, e.g. handicrafts, artwork and art of a community as opposed to say modern culture. Workplace culture is to do with the practices and ideas in workplaces, e.g. in a bank.

**3**
1 Mainstream  2 Football  3 Modern
4 Enterprise

**4**
- celebrity culture is the lifestyle that surrounds famous people such as singers, artists, footballers and actors
- street culture is the way of life of people on the street, such as activities related to the behaviour of young people
- mass culture is to do with the traditions and customs of the all the people in society
- contemporary culture is traditions and customs or way of life that are current at the present time

**5**
**Model answers**
1 In the present age of instant information, national cultures are being transformed gradually by diverse influences.
2 Mainstream culture is affected by a host of factors and changes gradually over time. It is dynamic, not static.
3 Academic culture can sometimes seem to be slow to embrace the changes that are occurring in the real world, especially the business world.
4 Sadly, local culture is often eroded by global influences.
5 Youth culture is an important influence on the media, yet it is often thought that it is the media that influences the young of today.
6 Consumer culture is a strong force which drives the economy of many countries in today's world.

**6/7/8**
Students' own answers

**IELTS Speaking Parts 1 and 2**

**1**
**Model answers**
1 What kinds of cultural activities/experiences would a visitor to your country expect to see?
2 How often do celebrations and festivals take place in your country?
3 When/At what time of year do celebrations and festivals take place?
4 Do you take part in celebrations and festivals actively/passively?

**2/3/4/**
Students' own answers

**5**
**Model answer**
I'd like to describe a large country house with extensive gardens in the southwest of England that I went to see with a friend last month. The house is situated by the sea and the gardens stretch down gently to the seashore. We went there by car, as it is quite difficult to reach by public transport. It was a great experience because we were able to visit the house, which was full of art deco furniture and artwork. The interior design of the house was really amazing with views looking out over the gardens to the sea. After visiting the house we wandered round the gardens, which were more spectacular than the house itself and very large. We really enjoyed wandering round the different types of gardens and taking pictures of the landscapes and the trees. We didn't walk right down to the sea and see very much of the gardens as that would have taken us a couple of hours more. But what we did see we really liked. It was good exercise climbing back up through the gardens again to the shop where we bought postcards and gifts. It is certainly a place to visit for someone who wants to have some exercise and a pleasant experience in the fresh air.

**IELTS Listening Section 4**

**1/2**
Students' own answers

**3**
1 all its forms  2 educational programmes
3 random encounters  4 3D pavement
5 realistic perspective  6 temporary  7 B
8 C  9 A  10 C

### Language focus: Defining and non-defining relative clauses

**1**
1 a, b: no; c: yes
2 a, b: yes; c: no
3 a, b: yes; c: no
a One non-mainstream way of drawing people's and especially children's attention to art, which is really intriguing, is random encounters with art in the street, so-called street art.
b Cities have always been full of street performers such as jugglers and singers, who add colour to otherwise drab environments, sometimes as part of festivals such as the Edinburgh Festival in Scotland.
c We've looked at ways that art can be used for therapeutic purposes with patients.

**2**

1 h  2 d  3 a  4 b  5 c  6 e  7 f  8 g

**3**

Students' own answers

## IELTS Writing Task 1

**1**

Students' own answers

**2**

1 no  2 yes  3 no  4 magazines, least for boys: poetry, least for girls: manuals or instructions  5 Equal re the types, but it seems girls read more overall.  6 websites, newspapers, comics and graphic novels, manuals or instructions and factual books  7 (the other) five

**3**

1  There is a ~~vast~~ significant difference in the reading patterns for boys and girls.

2  b is more expansive, but the paraphrase works

3  ~~Not as many~~ More boys ~~as~~ than girls read websites, approximately 58 per cent and 55 per cent respectively.

4  correct

**4**

**Model answers**

There was a noticeable difference between the proportion of girls compared to boys who read blogs or networking websites with approximately 50 per cent for the former and just over 40 per cent for the latter. Fiction books were more popular among girls than boys, approximately 50 per cent and 40 per cent respectively.

While factual books were the second least popular form of reading material for boys, they were less popular among girls than poetry.

**5**

**Model answer**

The chart compares the extra-curricular reading habits of boys and girls in England in the year 2007.
Overall, it is clear that there is a difference in the attraction of reading materials with the exception of websites.

**6**

**Model answer**

The chart provides information about a range of programmes on television watched by both genders in England in 2007/8.

Slightly more men watched the news and films, the most popular programmes for both genders, than women, 73 per cent against 71 per cent and 68 per cent against 64 per cent respectively. Likewise, the viewing tastes for men and women as regards wildlife programmes were very similar, 52 per cent compared to 50 per cent. While the proportion of women viewing soaps exceeded men by more than twofold (58 per cent compared to 29 per cent), the reverse pattern was seen regarding live sport coverage (72 per cent for men and 37 per cent for women).

As regards comedy, history and current affairs programmes, the proportion of male viewers surpassed female viewers, 64 per cent and 54 per cent, 44 per cent and 34 per cent and 36 per cent and 29 per cent respectively. By comparison, the programmes that were more popular among women compared to men were food and cookery (46 per cent as opposed to 30 per cent) contemporary or period drama (45 per cent as opposed to 25 per cent) and quiz shows (37 per cent as opposed to 31 per cent).

Generally speaking, there appears to be great variation in viewing taste between men and women, except for the news, films and wildlife programmes.

**7**

Students' own answers

## IELTS Reading

**1**

1 T  2 T  3 F  4 T

**2**

1  See paragraph 1, the first sentence
2  See paragraph 1, the second and third sentences
3  See paragraph 5, last sentence
4  See paragraph 6, last sentence

**3**

1 No  2 Not Given  3 Yes  4 No  5 No
6 E  7 H  8 D  9 B  10 G  11 I  12 D
13 A

## IELTS Speaking Part 3

**1**

1 a  2 c  3 b

**2/3**

Students' own answers

## IELTS Writing Task 2

**1**

**Model answers**

1 media/technology  2 technology/video games  3 running costs – fewer people attending  4 internet/business culture 5 internet/free newspapers
6 low cost of travel/people more mobile 7 technology/loss of interest in manual jobs  8 technology

**2/3/4**

Students' own answers

**5**

There are many <u>cause</u> (causes) of this situation, but perhaps the <u>main</u> (one) is the migration of people away from rural areas to the cities, (which) <u>tends</u> to occur mainly among young people. This process of urbanization is very damaging to local communities, as it means that only the older generations are left behind. With (such/the) <u>movement</u> of people, there is a good chance that many of those who move away will <u>loose</u> (lose) contact with their home towns and <u>tradition</u> (traditional) practices. They may also learn new languages and new customs, which may further erode the old customs and traditions. This may then make them feel their 'former culture' is old-fashioned and of less value than the new <u>cultur</u> (culture) they are experiencing.

**6**

Paragraph 1

1  a topic sentence:  There are many causes of this situation, but perhaps the main one is the migration of people away from rural areas to the cities, which tends to occur mainly among young people.

2  an evaluation of the situation: This process of urbanization is very damaging to local communities,

3  an explanation of the evaluation: as it means that only the older generations are left behind. With such movement of people, there is a good chance that many of those who move away will lose contact with their home towns and traditional practices.

4  a relative clause:  which tends to occur mainly among young people/those who move away/which may further erode the old customs and traditions,

5  a second cause: They may also learn new languages and new customs, which may further erode the old customs and traditions.

6  a conclusion: may then make them feel their 'former culture' is old-fashioned and of less value than the new culture they are experiencing.

**7**

**Model answer**

All areas of people's lives all over the world are undergoing rapid change and none more so than traditional ways of life such as festivals and celebrations, which are vanishing rapidly. This trend is the result of many factors and while the situation is serious, much can be done to address the situation.

**8**

**Model answer**

Most older people have seen life change dramatically compared to the younger generation, with some things emerging and others such as traditional skills and crafts declining. A number of causes have contributed to this latter situation, but it can be addressed by various steps.

The main cause, perhaps, is the rapid pace of development in modern life brought about by globalization. The world is now more connected than before, so new ideas and ways of doing things are spreading around the world rapidly. For example, while in the past basic materials like furniture and other household utensils were made by hand and the skills passed down from generation to generation, now these items like many others are mass-produced by machines in one or two locations and shipped around the world.

Another factor is that young people are required to learn new skills mainly revolving around technology and so older traditional skills lose their value. Hence, young people have no interest, as there is less need to learn these skills.

To help maintain the interest in traditional crafts and skills, the answer lies in focusing on the problem at school level. Like languages, if the skills are not used, they will decline and disappear. So, if children are taught crafts like making traditional items such as carpets and furniture by hand, there is a chance interest in these will survive.

Great value is often attached to items such as clothing, carpets and furniture that are hand-made. Therefore, with careful marketing and advertising coupled with apprenticeships and targeted funding, attention can be drawn to traditional skills and crafts and in many cases revived.

In conclusion, with care and attention there is no reason why traditional crafts and skills within all cultures should not survive, and indeed thrive.

**9**
Students' own answers

### Review

### Vocabulary: Collocations with *culture*

**1**
**Model answers**
1 meetings with clients, wearing special clothes like suits, going to conferences, attending parties, travelling nationally and internationally
2 shopping in person, shopping online, advertising, wasting resources such as packaging
3 team working, working with colleagues, making friends with colleagues, working practices

4 going to the cinema, theatre, attending sporting events, going to pop concerts, watching TV

**2**
**Model answers**
1 modern dance, popular music, video games, soap operas on TV, light entertainment
2 festivals related to the seasons, e.g. spring and harvest, wedding ceremonies
3 music such as hip-hop, modern jazz, music videos, video games
4 street dancing, street art, street sculpture, performing music
5 technology in all aspects of life such as tablets and smart phones, street culture as in 4

**3**
Student's own answers.

### IELTS Writing Task 1 (Using defining and non-defining clauses)

**1**
1 Concerts that/which are very expensive don't attract students or poor people.
2 Culture, which is very important for all of us, is often undervalued by the government.
3 Films that/which show a lot of violence should be banned.
4 Entry to museums, which are centres of education, should be free.
5 People who/that read a lot of books and newspapers are often well informed.
6 The arts, which reach a lot of people, need to be subsidized.

**2**
1 The least common type of reading material among boys was poetry (approximately 10 per cent), <u>which contrasted with manuals or instructions at around 12 per cent</u>. (Non-defining: additional information added to the sentence)
2 While the proportion of <u>girls who read emails</u> exceeded boys (about 60 per cent against 45 per cent), the reverse was the case regarding newspapers, with boys at just under 45 per cent and girls about 28 per cent. (Defining: to identify which proportion)

**3**
**Model answers**
1 Only a small proportion of people thought culture was too elite, posh or boring, which was quoted by about 2 per cent of people.
The idea that culture was too elite, posh or boring, which came at the bottom of the list, was quoted by only about 2 per cent of people

2 Literature, poetry, playwriting and authors, which was the second main association of the word *culture*, was cited by just under 25 per cent.
The second most popular association was literature, poetry, playwriting and authors, which was cited by 25 per cent of respondents.
3 History, which was quoted only by about 12 per cent of respondents, came seventh in the list.
Only a small proportion of people (12 per cent) quoted history, which came seventh in the list.

**4**
Students' own answers

### IELTS Writing Task 2

**1**
**Model answers**
the rise of technology, better home entertainment, video games, entertainment on the internet, social networking, online games

**2**
Students' own answers

**3/4**
**Model answer**
Perhaps the main factor contributing to a fall in people going to the cinema is the rise of personal entertainment systems. Nowadays, for example, people can watch high-quality films on laptops, tablets and mobile phones for less cost than going to the cinema. The latter can still have the 'wow' factor with 3D and large screens, but 3D televisions are now becoming more common and cheaper, thus increasing the appeal of home entertainment. Being able to watch a film on personal devices at any time is very convenient. So it is not surprising that cinema attendance is being affected.

## Additional material
## Unit 1

### Speaking Part 2

**1**
**Model answers**
1 Do you enjoy living in a city? Why/Why not?
2 How often does your family go on trips away from home?
3 Do you like modern towns or cities? Why/Why not?
4 What kinds of places do you visit in your country?
5 Would you recommend these places to tourists to visit? Why/Why not?

6 What is the most modern city you have visited?

7 Are old buildings important in your culture? Why/Why not?

8 Do you prefer modern buildings to old buildings?

**2**

Students' own answers

**3/4**

**Model answers**

town/city: noisy, overcrowded, dirty, too modern/old-fashioned, too many cars, poor transport system, too expensive, costly

modern building: bright, cheerful, welcoming, attractive, colourful, brightens up everything, made of glass and concrete, beautiful at night

**Vocabulary: Collocation with nouns**

**1**

Students' own answers – related to where they live or work or have visited, e.g. London

**2/3**

Students' own answers

## Unit 2

**Vocabulary 1: Collocations - multiple combinations**

**1**

1 evidence   2 records   3 studies/research
4 an investigation   5 history   6 research
7 analysis   8 (a) survey(s)/research

**2**

Students' own answers

**3/4**

**Model answer**

1 It is important to carry out archaeological research because it can tell us a lot about the past and confirm historical events such as battles and natural disasters such as earthquakes and floods. Such research is vital to help build an understanding of how civilization began and its development. This can improve our understanding of the modern world and develop and lead to a greater appreciation of the consequences of our actions. As archaeology is so important, funding at university level is essential to provide the experts that are needed in this field. Volunteers are useful to help do the basic groundwork, but training experts is essential.

**IELTS Writing Task 1**

**1/2/3**

Students' own answers

**Language focus: Using nouns to build ideas**

**1**

1 *The dramatic increase in new technology products* has made the choice for consumers difficult.

2 *The regeneration of old parts of towns* is needed to ensure *the preservation of important buildings of historical interest.*

3 *The impact of the study of history on young people's lives* must not be underestimated.

4 *The difference between conducting research on any subject at university nowadays and in the past* is enormous.

5 *The recent decline in reading newspapers and books in paper form* has been attributed to *the rise in ebook readers.*

6 *The range of products available for sale on the internet sites of major stores* is increasing on a daily basis.

7 *The rise in the number of tourists visiting national monuments such as temples and country houses* is causing *considerable harm to the fabric of buildings.*

8 *The number of TV programmes about history* outnumbers programmes about other subjects.

**2/3**

Students' own answers

## Unit 3

**Language focus: Prepositions**

**1**

1 with   2 in   3 from   4 with   5 from
6 on

**2/3**

Students' own answers

**IELTS Writing Task 1**

**1**

1 natural   2 both   3 both
4 manufacturing

**2**

1 B   2 A   3 C   4 D

**3**

Students' own answers

## Unit 4

**Vocabulary: Leisure and entertainment**

**1**

**Model answers**

street entertainment, leisure goods, leisure centre, leisure industry, entertainment industry, popular entertainment, leisure activities/pursuits, light entertainment

**2/3**

Students' own answers

## Unit 5

**IELTS Writing Task 2**

**1/2**

Students' own answers

**3/4**

**Model answers**

happier people
higher costs of care
greater demand on housing
overcrowding
longer working life
unhappier population
higher taxes

**5**

**Model answer**

Eliminating disease around the world is undoubtedly a worthwhile aim for all healthcare systems, but surely the prevention of illness and alleviating pain and suffering are also just as important.

Large sums of money are spent annually on finding cures for diseases such as malaria and lifestyle health problems such as heart disease and diabetes. Diseases like the former deserve to have money invested in them, because they are responsible for large numbers of illnesses and fatalities each year. Other health problems such as heart disease can also benefit from research to find a cure, but these illnesses are sometimes caused by people's lifestyles and can often be prevented through health education rather expensive research programmes.

## Unit 6

**IELTS Writing Task 1**

**1/2/3**

Students' own answers

**4**

**Model answers**

1 that took place around Tanton between the years of 1985 and 2010.
2 motorway had been built through the farmland
3 the spread of the town to the north
4 southwards
5 to the southeast mainly disappeared
6 shopping complex was constructed
7 being turned into a car park
8 was given over to the construction of a theme park
9 factories were constructed, while to the southwest of the village more farmland disappeared to build an airport

10 farmland and woodland being lost to development.

## Unit 7

### IELTS Writing Task 2

**1**

1 Browsing the internet can be fun, but it also wastes a lot of time.
2 People tend to be led by advertising when they shop, but it doesn't always affect people's shopping habits.
3 TV adverts during children's programmes should be banned, but this (strategy) is not going to stop the problem.
4 Some people think that children don't notice the adverts on TV, but they do. So parents need to be aware of this (problem).
5 Companies such as supermarkets carry out surveys to gauge shoppers' preferences. This is not the only practice that companies use to engage with shoppers.

**2/3**
Students' own answers

## Unit 8

### IELTS Writing Task 1

**1**

**Model answers**
1 Which age group is/are involved in acting the most?
2 Which is the most popular artistic activity for each age group?
3 Which is the least popular artistic activity for each age group?
4 What is the proportion of those aged 40–54 who do not participate in any artistic activity?
5 How does writing compare across the three age groups?

**2**
Students' own answers

**3**

**Model answer**
Decorating, handicrafts gardening:
1 Decorating, handicrafts and gardening were popular among the three age groups, with those aged 40–54 forming the largest proportion (just over 45 per cent).
2 While just under 30 per cent of the 15–24 age group took part in decorating, handicrafts and gardening, it was the second most popular activity in this group after photography and film at just over 30 per cent.

3 Of the three age groups, decorating, handicrafts and gardening (approximately 40 per cent) was the most popular among 40–54-year-olds.

## Writing bank

### IELTS Writing Task 1

#### Line graphs

The chart provides information about the number of teachers of both genders in nursery and primary and secondary schools in the United Kingdom between 1981/82 and 2007/8.

As regards nursery and primary level, while there were fewer teachers of both genders than secondary teachers overall for most of the period, female teachers constituted the largest number of teachers throughout at around 165,000 in 1981/82 and 175,000 in 2007/8. By contrast, there was a fall in male nursery and primary school teacher numbers from about 45,000 to about 35,000.

The pattern for the secondary level was markedly different with an inverse relationship between the two genders. For example, male teacher numbers declined substantially from about 155,000 in 1981/82 to about 100,000 in 2007/8, whereas there was a clear upward trend in female secondary school teachers from about 125,000 at the beginning of the period compared to approximately 135,000 in 2007/8.

Overall, it is clear that while nursery and primary school teacher numbers remained flat throughout the period, numbers at the secondary level declined, but with more teachers overall at this level.
Word count: 172 words

#### Pie charts

The charts provide a breakdown of the proportions of various types of fruit and vegetables produced along with the total amounts in millions of tonnes in the European Union in 2009.

Generally speaking, in terms of volume it is clear that considerably more vegetables (57 million tonnes) were produced in the EU than fruit (36 million tonnes). Of the former, the 'Others' category represented almost half of total production (46.7 per cent) with tomatoes at 29.5 per cent making up the greatest proportion of the vegetables listed. By comparison, while onions and carrots accounted for almost similar amounts (10 per cent as against 9.6 per cent), the production of lettuces was much smaller at 4.2 per cent.

Among fruit, apples accounted for the greatest proportion by far, amounting to 33.5 per cent of the total, clearly more than the proportion relating to 'Others' (30.2 per cent). The production of oranges (17.8 per cent), by contrast, was half that of apples, with fewer peaches and pears being produced, 8.2 per cent and 7.7 per cent respectively, while strawberries comprised 2.6 per cent of total fruit production.

#### Bar charts

The chart shows what children aged 8–16 in the United Kingdom thought about reading in 2009.

There was a greater proportion of girls than boys who enjoyed reading very much, approximately 28 per cent and 17 per cent respectively, with the latter being noticeably below the average for the age group of approximately 23 per cent. By contrast, regarding those who enjoyed reading quite a lot, the difference between boys and girl was less marked, although girls in this category still exceeded boys, at just over 30 per cent and 26 per cent respectively.

Approximately 43 per cent of boys enjoyed reading a bit, while 35 per cent of girls did so, with girls being below the average of around 38 per cent. The proportion of boys and girls aged 8–16 who did not take any pleasure in reading was small, around 14 per cent and 7 per cent respectively, with boys noticeably above the average of 10 per cent.

Generally speaking, it appears that girls in the 8–16 age group like reading more than boys, with the latter clearly disliking reading compared to girls.

### IELTS Writing Task 2

#### Discuss both these views and give your own opinion.

Gaining experience in the field of work is considered by some as mandatory for prospective university students, but there are others who feel that going to university immediately after finishing school is a much better option.

There is little doubt that gaining experience of work is important. Some people argue that such work gives young people valuable knowledge of the world, which in turn helps them to appreciate their studies and decide what they want to do in life. For example, if young people work for a year abroad learning a language, or in their home country in a foreign bank, it might give them a better understanding of the world and their aims in life. They should then see the significance of a university education.

Other people feel that prospective students will benefit from going straight to university, because they will finish their studies earlier than those who take time off. Moreover, they will enter the job market more qualified than those who delay their studies for a year and will earn more. Prospective students might also lose momentum by delaying their studies. For example, they might not want to go back to studying, thus missing out on a worthwhile experience.

In my own opinion, experience of work is crucial in the modern world, if anyone is to find a job. So I feel the sooner young people find out what work is like the better. However, I do not agree with work prior to university being made compulsory. Instead it should be encouraged, as it may not suit everyone, and also there may not be enough jobs to accommodate every young person. In conclusion, while work prior to going to university gives invaluable experience to young people, it should be optional rather than obligatory.

### In what ways … ? Has this become a positive or negative development?

Social media sites are a relatively recent phenomenon which have had a major impact on the way people communicate with each other.

The most important effect is that such media sites as Facebook have brought people together in ways never seen before. A good example is a student from Australia living, working, studying or travelling around the world. He or she is able to keep in contact with family and friends and to maintain friendships made during his/her travels. If recent photos and updates are posted on the site, this can then help keep friendships alive.

As with all good developments, there are negative impacts. Devoting too much time to developing 'electronic relationships' on social media sites can result in less time being spent on maintaining and starting 'real-life' relationships. The result can be a loss of social skills. This is a problem for people of all ages, but more so among young people, who should perhaps be developing more real friendships. Another effect is that social media sites can be addictive and interfere with studies and even work.

While social media sites may be open to criticism, on balance, I feel that they are a good development. They open up the world to people of all ages and help to bring people together. It is now possible to have friends all over the world, which for the young generation is very beneficial, as they can learn to interact with people from different cultures. Such sites can also be educational as people can contact each other in different languages such as Spanish and German.

As we have seen, despite the obvious negative consequences of social media, their use is a positive development.

### To what extent do you agree or disagree? What other measures do you think might be effective?

Investment in infrastructure can certainly have an impact on employment and hence enhance economic activity, but it is perhaps not necessarily the best method of doing so.

Large railway and road building programmes obviously stimulate economic activity, because they employ large numbers of people. For example, if roads are built, or improved, between major cities, this can lead to employment during the construction process. Further, as a consequence of better connections, there is a good chance economic activity between the cities will increase, leading to increased employment. The same applies to the construction of railway lines.

Another equally useful measure is to invest money in education at all levels. An educated workforce, for example in the car industry, can supply the skilled workers modern economies need, because even in times of unemployment there is always a shortage of skilled workers such as engineers, plumbers and electricians. Likewise, having a skilled workforce can increase productivity, as workers are likely to work more independently and efficiently.

Giving companies tax incentives to employ and train young people fresh from school or university is also very effective. Just like apprenticeship schemes, a business could be offered tax holidays if it takes on a young worker for say six months or more. If the job becomes permanent, then the business could be given further tax refunds. The same could also apply to businesses in areas of high unemployment to stimulate growth, but for both to work mentors to encourage to businesses are also necessary.

As we have seen, while investing in major infrastructure programmes is certainly a sound measure to help tackle unemployment and help the economy, it is one of many equally effective solutions.

### What do you think are the causes of these problems and what measures could be taken to solve them?

Some serious health problems such as heart disease, obesity and diabetes are a direct result of modern life, which arise due to a range of different factors. However, this is a situation that can be dealt with.

A major factor is technology at work and in the home, which has led to a sedentary lifestyle. This is clearly connected with obesity and, in turn, heart disease and diabetes. At work, for instance, people in many jobs such as banks spend large amounts of time at their desks looking at computer screens. This can mean that they rarely have to move around the office and, due to modern pressures, they may also spend their lunch break in the office. Home life is little different with remote controls, meaning people don't have to move to watch TV. Another factor is the endless home labour saving devices, for example, robotic vacuum cleaners.

Fortunately, there is much that can be done to solve these problems. Workers and students can be encouraged to take their lunch away from their desks. Even simple exercise routines like walking up stairs rather than taking lifts or escalators can help reduce the threat of modern diseases. Another measure is for all organizations to offer exercise through subsidized gym membership, which will pay back the investment through a healthy and productive workforce.

As increased wealth in many countries is also a reason behind modern diseases, it is essential to make sure that people do not overeat, and that they are conscious of the calorie content and the harmful fat and salt in food such as processed meals. Proper labelling, advertising and education from an early age can help with this.

As we have seen, there are certainly modern-day health issues, but with some encouragement the problem can be tackled.

Macmillan Education
Between Towns Road, Oxford OX4 3PP
A division of Macmillan Publishers Limited
Companies and representatives throughout the world

ISBN 978-0-230-43994-8 (+ key)
ISBN 978-0-230-43995-5 (- key)

Text © Sam McCarter 2013

Design and illustration © Macmillan Publishers Limited 2013

First published 2013

Design by xen
Illustrated by David Banks, Oxford Designers & Illustrators,
Seb Camagajevac
Cover design by Designers Collective

Author's acknowledgements

The author would like to thank the freelance editor for her
patience and guidance.

The publishers would like to thank Stephanie Dimond-Bayir, Jo
Preshous and Rachael Roberts.

**The author and publishers would like to thank the following
for permission to reproduce their photographs:**

**Apple Inc** p80(tr), **Alamy**/Arcaid Images p52(A); **Bananastock**
pp51, 59, 79, **BrandX** p17; **Corbis** p54(D), Corbis/Matt Gibson/
Loop Images p77(D), Corbis/Franz Marc Frei p68, Corbis/CDC
Phil p65, Corbis/Image China p18(D), Corbis/Richard Rancier
p86, Corbis/Alberto Lowe/Reuters p105(B), Corbis/Mario Secchi
p91, Corbis/David Sutherland p90(C), Corbis/Ron Watts p90(B);
**Digital Stock** p42(C); **Digital Vision** p81; **Ecole Polytechnique
Federale De Lausanne** (EPFL) p72; **Getty** pp46(B), 48, 52(C),
55, Getty/AFP p18(C), Getty/Henk Badenhurst p36, Getty/
Scott R Barber p78(B), Getty/Dan Bayley p74, Getty/Bloom
Image p44, Getty/C.Borland/Photolink p78(E), Getty/Peter Cade
p52(E), Getty/Toby Carney p30(A), Getty/Paul Chesley p66(C),
Getty/Martin Child p23, Getty/Comstock p52(G), Getty/Diane
Diederich p13, Getty/Domino p54(C), Getty Eschcollection
p77(A), Getty/Ed Freeman p6(B), Getty/Fotosearch p67, Getty/
Mitchell Funk p77(C), Getty/Alexis Grattier p6(D), Getty/
Jamie Grill p78(D), Getty/Tim Hawley p80(tl), Getty/Image
Source pp6(C), 24, 53, Getty/Kidstock p42(A), Getty/Mixa
p83, Getty/Leon p94, Getty/Norah Levine Photography p62,
Getty/Catherine MacBride p30(B), Getty/David McLain p78(A),
Getty/Johnie Pakington p6(A), Getty/Photoduo p52(H), Getty/
Photostock Israel p105(A), Getty/Tim Platt p46(C), Getty/
Science PR p54(B), Getty/Zen Sekizawa p96, Getty/Steven
Simpson p32, Getty Don Smetzer p78(C), Getty/Robin Smith
18(A), Getty/Andreas Strauss p54(A), Getty/Travelpix Ltd p9,
Getty/Visit Britain/Parvel Libra p98, Getty/Visit Britain/Grant
Prichard p18(B), Getty/Jack Wassell Photography p25, Getty/
WireImage p92, Getty/Yagi Studio p30(D); **Grapheast** p42(B,
D); **Image Source** p77(B); **Macmillan Publishers Ltd** p35;
**Macmillan New Zealand** p105(C); **Photodisc** pp56, 66(A); **J.
Rogers** p61; **Superstock**/Ambient Images p90(A), Superstock/
Cultura Ltd p52(D), Superstock/Robert Harding Picture Library
p19, Superstock/Imagebroker p52(F), Superstock/Photononstop
p42(E), Superstock/Pixtal p31, Superstock/Science Faction
p66(D), Superstock/Stock Connection p46(A), Superstock/Tips
Images pp66(B), 89, 91, Superstock/Marka p105(D), Superstock/
Giovanni Mereghetti p90(D), Superstock/Anton Vengo p30(C),
Superstock/View Pictures Ltd p52(B), Superstock/Felix Vogel/
Imagebrok p45.

**The author and publishers would like to thank the following
for permission to reproduce their graphs:**

ONS/DEFRA/ Costing potential actions to offset the impact of
development on biodiversity – final report p46, 47

ONS/ Lifestyles and Social participation: Social trends 41/Carla
Seddon pp108, 109

ONS-Social Trends No 40 2010 edition p82 (all), 84, 94, 95,110

Eurostat/European Commission/ Digital Agenda for Europe
201—2020 p10(t,b)

Eurostat/European Comission/ Youth In Europe: a statistical
portrait 2009 edition pp101(t,b), 103, 113

OECD.org/Health at a Glance Europe 2010 p62, 63

The author and publishers are grateful for permission to reprint
the following copyright material:

YouthNet UK for an extract adapted from 'Life Support: Young
People's needs in a digital age' www.youthnet.org, pp.4, 5, 10.
Reproduced with permission of YouthNet. Registered charity
number 1048995;

Stephen Jenkins, Watson and Jenkins Opticians Ltd for an
extract from "The History of sunglasses" by Stephen Jenkins,
05/08/2008, www.articlesbase.com. Reproduced with kind
permission of Stephen Jenkins, Optometrist;

Guardian News & Media Ltd for an extract from "The art of
slow reading" by Patrick Kingsley, *The Guardian*, 15/07/2010,
copyright © Guardian News & Media Ltd 2010;

NationMaster.com for statistics from "Media stats: United
Kingdom vs United States" copyright © NationMaster.com
2003-2012. All Rights Reserved

UNEP DTIE for material adapted from United Nations
Environment Programme, 2007, *Tourism and Mountains - A
practical guide to managing the environmental and social impacts of
mountain tours,* www.unep.org. Reproduced with permission;

AAAS for an extract from "'Electronic Skin' Grafts Gadgets to
Body" by Jon Cartwright, ScienceNOW, 11/08/2011, http://news.
sciencemag.org. Reprinted with permission from AAAS;

Guardian News & Media Ltd for an extract from "Swiss create
'janitor satellite' to clean up space" by Alok Jha, *The Guardian*,
08/03/2012, copyright © Guardian News & Media Ltd 2012;

Guardian News & Media Ltd for material from "Cheap clothes,
clean conscience" by Sarah Butler, *The Guardian*, 28/08/2008,
copyright © Guardian News & Media Ltd 2008;

Joshua E. Brown for an extract adapted from "Study: We May
Be Less Happy, But Our Language Isn't" by Joshua E. Brown,
12/01/2012, www.uvm.edu. Reproduced with kind permission of
Joshua E. Brown.

Printed and bound in Thailand
2017  2016  2015  2014  2013
10  9  8  7  6  5  4  3  2  1